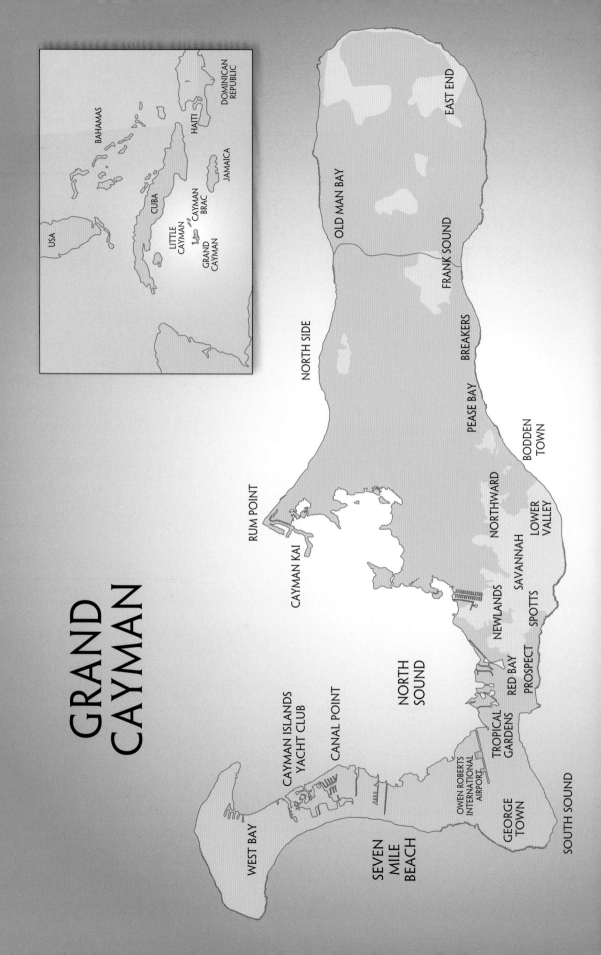

Hurricane Ivan

SURVIVAL STORIES

as told by the people of the Cayman Islands

by Terri Merren

THE MILL PRESS
KINGSTON, JAMAICA

First published in Jamaica 2005 for Terri Merren
by The Mill Press
184a Constant Spring Road
Kingston 8

National Library of Jamaica Cataloguing in Publication Data

Merren, Terri
        Hurricane Ivan : Survival Stories as told by the people of the Cayman Islands /
Terri Merren

ISBN 976-8168-12-9
A catalogue record of this book is available from the National Library of Jamaica.

Quantity discounts are available on bulk purchases of this book for educational or
gift purposes. Special books can also be created to fit specific needs. For
information, write to P.O. Box 31013 SMB, Grand Cayman, Cayman Islands;
or e-mail: supply@candw.ky

All photographs were taken by Terri Merren, unless otherwise indicated.
Additional photographs by permission of: Jennifer Godfrey, Dennis Mastry, Garry
Bosley, Christina Godfrey-Kirkaldy, Carole Kirkconnell, Ladner Watler, Rollin Ebanks,
Shelley Leonard, Ed Powers, Brenda Bryce, Robert Joseph

Edited by Mary Bowerman, South Sound resident, Grand Cayman
Cover designed by Shelley Leonard, George Town resident, Grand Cayman
Printed in the United States of America by Haff Daugherty Graphics, Hialeah, FL

Cover picture: "*Dead Fish*", North Sound, taken one week after the storm
Back cover: "*God's Rainbow*", taken four days after the storm

South Sound tree roots, taken by South Sound resident, Jennifer Godfrey

Highlights

"... those two doors burst into streamers!"

"... the dogs were swimming in the kitchen!"

"... more of the roof came off and we heard the most gigantic crash."

"We were ... watching all the cars floating across and the washers and dryers and televisions."

"... I seen one body ... It was a dead body ..."

"... We're going to drown over here ... There's no way we can get out."

"We tried to call 911 but could not connect."

"We are praying ... Oh God, do we have to die?"

"... the windowpanes exploded ... a piece of the glass came ... and licked me right on my eye!"

"... The house was full up with water up to our necks."

"... my wife ... was the first to get in the boat."

"... it took forever because the water was killing us. The rain was stinging us, pelting us like rocks ..."

"... the sand felt like someone was picking up big rocks and licking us with them."

"... when I looked, the house across the road was coming this way ..."

"... the truck was floating ... we were sitting in the back with our feet up on the seats ... We didn't think we would survive it."

"... the next door neighbours cried out that they are going to perish ..."

"... he had just then stopped breathing ... we basically dragged him ... into the hospital, unconscious."

"The whole top blew off ... the glass exploded."

"The screens and … all the doors are tearing off in all directions … it's bad. It's really bad. We're not going to make it."

"… the sliding door blew off … the hurricane was now inside the house!"

"Oh, Lord, how can we die by fire when we're in a flood?"

"… we were screaming and holding onto each other."

"… I heard BOOM! … I was thinking, 'Oh, why did I stay in this place by myself?'"

"Our roof has blown off and we are going to die."

"I don't think I'm going to make it … I really don't think I am."

"… I had the baby … and I cried, 'I'm drowning! I'm drowning!'"

"… the children are screaming and crying, crying and screaming …"

"I was smashed off my feet and swept right from the front to the back of the house …"

"… I saw a lot of people's bones … I even see somebody's false teeth …"

"… we were surrounded by ocean and we had no way out!"

"It sounded like screams - like witches' cackles."

"… the patio glass just exploded on us … my first thought was, 'Oh, Jesus, she must be dead.'"

"We could see that one side of her face was covered in blood."

"… we are underwater as all the sea has come in and is filling up the whole of the bedroom."

"… the waves were getting worse and … we were getting rammed up against the wall."

"… I couldn't breathe. I really, really, really could not breathe …"

"… I looked out the window and I saw the body of a dead man …"

"… we hit the ceiling and … In my head, I had this voice going, 'Get out! Get out! Get out!'"

"… we grabbed the tree and held on …"

Acknowledgements

To all the wonderful people who shared their stories, poems and pictures to make this book, thank you:

Donna Baxter • Martha Binns • DeAnn Blackman • Annette Blunt • Alex and Lisa Bodden • Mary Bodden • Zoe Bodden • Garry Bosley • David Bowerman • Mary and Mike Bowerman • Brenda Bryce • Mona Bush • Cleo Conolly • Frank and Alma Conolly • Max Consolini • Mirasol Deguzman • Monica Dehaney • Nalya Dixon • Nathan Dixon • Tina Dixon • Vernon Dixon • Rollin and Etta Ebanks • Theresa Foster • Louisa Gibson • Jennifer and Michael Godfrey • Maxine Harriott • Godfrey Harrison • Anthony Hurlston • Daniel Hurlston • Denham and Melva Hurlston • Harry Hurlston • Stephen Hurlston • Robert Joseph • Frank Kahoun • Christina Godfrey-Kirkaldy • Ryan Kirkaldy • Taylor Kirkaldy • Carole Kirkconnell • Ann Margaret Lauer • Wendy Lauer • Shelley Leonard • Barbara Levey • Wilston Levy • Carla Ebanks Martinez • Dennis Mastry • Shona McGill • Hebe McKenzie • Donnova McLaughlin-Christian • Bradley McLean • Bill McLeod • Merlyee Moore • Merlene and Keith Morrison • Pam Needham • Errol Nisbeth • Kathleen Oliver • Goldie Panton • Heather Panton • Robert Parr • Ed Powers • Rosanna Ridley • Aileen Samuel • Gordon Smith • Cecilia Solomon • Melligan Solomon • Nicola Sowerby • Ladner Watler • Michael Watler • Sophia Watler • Chip Whitney • Charron Whittaker • Catilda Wilson • Horace Williams • Grace Wright • Lindsay Wright

A project such as this takes many hands and heads, and sharing of responsibilities. I had the opportunity to share these responsibilities with family and friends (old and new), which made it such a satisfying experience. I especially wish to acknowledge these people, without whom this book would never have been possible.

ACKNOWLEDGEMENTS

I owe a tremendous amount of gratitude to my friends, Mary and Mike Bowerman, not only for their support, but for their generosity in offering their time and energy to edit the book for me. I realize what an enormous task this was and cannot thank them enough.

I also want to thank my new friends, Mrs. Valerie Facey and Professor Alexander McCall-Smith. I feel blessed and extremely fortunate to have met such incredibly knowledgeable individuals who cared enough about Cayman and its people to offer me guidance and expert advice so that 'Hurricane Ivan Survival Stories' could make it to the printers in a timely manner.

I would also like to express my appreciation to Mrs. Emma Dinwiddy for writing the foreward for the book and my friend, Shelley Leonard, as well, for designing the book's cover and assisting me in so many areas of graphic design and book making. Ales Cevela was also a huge help with his technological 'know how', and Haff Daugherty Graphics went out of their way for me. For this I am extremely grateful.

I thank my family in a big way - in particular, my mother and brothers, who were a great comfort to me over the telephone in the days and weeks following the storm. I also thank my parents-in-law, Helen and Edlin Merren, for their support in this endeavour and for always treating me more like a daughter than a daughter-in-law, my husband, Greg, for his support and love, and our children, Josh and Zachary, for their patience over the past few months while Mom spent hours on end working at the computer instead of out fishing with them!

And I thank God. If it had not been for prayer, I surely would have never finished this book! One of my prayers is that we never have a reason such as Hurricane Ivan to write another book of Cayman survival stories!

-Terri Merren

Table of Contents

TABLE OF CONTENTS

Aquart and Kirkaldy children walking along the 'broken road', South Sound.
Picture taken by South Sound resident, Christina Godfrey-Kirkaldy

Foreword

It is a very great honour for me to have been asked by Terri Merren to write the foreword for this moving and inspiring publication.

In the days following Hurricane Ivan numerous people spoke to Terri about their experiences before, during and after the hurricane. The result is this beautifully documented book, "*Hurricane Ivan Survival Stories*". Men, women and children speak about their experiences. Each account is unique. But common to them all is the spirit of courage, kindness and compassion, qualities that are so prevalent in these beautiful islands and which, in keeping with our long tradition, were just what were needed in the face of such an enormous challenge. People also spoke of their faith in God and of the great gift of life itself. There has been much suffering but I firmly believe that all those who survived have emerged stronger for the experience.

This book is not only an important historical document. It has played a key part in the recovery of the people. Talking to a sympathetic listener is a vital part of the healing process. I remember well the first time, while still in the fire station at the airport, that I spoke about how I actually felt following the storm. It was a great relief to unburden myself and gave me new strength. All too many people are still struggling to rebuild their lives after Ivan. But an enormous amount has already been achieved since the hurricane and I have great hope for the future.

I encourage everyone who knows and loves these islands to read this book.

Mrs. Emma Dinwiddy,
wife of His Excellency, the Governor of the
Cayman Islands, Mr. Bruce Dinwiddy

The Citrus Grove Building sheltered and saved the lives of hundreds of grateful people on the island during Hurricane Ivan, including the author of this book and her family. Many thanks to Maxine, Maureen and Attlee Bodden, Pansy and Andy Anderson and family for their usual, kind generosity, and also to the Uglands, McAlpine Ltd., and DeLoittes, who went out of their way for the safety and comfort of others!

Home Alone
- Bodden Town

When Merlyee Moore's boyfriend, Melligan Solomon who works the nightshift at CUC, left for work late Saturday evening, 11th September 2004, Merlyee wondered how bad the hurricane might be, as she knew she would be there in the *home alone*. Having grown up in her house and weathered many storms, she never imagined it would be as bad as it was. She told of her fight for survival many weeks after Ivan left Bodden Town and her home in a shambles. Melligan never thought Merlyee's life would be in danger after he left ... but little did he know. The following is their story in their own words:-

Merlyee Moore and Melligan Solomon

Merylee: Sunday, September twelfth was my birthday and I spent it in a clothes closet!

It all started around six-thirty Saturday night. I was wondering what was going to happen if we didn't get boarded up. I kept saying to Melligan, "Time is running out, the hurricane is coming and we need to board up." He was like, "No, nothing is going to happen." I said, "The wind is going to be bad. We have to board up." My house doesn't have any houses close by to protect it; it is just open for the wind. When I started panicking, Melligan finally said, "Okay, we're going to board up." A neighbour came to help him. I was there telling them which windows to board. When they finished putting the boards on the windows, I said, "Well, my nephew, Kevin, is coming to be with me so I'm going to be fine." Every five minutes, I was calling Kevin and saying, "Are you coming?" and he said, "Yes, Aunt Mimi, I'm coming, I'm coming." Eight o'clock … no Kevin. Nine o'clock … no Kevin. Ten o'clock … no Kevin. I said to Melligan, "Melligan, Kevin not reach here yet." Then, around eleven o'clock, Kevin, who was on his way from George Town, called and said, "I can't make it. I can't make it. I have to turn back. The wind is getting real bad." I started to get really disheartened then and I said, "Melligan, are you still going to work?" He said, "Yeah, I have to go in. They need me."

It was about eleven-fifteen when I heard the guy come and blow the horn and Melligan said, "Well, I gone," and I said, "You gone and leave me by myself?" He said, "Yes, I have to go." When I saw the tail end of the vehicle, I said, "Oh, my goodness. I'm going to have to ride this hurricane out by myself!"

Melligan: I HAD to go to work. I left my car in Bodden Town and carpooled with a group of guys. I left Merylee by herself in the house there, thinking it would just be a normal hurricane.

Merlyee: I went inside and closed the door. I looked around and knelt down and said a prayer. Then my cell phone started ringing. It was my sister in Philadelphia. She said, "Mimi, you know what you do. You go into the smallest room in the house." Around twelve o'clock I could really hear the wind but I didn't look outside again from the time I shut the door. I just lay down in the room and thought, What is going to happen to me? What is going to happen to all of us in this hurricane? I said, "Lord, just make it pass us and disappear."

At about twelve-thirty, I got a call from my nephew, Phillip. He asked me if I was going to be okay. He told me, that if he had known Kevin wasn't going to come to me, he would've come. I told him it was too late – that nobody could reach me now – and that everybody must just stay where they were and pray. I kept calling Melligan and I said, "You know, Melligan, I'm really scared. I'm really scared here by myself." He said, "No, don't worry. You going to be okay." So I hung the phone up and it rang again and it was my nephew, Phillip, again. He said, "Aunt Mimi, I'm going to call you every five minutes," and he did. My sister kept calling too.

Melligan: On Sunday morning at two o'clock, we start feeling the breeze. We were on North Sound Way and I was in the engine room. In there with me was Shane Williams, Marshall Watler, Marlon Smith, Shawn Miles, Sheldon Watler and then there was another group of guys.

When that breeze start, the sound that we hear in that engine room was like men crying. You never heard sounds like that. It sounded like what you would hear in Africa, in the jungle. Then it sound like somebody bawling, like a woman giving birth. Around three or four o'clock, water start coming into the engine room, doors start busting up and the building start shaking. We had to shut down everything and run to the control room. That's where we passed the time; in the control room, watching the seawater coming through the engine room. I couldn't say how fast it was coming but it was just so fast!

Merlyee: When the wind really started getting bad, I knew I was going to lose the roof. I went into the front bathroom with a pillow, a comforter, a bottle of Lucozade, a little radio and my cell phone, and I lay down. Every ten minutes, I was calling Melligan. At one point, I couldn't get him and I wondered what had happened to him in town. He was right up in the sound and the sea was right there. I thought something must've happened to him and I really started panicking. I was getting really nervous and started praying again.

Around one o'clock or one-thirty, I heard banging. I have a palm tree right by the front window and it was banging, banging against the house! I thought I should've cut that tree down. Then I heard the water shooting through the eaves of the house and the sheetrock start falling. I said, "Oh, my goodness! What am I going to do?" I called Melligan again and said, "The roof is going! The roof is going!" He told me to just move and go somewhere else. Now my cell phone was starting to die.

After the sheetrock start falling in that bathroom, my nephew called again and asked me if I was okay. I said, "No! Phillip, water is coming in. The water is coming into my bathroom!" He said, "Go in the next room, Aunt Mimi!" I could hear the fear in his voice.

When I came out of the bathroom, I was backing the pillow, the bottle of Lucozade, the radio, the flashlight and everything. I was holding all of this in my hands. I went into the smaller bedroom to lie down and the wind was humming! It was moaning! It was singing! It was so awful that I couldn't take it in there. So I moved out of that room and went into the smaller bathroom.

When I got in there, I was so tired. I just put my head down on the floor and lay there. Then I started to feel cold and realized the water was coming up through the tub and over it. I heard the front door start banging so I called 911 and told them that the wind was going to burst my front door in. I told the man I was by myself in Bodden Town. He told me not to come out of my house. He said, "Stay inside. Get a mattress and put it over your head in case the roof goes."

At this point, my phone went dead and I knew I had lost all contact. That's when I really started to panic! I then took the couch and pushed it in front of the door and went into the laundry room. I have an extra closet door so I put that across the door too. I pushed another couch against it but it was still moving so I had to get something heavier. I went and got Melligan's weights from in the room. I picked those weights up like they only weighed an ounce and I put them across the door. Then I felt some coolness by my feet and I knew the water was coming in under the door. It was saltwater coming in. So I got some towels and packed them up by the door. I got some tape and taped all around it. By the time I could tape that, I heard BOOM!

When I went in my room, I didn't see anything at first. So I opened my closet door. When I looked up, I saw that a big hole was in the roof and the water was just coming down and the sheetrock had dropped! I got a garbage bag and wrapped it around a broomstick. I got up on a chair and pushed that bag up into the hole. As soon as I pushed it up, it just took off. The wind just took it. But I didn't give up. I got another garbage bag and a towel this time and wrapped the bag around the towel. I got on the chair and pushed it up and it stayed that time! I was very determined to make sure I was safe.

As soon as I got out of that room, I heard this thing spinning. The trap door to get into the ceiling had lifted up and was spinning. It was spinning so fast ... like a top! Then it turned crossway and jammed. I said, "Thank You, Lord." Then I climbed up on a chair with the broomstick. I straightened it out and brought it back down flat.

I started praying. I said, "Lord, it's You and me and my mother in this house tonight," because my mother is dead. I said, "Lord, You are here with me and only You can guide the wind and control the sea." I was so scared but I knew the Lord was going to see me through.

After that, I went into the living room and sat down. I was talking to myself. I thought I was going crazy or something. I said, "I'm in this house. I don't know what's happening outside." Then I heard the big picture window start banging. Even though it was boarded up, it was banging, banging! I thought, Oh, my God. I told Melligan to put that board lower down! I was going crazy! The wind was getting under the board. Then I heard the screen door start banging really fast. I said, "Well, if the door bursts open, I'm going to the north room in the house."

Then, all of a sudden, the wind must've shifted. I heard the north window start moving. I went into the kitchen and saw that the wind had pushed out the window. I had a candleholder and I jammed the window with that and it held. But I was thinking, Oh, why did I stay in this place by myself?

Melligan: We lost communication sometime after four o'clock in the morning. One of the last phone conversations I had was Sunday morning around four with Merlyee. She was crying and saying that things were really getting rough and she didn't know why I had left her by herself.

But the very last people we managed to get a connection with told us what they heard was that, in Bodden Town, seawater was washing all over everything and that

Bodden Town was washing away. That's when the guys start worrying because we had men who couldn't get in communication with their wives and children. That's when I see men that have hearts like lions - tears coming out of their eyes.

I was thinking about all the bad things I ever said to my girlfriend and I was wishing I could take them back. I felt so worried for her in the house all alone. My heart was pounding so much that I didn't know what to do. I could've taken a bottle of rum and put it to my head at that moment, even though I don't drink anymore. Then we found some little jokes to say about somebody and we all burst out laughing and that took a little bit from our minds. I have to say, there was this young guy there with us, younger than me, Shane Williams. He was second to the captain. He's what kept us going. He was encouraging us and saying we were going to get through this thing. He was really good for such a young guy.

Merylee: Around four o'clock, I decided that I could get out of the house through the back. So I went and opened the back door and the water gushed right through. My little cat was in the washroom and I was calling him, "Come, kitty, kitty, kitty." I could hear him bawling but I couldn't see him. I thought he was going to drown because the water was so high in the washroom. I couldn't get the door closed because the water was hitting the door and it was starting to swell.

Before I knew it, water was all through the house. I tried sweeping and I used up every towel I had trying to keep the water out of one room but I couldn't stop it. All the carpet just started swelling. My computer was in the water. Everything was in the water and it was just me one in the house. I just had to leave it because, alone, I could not do it.

When the wind start getting bad again, I went to the middle room of the house. I was very tired. I was so exhausted! I went to lie down on the bed and I looked up and saw a strip of the sheetrock but I thought it was okay. But, as soon as I put my head back on the pillow, the sheetrock just flew off! It missed me by a fraction of an inch. It came down with a force … with a force! If I did not move my head, I would've been in there and nobody would've found me until it was too late.

The wind was really bad outside. I was walking in water in the house and the roof was gone, so I went into the closet. I got two plastic chairs and put my head on one and my feet on the other with pillows in the middle. I just pulled the clothes across and closed the closet door. I took my radio earphones and put them in my ears so that I couldn't hear the wind. I couldn't take it anymore! It was so bad.

I put my Bible on my chest and said, "Lord, they said this hurricane developed around Africa. Lord, these are the cries of Africa. These are the cries of those people suffering," because the wind was moaning and it was talking. The sound was just unbearable. I said, "Lord, You take control of this. You can calm this wind and You can take this water back."

I pulled myself up and I put my feet on the floor and it was a miracle. The water was gone and all that was left there on the floor was the mud. Then I hear this humming like 'M-m-m-m-m. M-m-m-m-m. M-m-m-m-m' and that was the sea going back. It was receding. God was pulling it back. I said, "Lord, You took control." I took the flashlight and started to read the Bible and I said, "Thank You, Lord. Thank You." But I stayed in the closet. I went in there about six in the morning and stayed there for hours because the wind was still so strong.

When my clock would chime, that was what kept me going. When it chimed eight o'clock, I thought, Melligan should soon be here because that's what time he comes home. But … no Melligan. I was so worried.

Then I thought I heard voices and I wondered if someone needed help but I knew I couldn't open my front door and I was hoping that, if someone was there, they would remember that I had a back door. I listened but I didn't hear anybody again and I started crying.

Melligan: On Sunday, about eight o'clock at night, we tried to see if five of us could go to Bodden Town with different trucks but we could only get as far as by Biggie's tile place and we had to turn back because the water was so high. Shane Williams was so worried about his family and his children that he wouldn't give up. He wanted to take a try with a bigger truck but, when he came up to Ocean Club, he couldn't pass there because a house was blocking the road. He had to turn back. We couldn't rest all night.

Merlyee: When I came out of the closet, I had lost all track of time. I didn't know what day it was.

Melligan: On Monday morning, at four o'clock, we were up. We had just had about a five minute nap. Some of the guys just had no sleep at all. We were going to take a try again. We had to detour all the way because, coming by the airport, it was like the ocean. You couldn't believe there was any land there! And the homes were in such destruction that it made us wonder, if it is like this in town, what is left of Bodden Town? The surprise that we get, you had to have a good heart to take it because you couldn't tell it was Bodden Town. You couldn't tell at all that it was Bodden Town! There was all the sand, all the gravel and all the rocks. A buddy of mine had his house right by the church. When we got there, we couldn't find which road we had to turn into. He was asking where his house was.

Merlyee: Inside, the water had gone but, when I looked out through the window, the water was up to my window outside. I saw trees down and everything. Then I heard voices. It was my next door neighbours and they were outside so I knew that the storm was done and had passed. I took my flashlight and blinked it at them and they saw. They waved to me and said, "It gone! It gone!" I said to myself, "People are alive! They are out there!"

I opened the door that leads to the washroom and went to the glass door and looked out. Debris was everywhere. I saw zinc ... every tree was down ... power lines ... nails from the roofs ... everything that could be there! It was like the dump. There were so many things in the way that I couldn't get out of my house. When I went and pulled the front door open, I hear all the neighbours talking. To me, what they were saying didn't make sense. They were just gabbling on and on but everybody was okay. Everybody was fine!

Melligan: When I came to my home and saw the ocean, I start worrying because I didn't see NO sign of Merlyee and my heart start beating even more harder.

Merlyee: When I looked out through the front door, I saw people trying to make it through the water. There was so much zinc you had to be careful where you put your feet. My nephew, William, was coming through the water. They had to move all the power lines and zinc to get through. And, when William saw me, he said, "Oh! Aunt Mimi, you okay! You okay!"

Melligan: Thank God, when I got there, there she was, and she was alive!

Merlyee: Then I saw him! I saw Melligan! Oh boy! I was so overjoyed! And he was really happy to see me.

Melligan: Through this hurricane, my wish is that, a lot of people who had all the hatred and the families that lived with a malicious way - I pray in God's name that they will forget all that and live better because we lost material things, but it is life that is always important!

On Call
- Webster Estates

On Saturday night, 11th September 2004, Dr. Gordon Smith started out alone in his home in Webster Estates as his wife and children were already in Miami prior to Ivan's approach to Cayman.

As the night went on, Dr. Smith ended up with four visitors, one of whom was his father-in-law, Mr. John Franklin Bodden, who hadn't been well and whose life was in danger by mid-morning of the storm. The following is Dr. Smith's family's story of survival:-

On the Saturday night, my wife and two children were in Miami so I was just there, at the house on Webster Drive, on my own. My in-laws, Lilymae and John Franklin Bodden, arrived about eight o'clock that night because they had been persuaded by their family to leave their house which is only a hundred

Dr. Gordon Smith, in his office on Smith Road, George Town

yards away from my office on Smith Road. My father-in-law, John, is a dialysis patient and about three weeks prior to the storm he had been admitted to hospital with fluid on his lungs. In the end, it's a good job they did leave their house, as it lost its roof during the storm and had about four feet of flooding inside.

They arrived at my house about eight o'clock Saturday night. Shortly after that, my receptionist, Annisa Wood phoned. She used to live at a place called Woodland Glen just by Marina Drive. She called to ask me to come and pick her up because she was afraid the place might flood and she didn't want to drive in the bad weather conditions. So I drove through South Sound and even at eight o'clock Saturday night, the rocks and sea were coming across South Sound Road. I went up to Woodland Glen and came back down via Crewe Road. There was not too much flooding there at that stage.

So everyone got sorted out. Lilymae and John were in my bed and I slept in my son's bed. Annisa and her nine-year old son, Daniel, were in the guest bedroom.

I was looking out the front door at about half past three on Sunday morning, just watching the storm, and Lilymae came through from their bedroom and said, "John's feeling breathless and I think you better come and have a look at him." When I went to see him, he was sitting by the window trying to get some air because, of course, there wasn't any air conditioning by this time. I asked him, "How do you feel compared to three weeks ago when you were admitted to hospital … about the same?" He said, "Yeah, almost as bad." I knew immediately that we had to get him to a hospital within a half an hour because he had fluid gathering on his lungs and was basically drowning in his own body fluids.

I phoned 911 but the operator said, "The winds are too high and the ambulance can't come out. It would topple over and we would lose an ambulance."

Early on in the evening, Lilymae's car was positioned in front of the two garage doors. I had asked her to move it so that we had one car, just in case we needed to make a quick getaway, which we now did. We got John into the garage and into my wife's Jeep Cherokee and reversed out. Then I got out and closed the garage door down, left Annisa and Daniel at my home, and drove Lilymae and John to the hospital, along Walkers Road.

At that time, between half past three and four a.m., there were already a few trees down and I had to leave the road about three times to avoid them. I was trying to get to the hospital as fast as I could but not putting our own lives in any more danger than we were already in. There were a couple of big puddles along the road and some quite high winds but I'm from Scotland and we're kind of used to high winds and rain. The road by the four-way stop by the hospital was dry at that stage. We pulled into Casualty and beeped the horn. They were amazed to see someone arriving at the hospital but they opened the door for us.

I had been talking to John all the way along. Then he went quiet. When I went to get him out of the back of the car, I realized that he had just then stopped breathing. He had what we call a respiratory arrest where his lungs had stopped functioning but his pulse was still okay. I couldn't get him over my shoulder so we basically dragged him into a wheelchair and then onto a trolley and into the hospital, unconscious.

There was Dr. Fiona Robertson and Dr. Denise Osterloh to look after him. They gave him some oxygen and he responded but not all that well. His pulse never stopped.

So they intubated him, put him on a ventilator and took him upstairs to the ICU. About one or two hours after we arrived in ICU, there was an announcement on the tannoy saying that the emergency generator would now be switched off because of rising flood waters at the back of the hospital. I thought, Well, what do we do now for people who are on life support machines? The answer then was that every nurse in the hospital would take turns at 'hand bagging' them for fifteen minutes to a half an hour per session. It was a very precarious situation. John was hand-ventilated for about twenty-four hours - one nurse after another for about fifteen minutes each. All the nurses from Maternity, Pediatrics, Accident and Emergency, Surgery, off duty people … everybody helped.

After about twenty-four hours, the hospital got a small battery operated generator but there still weren't any lab facilities to monitor John's sodium and potassium, etc. and there wasn't any clean running water to dialyze him so it was very dodgy.

Sunday morning, once I had arrived at the hospital, I was tempted to go back home, since I had left Annisa and her son there. Then I thought that would be a rather hairy drive along Walkers Road and I had better preserve my own life and not risk the drive back. Late Sunday afternoon, about six o'clock, I attempted to walk along Walkers Road, as the storm had died down. But, outside Health Care Pharmacy, the water was still up to almost waist-high. There was about three or four feet of water there so I decided to overnight at the hospital with Lilymae. We camped outside of ICU.

On Monday morning, I got up at half past five as the sun was coming up. My car was okay because I had parked it in a good spot outside Accident and Emergency. It had a few scratches on it from flying shingles but it didn't get flooded. The front and side of the hospital were okay but the back of the hospital had four or five feet of water. I drove along the coast road, through George Town, and around past Smith Cove car park, to go home. There was a lot of debris; light poles, power lines, plywood, trees and everything in the road. I managed to somehow drive my way through but I couldn't get into my road. So, to get back into my house, I parked at Smith Cove car park and jumped over the wall and then into the garden.

There were tarpons swimming in the road but we were fortunate. When we were building the house, after getting some advice from APEC, we built eight feet above sea level. So we had no flooding inside the house.

After I jumped over the wall, the first thing I saw was one of my kid's toys, which had previously been in the garage. So I knew that there was some damage but was greatly relieved to see that the roof had stayed on and the people inside were okay.

The medical and nursing attention that my father-in-law received at the George Town Hospital was second to none so we are very grateful to everyone that saved his life.

A Strong Foundation
- Tropical Gardens

Rollin and Etta Ebanks built their house in Tropical Gardens many years ago and had stayed there during Hurricane Gilbert and other hurricanes. Rollin's sister, Christine Smith, a well-known Cable and Wireless telephone operator for thirty-one years, decided to ride out Hurricane Ivan with them, rather than being alone in her own home in the same neighbourhood. Four months after Hurricane Ivan tore the roof off and flooded their home of twenty-one years, Mr. Rollin and Miss Etta told of their horrifying experience:-

Rollin and Etta Ebanks

Mr. Rollin: We were hearing about Hurricane Ivan for a whole week. I think most people on the island were down in prayer, praying that it wouldn't hit us. Everybody was hoping it was going to be like all the other hurricanes, like Gilbert and a couple of others that have passed this way. Those all just came down and, in the last moments, they just fell off from us. I really thought that was going to happen again until Saturday night, when I realized we were going to get a big hit.

Miss Etta: Some years ago, when Gilbert was approaching, one of my sisters came to stay with us. She asked me then if I was scared and I said, "No, as long as Rollin is with me, I'm fine. If we're going to die, we're going to die together, holding hands."

Mr. Rollin: We had prepared the house so there was nothing else we could do but sit and wait, and ask God to take care of us. My wife, Etta, my sister, Christine, and

11

I were in our house. Christine came over to stay with us because there was no one in her house with her, as her husband had to work at the hospital. I built the foundation of my house very high because I know that, when you build in a new development with an unfinished road, you shouldn't build too low because, as the years go on, the roads keep building up. After awhile, if the house is too low, the road would be above it and the house would flood. So my foundation is about two feet above the road. When Gilbert passed through, I think about one hundred and twenty-five miles southwest of us, we had water in the yard up to the second step. I always told people, "Well, the day that you see a hurricane come and hit Cayman and the water come up and into my house, I think the whole island is in trouble."

Saturday night, we were in the den, playing hymns and drinking coffee, when the lights went out. I could hear the sea outside slapping against the foundation and I looked out and said to my wife, "Honey, this time I think the sea is going to come in!" It was then up to the level of the porch outside. We just sat in there, comforting one another – the three of us … and God. I always say that, once He's in the boat, we know we're going to get to the other side.

The storm was bad but the scariest thing for me was having the two women with me and knowing that my wife can't swim and not knowing how much my sister could. So my thoughts were really on trying to protect them.

All through Saturday night we didn't really get a good sleep but we dozed off a little. Sunday morning, we had tea around four o'clock. After that we were just listening to the wind howling and the water splashing outside. We were looking out and seeing our CRV floating up and down, all over the place. We could hear the shingles from other houses and some debris blowing around.

Miss Etta: When we got out of bed Sunday morning, we sat out in the living room. Paulette was playing some beautiful hymns on Radio Cayman. I had boiled water the evening before and had filled a thermos. So a little while later I made some tea for Christine and myself, and a cup of coffee for Rollin.

Mr. Rollin: Around eight o'clock was when the water really started to come in. The water was high outside, up to my window level, but we only had about two feet of saltwater inside the house. The wind had shaken up the window and the water was coming in through there. The doors were very tight so not too much water came in under them.

My house has this porch that goes right around and it was encased on the outside with sheetrock. Sunday morning, around nine o'clock, I could hear that sheetrock dropping as the wind was blowing the rain and the seawater up into it. When that sheetrock got soaked and dropped, I told my wife and sister, "I think we're going to have big problems now because that wind is going to get directly inside the roof."

Sure enough, that's what happened.

Miss Etta: Christine and I were having our tea. Rollin never even finished his coffee. All of a sudden, he said, "Honey, the fans are shaking. Let's get up from here before the water comes in and go to the bedroom."

Mr. Rollin: The wind had got inside the roof and was shaking the whole house.

Miss Etta: So all of us went to the master bedroom and sat on the bed. When the water reached my ankles, I said to Rollin, "Go to the kitchen and bring me some garbage bags." I emptied the three lower drawers of my dresser and the bottom drawers of Rollin's chest of drawers into the bags.

Mr. Rollin: About three gusts of wind came through and, each time, everything was rattling – all the ceiling fans were rattling. When the fourth gust came through, that's when we heard crashing and the whole roof just ripped off – not just one sheet of plywood at a time - the whole roof just ripped off and flew over into Rollin and Christine Jackson's yard, about two hundred yards away from my house. It just missed their house. God blessed them that the direction of the wind blew it more to the south. If it had landed on their house, their whole roof would've been gone too.

Rollin and Etta Ebanks with Christine Smith (right)

Miss Etta: Rollin had warned us to stay away from the window but Christine walked to the kitchen to look out. That's when we heard a big bang and she screamed. The sheetrock had fallen within inches of her head so she rushed back into the room with us.

Mr. Rollin: By the time she moved from the kitchen, almost the whole ceiling went. Everything just dropped down. So I told them, "Let's get into the smallest part of the house," which is the utility room.

Miss Etta: We hadn't quite reached there when we heard a big BANG and water started to pour down on us. I was frightened but I thought, The Lord has promised never to leave us or forsake us. I kept saying this in my heart. Rollin looked up and said, "Christine, you and Etta get the chair and put it over your heads and I'm going to stand in the doorway to break anything from falling on you." I was really scared then because I didn't want to lose him. [Fighting back tears] I said, "Okay, if we're going to die, we're going to die together." So I coaxed him to join us. We pushed the

Picture taken by Rollin Ebanks

Rollin and Etta's bedroom after the hurricane

washing machine away so all three of us could stand there together.

Mr. Rollin: The three of us got inside and stood there from ten o'clock in two feet of water. I opened the door that leads outside so I could see out. I could see that the fence between me and Rollin Jackson's house was underwater. There was five to six feet of seawater just going right through. It was hard to see through the wind, salt spray and rain. It was just like a white fog outside there!

Miss Etta: Rollin looked up and said, "This sheetrock is going to fall as well. What are we going to do then?" So Christine called Radio Cayman and said, "Our roof has blown off and we are going to die." Then a portion of the sheetrock in the corner fell and Rollin could now see in our bedroom and could see that God had saved a spot for us in there.

Mr. Rollin: We were just standing and standing for so long, watching the sheetrock drop down off the wall and off the ceiling in there, and the rain was getting to us. I looked at my wife and she was so blue that she was almost purple! She was cold and shivering. I was shaking too and kept having to move my arms up and down because they were starting to cramp. I had been holding a steel chair in front of me with the two of them crouching in a corner using the washing machine and the steel chair to keep any wood or debris from hitting them. It wasn't much protection with the way the wind was blowing and things were blowing so fast.

Around eleven o'clock, when the wall between the utility room and my bedroom dropped down, I could see that just one little corner of the roof was left in my bedroom. Our bed-head was high so I said to them, "All right, the only place to get protection is in there." So, one at a time, we would take a peek and, when the wind would ease off a little,

Picture taken by Rollin Ebanks

Rollin and Etta's kitchen after the hurricane

14

we would run and get behind the bed-head. I took a lawn chair so they could sit down.

Miss Etta: We sat on the chair and I put one of our pillows over my head and gave one to Christine. Rollin was very, very protective of us. He said, "You two stay there." The blinds were banging and a portion of the drapes were torn, so he tore the rest of them off.

Mr. Rollin: I was going to try to move the mattress. Everybody had been told that, in a hurricane, you should get a mattress and put it over you but we had a king-size bed with a king-size mattress. It would've taken ten people to move it because it was soaked with rainwater, plus all of the sheetrock had dropped down on it and the fiberglass insulation was down amongst it.

The fiberglass was killing us. My sister, Christine, nearly went crazy with that! At one time, I was so worried about her that I said, "Christine, do you think you're going to make it?" She said, "No, I don't think I'm going to make it, Rollin. I really don't think I am." Then I said, "Lord, help me because, if anything happens to her, I know she's going to die because we can't get her to a hospital. Help me that she can make it." She has diabetes and things like that. She had these chills and this fiberglass was sticking in her. There was nowhere for anybody to lie down or, much less, sit down properly.

We stayed there in that position until sometime after twelve o'clock. About that time, the blinds were banging and I went to pull them up. About ten minutes after that, I looked out and saw two men standing outside my bedroom window with motorcycle helmets on! The first thing that came to my mind was, Well, I know that they did not come here on a motorcycle! I pushed up the window and found out that one of them was my neighbour's son from two houses above me. He had come over with a friend of his and said that his mother wanted us to come up and shelter with them. She had about three feet of water in her house, which by now had receded, and their roof was intact.

Miss Etta: So we were rescued but the way the rescue came about was that, Saturday, our neighbour, Lindsay, had come by and said, "Rollin and Etta, this doesn't look good, you know. What are you going to do? Are you staying here or are you going to a shelter?" We told her we were going to stay here. She said, "Okay, we are staying home as well because our house is two floors and, if anything, we can go upstairs." That was what prompted her to send her son and his friend to check on us.

Mr. Rollin: We were so glad to see somebody and to get out of our house! By that time, since we had moved from the utility room to the bedroom, I forgot that we had left the door open there and we went out through the living room window! There was so much wood against the front door that we thought the window was the only way out. We grabbed up what we could – mine and my wife's medication and things like that and we went out with the two young men. We had to bend down to keep ourselves from being blown away because the wind was so strong. It was a good thing that the water had gone down a bit because, at this time, it was still up to about four feet. If it was as high as it had been, we would never have made it. One of the boys took my wife, and the other one held my sister. I went by myself because I was carrying the things that we grabbed up.

Miss Etta: It was very difficult walking down because the wind was very strong. I get palpitations sometimes so I kept my mouth open to get enough oxygen. May God bless Lindsay's son, Chipper, who helped me. He was very protective of me and had a very tight grip on my arm. I did not know who he was until we stepped into Lindsay's yard. I looked up at him and said, "Oh, you're Lindsay's son, Chipper! Thank you for rescuing us!" Lindsay and her daughter-in-law had huge towels and wrapped us up because we were cold. Then we rested.

Mr. Rollin: Thank God for good neighbours! I love all my neighbours around me and I'm sure that they all love us. We sheltered there with them until Thursday.

I have apartments on Ryan Road and, on the Wednesday, one of my tenants came up to check on us. When she saw the devastation to my house, she invited us to stay with her, so we did for a week.

Christine's house only had minor damage compared to ours. Although she had water in there and a lot of her sheetrock had come down, her roof was still intact. So we've been staying with her since then.

Our apartments on Ryan Road didn't get damaged so the Lord blessed me there. It would've been too much on me to have to rebuild there and to rebuild my house. Everything in the house is gone – everything, that is, but the kitchen sink! I still have that.

Miss Etta: When I went by our house Monday morning and reached halfway into the living room and saw the devastation, I cried. But God is an awesome God. We have lost a lot but, like someone told us, He didn't promise to bring us this far and leave us. He never left us. His hands held us and protected us. We were soaking wet and we were in the fiberglass but we did not even sneeze!

Picture taken by Rollin Ebanks

Rollin and Etta's house, Monday, 13th September 2004

An Angel Watches Over Us
- South Sound

Barbara Levey and Ed Powers, owners of the Book Nook in the Galleria Plaza and Anchorage Centre, have resided in South Sound for over twenty years. Because they have five small dogs, they felt they needed to stay in their home for the hurricane instead of going to a shelter. The following is their story of survival:-

Barbara Levey and Ed Powers with a couple of their dogs, at home in South Sound, four months after the storm

Ed: We have been living in our house on Mary Read Crescent for fourteen years. Just before Hurricane Charley, in August, for the first time, I had hurricane shutters installed on the house. After Charley, I was saying how not one leaf blew off our trees and we went to all the trouble of putting up those shutters! I wasn't in any hurry to put them back on again for Hurricane Ivan, but I did it anyway.

Barbara: On the Saturday night of the storm, we drove down to the South Sound dock. The water was coming over the dock then but we had no idea it was going to get as bad as it did. We woke up Sunday morning at seven o'clock. Although it was blowing hard, we called relatives and said, "Don't worry. Everything's fine." Within an hour, the water started coming in under the side door of the house. It was rising so quickly. I told Ed that the showers were making a funny bubbly noise.

Ed: I knew right away that the septic tank had come up but I didn't tell her that. Once I saw that the water was up to the first panel of the glass on the French doors, I knew we were in trouble. I was scared, as I knew at that point we were surrounded by ocean water. I didn't want to get Barbara panicked but I knew I had to get her and the dogs up into the attic.

Barbara: So he pulled down the attic stairs and helped me get up into the attic with our five dogs. I wasn't really scared at this point.

Ed: After Barbara was up there, I handed the dogs up one at a time, together with a few bottles of Evian and our important papers. I took up with me an ice chest, a twelve volt light so we could see, and my tools just in case we needed to break through the roof, as we had no idea how high the water would rise.

Barbara: From up in the attic, we were watching the water come up the wallpaper on the wall downstairs. It quickly got up to about four feet. So Ed said, "Okay, we're going to leave the dogs in the attic and we're going back down." They are little dogs so we were afraid they would drown.

Ed: I was thinking, Do I want to get killed by the rising water downstairs or do I want to die up here in the attic when the wind blows the roof off? The roof tiles were breaking off not only from our house but other houses as well, and skipping across our roof. They were making the most horrible sound I'd ever heard and the wind sounded like very loud, low, deep rumbles! Then a big blast would hit with percussion and the house would shake. There were also these fast bursts that sounded like bombs or cannons going off. It was really very scary! At that point, I just felt sick inside. I really thought that was it for us but I was trying to remain calm for Barbara's sake. I was thinking to myself, I'm going to die. All the years and everything I've done in my life has come to this. In five minutes, it's going to all be over.

I didn't know if a tidal wave was going to come or if the wind was going to take the roof off so I made the decision that we had better get out of the attic. I thought our chances of living were better if we floated on cushions rather than staying up there. We had no choice but to leave the dogs so we left them there with the twelve volt light on.

Barbara: When we got downstairs, we looked out the side door, which was the only door that wasn't covered with hurricane shutters. It was a steel door and by now it was bent almost in half from the force of the wind and seawater. When Ed went to straighten it, it fell off so now there was no door there at all! We were now debating on whether we should leave the house or stay. Ed said, "Maybe we should go. It might rise as high as the ceiling," but I said, "Ed, they said not to leave the house even if it gets bad and I'm not going out there in that," as there were whitecaps in the carport. Ed had gotten sofa cushions for each of us in case we had to float. We decided that, since there was no place to go other than to float on those cushions out in the swamp, we'd better stay inside! I was getting a little scared then and even asked Ed, "Are we going to die?" and he said, "I don't think so."

Picture taken by Ed Powers

Barbara and Ed's cars after the storm.

Ed: I really thought we WERE going to die but I didn't want to tell her that.

Barbara: By that time, which was about nine-thirty, everything was floating. The fridge was floating, and the clothes dryer had broken free and was floating through the house. The water inside the house was black, a combination of seawater and sewage! Ed pushed the clothes dryer down in the dining room and helped me up on top of it. Then he sat on top of two tables, which were stacked on top of one another. We sat like that, with the five dogs up in the attic, for eight hours until the water got low enough to let the dogs down. When the dining table, which had been submerged, floated up, we climbed onto that and had a little nap.

Barbara: Our two cars, which had been parked in our garage and the van in the driveway were all ruined by the saltwater. The neighbours' SUV, which was parked in front of their house across the street, floated into our driveway, smashed into our car and turned it around.

On the Tuesday after the storm, since we now had no vehicle, Ed rode a bicycle to our partner, Jeanne Brenton's house which is next to the Grand Old House and borrowed her car to go and feed our parrots in the store. The parrots miraculously survived the hurricane. The store did not.

Picture taken by Ed Powers

Barbara and Ed's back garden,
Monday, 13th September 2004.

To me, the worst part of the hurricane was the aftermath! The nasty water had soaked into our couches and all our furniture. It had gone into our dresser drawers so all our clothes were wet. The beds were all wet so there was no place to sleep that was dry. We had towels that had been up high and stayed dry but as soon as we put them on the bed, they were wet too. We couldn't dry the clothes inside so we put them out on a line to dry. As soon as we brought them back in though, since the house was so damp, they were wet again. No matter how much we cleaned and mopped out the house during the day, the nasty water which had been absorbed by the walls would seep back out onto the floors during the night. That went on for days.

There was no electricity, no water, no telephones, no cars … nothing. Everything was so primitive. It was like we were starting over. The streets were covered in sand and looked like the beach. Most of the trees were down so, when people came to see us, they couldn't find the house. All the usual landmarks were gone.

Ed: After the storm, our friend and co-worker, Winsome Prendergast, came to visit and to bring supplies to us like food and water. The only way she could get to us was to wade through the swamp water. We were very grateful to her and in return for her thoughtfulness, we let her siphon gasoline out of our cars, which were no longer of use to us.

Barbara: Our cars were destroyed, our house was badly damaged, and our store, Book Nook at Galleria, was totalled. The water came up to at least four to five feet high and it lost its roof. Other people had it a lot worse than us though, so we feel very fortunate. Someone told me the other day that there's an *angel watching over* us and I said, "Yes, we've always believed that because of my daughter, Julie, who we lost in a diving accident in August of 1979. It's like she watches out for us." Things have happened over the years that made us say, "She's at it again." When we look at our house and compare it to the other houses in South Sound, we feel fortunate and think she was watching out for us THIS time too!

LEFT: *Barbara and Ed's pool BEFORE the storm*
BELOW: *Barbara and Ed's pool AFTER the storm*

Pictures taken by Ed Powers

Saving Mrs. Harquail
- Whitehall Gardens

On the Saturday when Hurricane Ivan was slowly making its approach to Cayman, a Filipino couple, Cecilia and Alberto Solomon, together with their aunt, Mirasol Deguzman, a brother-in-law and a nephew, decided to take refuge in their small home on Mrs. Helen Harquail's property to make sure that Mrs. Harquail survived the storm. Cecilia and her Auntie Mirasol fought back tears as they recalled the events that unfolded during the early morning hours of Sunday, 12th September:-

Picture provided by Cecilia Solomon

Alberto and Cecilia Solomon (left), with Mirasol Deguzman

Cecilia: We knew the hurricane was coming and my husband, who works for Mrs. Harquail, decided we should stay by her so she would be safe. So on Saturday morning, I phoned my Auntie Mira to ask her to stay with us because she told me that she would stay in her apartment on Eastern Avenue but the apartment is not very strong. She said, "Okay."

My employer, Miss Jan, phoned me in the afternoon encouraging me to go to the Hurley's shelter with her family. She was asking me where we were going to stay when the hurricane came. I told her the house where we were going was okay. When I get home, I asked my husband if he wanted to go to the Hurley's shelter and he said, "No, we have to stay here with Mrs. Harquail because she doesn't want to go out. She wants to stay here."

Because my husband is an employee of Mrs. Harquail, we live on her property in a separate house. Five of us were in our house: my husband, Alberto, my Auntie Mira, my brother-in-law, Franco, and our nephew, Roberto. Mrs. Harquail will be ninety-two years old in December, so we didn't want to leave her. She was in her house, on the same property, next to us.

On Saturday night, we were just telling stories and phoning Mrs. Harquail all night to see if she is okay. We just were sitting and listening to the sound of the wind and waiting for the hurricane. We didn't have boards on the windows so we could see out. That night, our neighbours are moving to the shelter and they are beeping their car horns very loudly indicating for us to come.

Mirasol: We didn't sleep all night but, on Sunday morning, we went to sleep about five o'clock and then they woke me up around six o'clock. We were having our breakfast and looking out the window and we see that the wind is so strong. About eight o'clock that morning, Cecilia's brother-in-law said, "Look, outside the water is coming up!" Then we decide to pack our things and go over to Mrs. Harquail.

Cecilia: The water started to come inside our house and we were panicked and decided we need to move. By now, the water was above our knees outside the house.

In plastic bags, we grabbed lots of things, like clothes, laptop and passports. We were very scared. Mirasol was the one to go out first but, when she opened the door, it hit into her face and knocked her down to the ground.

Mirasol: The wind was so strong. The door hit me and I fell. Now the water was really coming into the house. I was so nervous at that time that I didn't realize the door had hit me. My eyeglasses were lost. I found them three days later.

Cecilia: We walked to one side of the house holding onto each other and we need to grab onto the trees and the fence because the wind and the water were taking us.

Mirasol: It took us fifteen to twenty minutes to walk across because it was so hard to move. The wind was coming in so strong this way and we were going that way. We were going against the wind.

Cecilia: After that, we were at Mrs. Harquail's and we knocked on the door. It took a long time because everything was so loud and she was busy inside. We knocked on the door for five minutes and then the dog started to bark and that's when she came to the door and let us in. She had been holding onto the window inside because it was shaking and trying to blow in. It sounded outside like "wh-ew-ew-ew-ew-ew-ew" and it was raining.

Mirasol: When we got in, Cecilia told her brother-in-law to hold that window for Mrs. Harquail. Then my nephew, Roberto, found a string to tie the window but it didn't work because the wind was too strong. We were in the house maybe an hour, around nine o'clock, when the water really started to come in.

Cecilia: Then the door in the back of the house broke open and the water started coming. Now we panicked again. The water was up to our chests so we planned to go up in the attic in Mrs. Harquail's bedroom but she did not want to go. So my husband and I went up there in the attic with our things but it was very dark. I said, "I don't want to go there. I want to stay down in the home and maybe we can pass the water out." I didn't want to be trapped in the attic if the water kept going up. It's very dark there. So we just put our things up there and decide not to stay there.

Mrs. Harquail walked slowly and her furniture and everything was floating and she wanted to save all her things, like lampshades and things. But we said, "Madam, just leave it. Let's go." And then, when we were in the door, my brother-in-law said, "Oh, I know one more attic," and so he went outside on the side of the house to look. We were lucky because Mrs. Harquail just built this new roof so there was a new attic.

After we decided to go there, Mrs. Harquail said, "Oh, my purse!" So my husband went to go look for the handbag of Mrs. Harquail because her passport was there. He came with the bag and then he said, "Okay, here's your bag." Then Mrs. Harquail said, "Oh, Mitzi!" That's Mrs. Harquail's dog. She said, "Oh, Mitzi! Get Mitzi!" So my husband went back and got Mitzi. He found her on top of the table because the water was so high.

Mirasol: When we went out there, they got a ladder but it was very hard to go up because the ladder was short and it was in water.

Cecilia: My nephew, Roberto, was leaning against the ladder, holding it, so that it wouldn't float. It was so short that it was hard to get up into the attic. My brother-in-law, Franco, went into the attic first and then Mrs. Harquail went up the ladder. Then my husband, Alberto, had to go up the ladder under her. Mrs. Harquail put her feet on his shoulders because she wasn't high enough to reach the attic. Alberto climbed up and hoisted her up while she was standing on his shoulders. Then my brother-in-law pulled her up into the attic. That's how we all got up. After my husband was in, he tied the ladder with Mitzi's dog leash so it wouldn't float away.

Mirasol: We tried to call 911 but could not connect. So that's where we stayed from about nine o'clock until about two o'clock … waiting for a rescuer.

Cecilia: Before we went up, I phoned my brother-in-law, who works for Mrs. Olde. I wanted to know if they were okay because we were not okay. His phone would ring, but if they answered it, the line would cut off. I was worried because they were by the sea in East End. Mrs. Harquail kept asking, "Did you phone them? Did you reach them?" She kept asking me that.

When we were in the attic, the roof was shaking. We were thinking that it was a tornado because the roof was shaking so much. We were crying. We were praying. I was saying, "Oh God, do we have to die? I want to see my children. We are here to work for them." It was a long time we were crying. We had a chair up in the attic for Mrs. Harquail to sit on … and she was crying too. You didn't hear her but you can see the tears in her eyes.

While we were there and I was crying and praying, my husband said to me that if it got so bad, I must save myself. One of us had to survive for the children. It was very long that we were in the attic and the wind and rain were so strong. We thought it was never going to be stopped.

The wind sounded like "Z-z-z-z-z-z-z-z-z" and the roof was shaking all the time. I was so worried about my nephew, Roberto. We were worried that he was going to die before he could see his new baby that was just born. It was already Monday back home and his wife had already given birth. Early Sunday morning, when I saw Roberto's cell phone, there was a missed call from the Philippines so he tried to phone back but he could not connect. We knew they phoned to tell him that the baby was born. Days later, after he talked to them at home, they told him they named the baby 'Ivan'.

Around two o'clock, the men went down and said that the water was going down and they would go and look for a higher ladder but it was in Mrs. Harquail's garage and the wind was still too strong. The ladder we had was too short so we had to hang down to almost the ladder and let go and jump down.

After the hurricane, I called my children and told them what had happened to us and they asked why I didn't come home and … [long sobs and silence]. I just thank God that we survived and want to forget that it happened.

Mirasol: Mrs. Harquail … she loves gardening but now her garden is all destroyed. All of the trees are down. Alberto and Franco are working hard to fix it back up. Mrs. Harquail's truck and her Toyota were flooded in the hurricane. We all lost our cars. There were five of them.

Cecilia: Mrs. Harquail stayed in her house that night and we stayed in our house. All our things had flooded and were wet. We lived there that night in our wet bed with plastic garbage bags over the bed but we didn't sleep at all. Before we went to our house, we knew that Mrs. Harquail was hungry so we gave her hot noodles – Chicken Noodle Soup. Then, early Monday morning, my nephew saw some light. It was Mrs. Harquail outside shining her flashlight. So my nephew said, "Maybe she's calling because she needs to be rescued." So my husband went there and made coffee for her. She had slept in a chair that night.

That day, Monday, my husband told Mrs. Harquail, "We only stayed here for you. We wanted you to be saved because we love you." Mrs. Harquail was very thankful. She said, "Thank you." When people came by the house after the hurricane and asked, "Where is Mrs. Harquail? Is she okay?" We said, "Yes, she is okay because we saved her."

A River Runs Through It
- South Sound

While preparing for Hurricane Ivan on Saturday, 11ᵗʰ September 2004, Alex and Lisa Bodden knew they were in for a bad storm. They just did not know HOW bad. They, together with their twenty-four month old daughter, Stephanie, endured nineteen long hours in the attic of their home, with their two dogs, after the sea came crashing through their bungalow on The Avenue in South Sound. Fighting back tears, Lisa, together with Alex shared their amazing story of survival:-

Alex: We live in South Sound on The Avenue. Our house faces South Sound Road and is approximately seventy-five yards from the waterfront.

On Saturday, 11ᵗʰ September 2004, we took care of our business

Alex and Lisa Bodden with their daughter, Stephanie.

interests in terms of going to our offices, securing our computers, etc. Then we went home. During the day, we were keeping an eye on Ivan's track on-line. It continued to get worse with every update.

As the storm was approaching, the winds were really intensifying across the whole island. We were at home from lunchtime on Saturday. We had no real thoughts of leaving the house although family members had asked us what we were going to do.

25

Some family members were going to Lisa's parents' house but we decided that we were confident enough to stay in ours. We thought we would be okay. Saturday afternoon, we had a family meeting at Lisa's parents' house and then headed back home, which is about a ten minute drive. As we started to drive down South Sound Road, at the corner of Old Crewe Road, seawater was already starting to wash across the road. We had seen this with previous storms so we weren't unduly worried. We just knew we were in for a reasonably bad storm. When we got home, the first thing we did was close the garage doors and back the cars up against them to provide support for them. We then started to get our supplies together in terms of organizing them in the house. We had purchased a portable gas cooker and sat that up on the kitchen counter. This would later prove to be an absolute blessing for us.

We lost our main water supply at about five-thirty in the afternoon and the power went off at about six forty-five in the evening. The winds were continuing to get stronger but incredibly both the landline and cell phones were still working. This enabled us to keep in contact with family and also to keep track of the storm up until late in the evening. As the storm continued to get worse through Saturday evening, we decided to go to bed early because we thought we might have trouble sleeping and we didn't know what time we would be up on Sunday morning. We never got any proper sleep because the winds were very, very strong. The sounds were getting incredibly loud. At approximately four a.m., due to the noise, we were up. Our daughter, Stephanie, couldn't sleep either.

Once it got light and, whilst Lisa tended to Stephanie, I took the opportunity to start videotaping out front and at the back of the house. It never really got fully light, as everything looked gray outside. By seven a.m., the wind and rain were howling and screaming across the house. Out front, South Sound Road, about thirty yards in front of our house, was a raging *river*. All sorts of debris like kayaks and whatever were washing by but there was no water actually on our property yet.

Lisa: While Alex was videotaping, I was in the kitchen finishing off breakfast with Stephanie. I will always remember that moment, looking out through the kitchen window into Sidney Coleman's property. It was amazing just watching the water as it started to creep onto the property.

Alex: At about eight o'clock in the morning, I was continuing to tape from the shelter of our entranceway out front. I was filming huge, mature coconut trees being blown over, our hedges being flattened and our garden just basically being destroyed. The wind and rain just kept getting stronger and stronger. It was at this point that water started to come onto the front and rear of the property, and our garden became flooded. I went out to the back porch where there is a substantial wooden structure and the wind just started to rip it apart like it was matchsticks.

At nine a.m., the front yard and back yard were completely flooded. At this point, our toilets started to back up and I told Lisa that I knew we had real problems, as the water table was now above ground level.

Lisa: It was at this point that I phoned my father to inform him that the property was flooded. We didn't yet have any water in the house but given what we were seeing on the outside, I called to tell him that we could not escape from the home and that our backup plan would be to go into the attic.

Alex: At nine-thirty, water started seeping through the front door and the garage door. I started grabbing towels and whatever I could to plug the gaps around the doors. I felt like King Canute, trying to hold back the seas but nothing was going to stop it. It was at this point that I felt like crying, as I knew the house was in serious trouble, let alone the potential problems there might be for my family and myself.

Lisa: During the preparation time before the storm, we had made a note of important documents and essentials that needed to be packed for the baby and ourselves. This was when Alex nodded to me indicating that I should get the things together. I had the baby with me in the master bedroom putting together all the important documents and grabbing all of Stephanie's things as well. I went back into the kitchen, put everything up on the kitchen counter and also a cooler in which we had packed extra milk for Stephanie. This is when both Alex and I knew that we were in trouble.

Alex: It was now about ten o'clock on Sunday morning. Our house had a big, heavy wooden door but it was no match for the sea. I was trying to jam the door with a sofa wedged against the wall behind it but it was hopeless. The water was pouring in and the level was rising rapidly up to my knees, then up to my waist. I checked on the other end of the house. The water was pouring in through the garage door. It opens outwards and was jammed. At approximately ten-thirty, the water was up to about three to four feet. Lisa, Stephanie and one of the dogs went onto the kitchen counter. We have two dogs but could only find the one which we have had for ten years. I eventually found the dog at the far end of the house floating on a piece of furniture and got her into the kitchen. So the four of them were on the kitchen counter as the water continued to rise.

I was trying to move things of importance up, like photo albums and such. I had given up on the hi-fi and T.V. and everything. I was just doing what I could to save whatever I could at this point. It was an almost impossible task.

At just after ten-thirty, the front door completely ripped open and the sea came rushing in. I was smashed off my feet and swept right from the front to the back of the house by this wave. I had no control. The water took me straight past the kitchen and past Lisa and Stephanie. I was scrambling, trying to regain my feet, trying to grab hold of something but I couldn't. I could hear Stephanie starting to scream. I was just trying to stop myself. What stopped me were the sliding glass doors at the back of the living room. I slammed into those and they didn't give way. That was the only thing that stopped me from being washed outside through the back of the house.

Lisa: I can honestly say that this part of the hurricane was the scariest part for me. It was so difficult watching Alex helplessly float around in the back of the house while Stephanie was in my arms literally squirming and screaming for her daddy. She was a bit wet because of all the salt spray from the waves, which had come through. The two dogs were frantic on top of the kitchen counter. I was trying to keep hold of our cameras, photos, passports, food … you name it.

Whatever we had put on the kitchen counter to keep safe, I was there in the middle of all this trying to keep calm whilst potentially losing my husband. I just thank God that I still had Stephanie in my arms trying to keep her calm. This was the only time I can remember her crying. She had kept calm throughout the buildup to this point in the storm. Eventually, when Alex was able to hold onto a piece of furniture, he was able to meet us back at the kitchen counter and to reassure Stephanie that he was okay. But this was not the end of it.

Alex: I sustained just a few cuts and bruises so I was very lucky. When I was being carried through the house by the sea, I had to subconsciously make a decision about what to do next. I think that, in a situation like that, human nature kicks in and you just go into a sort of auto-pilot mode. You've got responsibilities so you can't give up.

After the waves calmed down, the water was obviously continuing to rise and I noticed that the water level outside at the back of the house was about a foot higher than that inside, so I decided, whether it was wise or not, to equalize the levels. I thought that if I didn't, the sliding doors might disintegrate and I didn't know what sort of problems that would then cause. So I made the decision to open one of the sliding doors and, instantly, the doors just popped out and fell straight out into the water outside. I clung on and didn't go with them. The water rushed in and that took the level up to the edge of the kitchen counters with additional surges. This was at about eleven o'clock in the morning.

At this point, we made the decision that we had to get up into the attic. I went to open the garage door because that's where the attic door is but I couldn't open it. It was jammed. The water had started to rip into the sheetrock wall beside the inside garage door. The bottom of the wall was starting to pull away. The only way to get into the garage was for me to smash the rest of that wall out, which I did with my bare hands. In normal circumstances, I might not have been strong enough to do that. I made a hole big enough above the water level for us to climb through in order to get out into the garage. When I did this, I found that the garage door had been jammed tight by the hot water tank, which had been ripped away from the wall. This was wedged against the door with all the debris from the garage smashed against it.

As I climbed out, I saw that the garage doors had gone. Our two cars were floating around in the garage. The only way up into the attic was to climb onto Lisa's car and reach up and pull down the attic ladder. Lisa's car was bobbing around like a duck. It was very tricky and I was concerned about how I was going to get both Lisa and Stephanie up there. I got the ladder down and went back inside the house to the kitchen and grabbed Stephanie and led Lisa through the house in chest deep water to the hole I had made. Lisa climbed through first. Then I passed Stephanie to her. Then I climbed through.

The situation was just plain dangerous but it was the only way. It was very wet. The wind was howling and the rain was coming straight through the garage. The side garage door had been blown out so it created a sort of tunnel effect for the elements so it wasn't as if it was calm in there. It was almost as if the storm had intensified. Lisa climbed onto the hood of her car and up into the attic. I then managed to climb up onto the car with Stephanie and, since I couldn't reach up far enough to hand her up, I literally threw her through the attic opening and Lisa caught her. After I had Lisa and Stephanie up there, I threw the dogs up into the attic as well. During the course of the next hour or so, I continued to go around the house collecting things like pillows, important documents and food. I was doing shuttle runs between the house and the attic with anything I could get up there, both for our own comfort and simply to save things. What was very depressing was that every time I went back into the house, like into the living room or our bedroom, something else had gone underwater or had just disappeared. I lost track of what used to be there, let alone what still was there.

From lunchtime on Sunday, Lisa and Stephanie were up in the attic and I was up and down, as the water level did not appear to be getting any worse. I was continuing to do what I could downstairs which seemed to be a thankless task. I even managed to cook us some lunch, well some soup, on the gas cooker. In the attic, we were praying that the roof would hold. All the internal walls were being ripped out. About ninety-five per cent of our belongings were just being destroyed and washed away. The house looked like a bomb had gone off in it.

Up in the attic, the noise was incredible. It was just relentless! The roof was groaning and creaking. We just didn't know what was going to happen. We have very heavy, concrete roof tiles and they were just being ripped off. Whenever one was blown off, as it rolled across the roof it sounded like a machine gun being fired right next to our ears. It was so scary and so loud that it is hard to put into words. What I didn't mention to Lisa at the time was that we were sitting on the plywood floor of the attic next to the garage gable end which is only constructed of cement board. So throughout all of this time in the attic only a couple of inches of material was separating us from this howling storm outside.

What we continued to find amazing was that our cell phones continued to work, albeit erratically.

Lisa: I managed to get through to 911 and they told us to sit tight on as high ground as possible and ride it out as there was no chance of anyone getting to us. We also had text messages from family members giving us the same information, as they had also managed to contact 911.

Alex: Stephanie remained amazingly calm throughout this time and the rest of the day and night. We were, and will always be, so very proud of her for how brave she was during this horrible time. It was impossible to relax but we tried to close our eyes, as we were mentally, physically and emotionally exhausted. We didn't manage to get much rest, let alone any sleep that night. We kept the attic door partially open to avoid any potential vacuum problems, which obviously left us more exposed to the elements.

We were fortunate that we had had the space above the garage converted into an attic storage space only a couple of months before the storm. Otherwise, I'm not sure what we would have done because our home was being destroyed beneath us. We are grateful to the person who built the house because the roof structure somehow held, despite everything.

In the early morning of Monday, September 13th, we received either phone calls or text messages from family members saying that they would be trying to get to the house to rescue us if at all possible. At six a.m. when there was light, the winds had subsided and the water level had receded. I climbed down from the attic and ventured outside. The metal garage doors that had been ripped from their frames had been tossed to one side and just scrunched up like tissue paper. I looked around and the house opposite ours, belonging to Mr. Lawrence Thompson Sr., was gone. I very quickly realized that a large quantity of debris in our front yard was in fact part of the remains of his house. It was completely destroyed with only the concrete foundations left on the land. I looked around the rest of our property and there were bits of roofs, walls, appliances and personal belongings of unknown people everywhere.

I then walked back through The Avenue to see if it would be possible to get through the back of Ithmar Estates to the relative safety of a nearby family house which was on higher ground. We had heard that they were okay and their home was relatively undamaged but it was impossible to get through. As I walked around, other people were doing the same. Everyone had a sort of "shell-shocked" look on their face but in a subdued way everyone was glad to see both familiar and unfamiliar faces. South Sound Road itself was not visible, as it was covered by sand dunes washed up from the beach. I had to be quite careful walking about due to the wires and other debris.

Around seven a.m. I continued to walk down South Sound Road and finally met up with our brother-in-law, Tom Parsons, and his brother, Brent. We were so glad to see each other and were so grateful they were able to get to us because we could not risk, at that moment, taking Stephanie away from the safety of the attic. I, along with Tom and Brent, went to collect Lisa, Stephanie and the dogs. We walked about a mile down South Sound Road towards town to the nearest point that Tom could get to in his SUV. At one point on this walk, the sea had broken through and forged a *river* into the interior of the island. We, like many others, had to wade our way through this river.

As the days passed following the storm, we realized that basically the south coast of the island got hit the hardest. Everywhere got hit hard, but the south coast got the sea surge. I suppose we were just in the wrong place at the wrong time. Everybody suffered, though. To this day, however bad you think you had it, it's amazing the stories of others and what they had to endure and experience.

I think that in a way, Cayman was both cursed that weekend but at the same time blessed, because of the fact that there was so little loss of human life. It's just incredible that we're all still here. It's impossible to fully comprehend and appreciate the strength and intensity of Hurricane Ivan. While I was videotaping, I was trying to describe what I was seeing and most of the time, words failed me.

The storm brought out the best in people on the island, both Caymanian and expat, over the coming days and weeks. Without dwelling on the problems of looting and other minor social disorder problems, it is incredible how strong and caring people in the community were to both friends and strangers alike. It is best to focus on the life changing events that brought about a common bond which we believe in the long term will make this island a stronger and better place to live.

Lisa: We are so very thankful for the generous support and outpouring of love we were shown and are still being shown by our family and friends, in particular to Lori and Tom Parsons. They welcomed us with open arms to a very warm, comfortable and loving home after we had

The back of Alex and Lisa's house after Ivan

been through such an awful experience. Words cannot express how deep our feelings are on this point but we can only hope that everyone knows how truly grateful we are for the help we received. We hope to be back in our rebuilt home by Christmas 2005 and we truly hope that we never have to experience anything like this again in our lives!

A Wild Party
- Tropical Gardens

DeAnn Blackman, together with her parents, Randy and Lorna, stayed in their home in Tropical Gardens during Hurricane Ivan. They realized in the early morning hours of Sunday, 12th September, just how big a mistake this was. The following is DeAnn's recollection of that terrible morning when Ivan wrecked their home and separated her family for three long months afterwards:-

DeAnn Blackman, at home in Tropical Gardens

On September 8th 2004, everyone was shaking knowing that a Category Five hurricane was coming towards the Cayman Islands. Many people were making plans to fly off the island to other places to be safe from the hurricane. On Thursday, September 9th, I went to school and most of my class was gone. Most people were either preparing to leave or had already left the island. We left school at noon. At one o'clock my daddy and I went to A.L. Thompson's to buy some ply board to board up the windows. We also bought concrete nails and batteries. My mom was at her school storing and covering things, preparing for the hurricane. We made sure we had enough tin food, water and three flashlights. My dad had one big flashlight and my mom and I had two small ones. My mom and dad stayed up for most of that night putting up the ply board with the assistance of our neighbour. His daughters came over and we watched movies and ate popcorn until late while they were battening down the windows on my house.

On Friday, September 10th, the neighbour's wife and two daughters left to fly to Miami to escape the hurricane. That morning, my parents got enough water to last through the storm. Saturday morning, our neighbour left to go to the Cable and Wireless building where he works to take shelter from the storm. He left behind his sister and her family, together with the helper, a friend and the dog, Max. Just before he left, a line fell. Imagine the wind being that strong to blow a line down and it wasn't even the hurricane yet!

After that, my dad drove the car into the garage. Then my mom did the washing so that we would have clothes to wear before and after the storm. Just in case anything bad happened, my mom packed a small suitcase with clothes for the three of us. Day went and night came. We all stayed in my room. Since it was the farthest away from trees, we figured it was the safest room. During the night we heard so many different noises. The noises were so scary. They could scare a cat out of its fur! Every time I heard a noise, I ducked my head under the comforter and sheets. Outside sounded like the island was whistling a song that everyone was scared of and a sign of danger was coming. Around twelve o'clock, we looked out in the back yard and were shocked at the first tree that fell. It was a large almond tree to the right hand corner of our back yard. We were surprised at the way it fell. It could have fallen on our garage or on the house behind us. Instead, it fell between the neighbours' house and their shed, crushing the fence. After seeing what the wind did, I had trouble falling asleep. I didn't stay asleep for long though because I kept being awakened by the noise outside. We kept the radio going to keep our minds off it.

Around six or seven o'clock Sunday morning, September 12th, I woke up and saw my parents spreading towels and sheets on the floor trying to soak up some of the water that was blowing inside through the seals of the door. My mom and I moved our couch so it wouldn't get wet. Before the hurricane, my mom roasted breadfruit, so she put it in the oven to keep it warm. While having that for breakfast, all of a sudden we heard a noise coming from the garage. It sounded like the ceiling had collapsed.

I was extremely scared because, before the hurricane, I relocated my turtle from the back porch to the garage. I was so worried that he might have been killed. When I went to open the garage door my dad told me not to, because he was unsure of what was going on in there. We looked through the kitchen window and saw zinc flying off from the shed belonging to the people who lived behind us. I saw the wind tossing and turning like the island was having *a wild party* with no care in the world. At the same time, I realized that all the trees in my back yard were blown down and none of them fell on the house.

In quick time, I went to change my clothes because I was still in my pajamas. My mom, dad and I each had a flashlight for our self. Instead of staying in my room we all stayed together in the living room. My mom had our cell phones, in case of anything. My dad kept his phone in his pocket. We had the radio on and our emergency suitcase ready. In my hands, I held a towel and my flashlight. My mom went to try and mop up some of the water in the passageway. My dad went back to try to push the towels and sheets in the door. Then all of a sudden I saw a crack starting to form over his head. I shouted after him, not knowing if he saw it, but then I realized that he heard it. I just started to panic. He grabbed me and we started heading towards the passageway where my mom was supposed to be. She didn't know what was going on. All she heard was the noise and my dad calling her name. Then she started calling his.

DeAnn's parents, Randy and Lorna Blackman, standing in front of their damaged home on Monday, 13th September 2004

Our house isn't that big, but with everything happening all at once, it seemed like we were lost in our own house and didn't know what to do or where to go. We did end up somewhere though - in my parents' walk-in closet. With me crying my heart out and my mom holding me in her lap, my mom repeated scripture verses to comfort me. Then she called her brother in Jamaica and told him that we were in the closet and the ceiling was collapsing. Then we called our neighbors and told them what was happening and that we might be coming over. While my dad was on the phone with his sister, we heard the ceilings in the guest room and my room collapse. Hearing that, I was scared even more and knowing that my parents' room was the only room that the ceiling hadn't come down on yet. I had a feeling it was going to be next.

Then we moved to my parents' bathroom. My dad moved the dresser in front of the door just in case the door blew in. We found a garbage bag and placed a few items in it that could keep us until the following day. While holding me in her lap, my mom called our pastor and told him what was going on. Then I started saying how I wanted to go next door to the neighbours' house, as we could see that their roof was still on. We prepared ourselves to go outside in the middle of the hurricane. I placed the towel and my flashlight in the garbage bag. Then I held the comforter in my hand. My dad found two jackets and gave one to my mom and then placed one on me. Since I was wearing slippers, I had to put them in the garbage bag and then put on my mom's sneakers to cover my feet. When we went out of that room, my dad realized that a beam from the roof had come down, along with the sheetrock. Now we were trapped inside the house!

My dad tried to move the beam and the sheetrock so we could open the door and get out. It was very hard for him because, since the roof by our front door was gone, the wind was blowing so strong that it was almost blowing him away. But he got through. He called my mother and me and we walked over to the door. Just walking to the door was hard because the wind was blowing in our faces. We finally got outside and my mom held on to me while my dad tried to shut the door. Then we headed on our way to our neighbours' house. My dad held on to me now because if he didn't, I would have probably been blown away.

It was an experience of a lifetime to see and be outside in the middle of a hurricane. Trees were swaying, the wind was just blowing in our faces and surprisingly the seawater was blowing. It wasn't exactly rushing over or flooding our house but the air just carried water along with it like it was drinking water and hadn't seen any in days. While walking over, my mom was carrying a pillow and it blew out of her hand. Surprisingly, she turned back and went after it. When she did this, I was very scared of what would happen to her. But she caught the pillow and caught up with my dad and me, not knowing that her Bible had fallen. We made it next door safely around ten a.m. with no one injured or hurt except for me. I caught the cold.

When we got to our neighbours' house, they were glad we made it over in time and safely. I was too. After we arrived, I went into the bathroom to look out the window to see what was going on at our house. It looked really bad. Part of the roof was gone, ceiling and beams came down on the car and all the trees were down. My parents think that there were little mini-tornadoes in the hurricane. I think so too.

While we were at the neighbours' house, we had to bore holes into the ceiling for the water to come through in order to prevent the ceiling from collapsing. My dad helped our neighbour by using a dustpan to scoop buckets and buckets of water from the floor, which came from the ceiling. We tried to locate Radio Cayman on the radio to hear what was going on, but we were unable to because something happened to the station. Suddenly there was a loud crash. The ceiling with the chandelier came crashing to the floor. We were so frightened! We prayed and hoped that the rest of the ceiling would stay up and not come down. Then we decided to cook. The meal of the night was white rice and corn beef, with water or juice. After dinner, my dad assisted our neighbours in moving a bed from the bedroom to the living room in order to protect it.

We made ourselves comfortable either on the bed or the couch for the long scary night ahead. It was the longest night in my life! For once, I wished morning would come early. I had trouble falling asleep. I kept watching the ceiling, fearing it would collapse. I finally fell asleep - surprisingly after how scared and worried I was after hearing the rain pelting down on the roof like it was playing a Congo drum and the wind blowing its harmonica to the beat of the drum like an African song.

Around seven a.m. on Monday, September 13th 2004, my dad and the neighbour's brother-in-law went over to our house to see the final damage of what used to be our happy, cozy, loving home. It was a disaster and devastating to see. Some of our other neighbours came to view the damage that was done to the neighborhood, especially to our house. Everybody agreed that there were tornadoes within the hurricane. A clear path could be seen where the monster had traveled. That day, one of our neighbours offered me to stay at their house while my parents sorted out ours. While at the neighbour's, we tried to drive to North Side but the road was blocked. A house had blown from one side to the other and flipped over. Another house got lifted onto the road. I felt really sorry for those people and how there was nothing left for them. On the other hand, my family and I still had our walls up and part of the roof, and so some of our things were saved or not badly damaged. I just thanked God we were alive.

On Wednesday, September 15th, I boarded Air Jamaica after spending six long hours at the airport. I was on my way to be with family and friends. I was happy to see my uncles, Dougie and Vern, aunties, Claudette and Theda, and my cousins, Kriste-Kaye, Brandon and Chevaughn. Best of all, I now felt safe with relatives and friends.

After experiencing Hurricane Ivan, I would not like to experience another Category Five hurricane again - especially in my house, although it was an experience of a lifetime! Only two deaths were reported due to the hurricane but people started dying all of a sudden after it was over, from stress and other things.

While I was in Jamaica, my mom called and told me that my dog and turtle had died. I felt really bad because my dog, Pebbles, had been my first dog and my turtle, Timmy, was the first turtle I ever had.

I enjoyed my three months stay in Jamaica but I really missed my parents. Being away from them for so long was really something! I never want to leave them again and especially because of another hurricane!

Ignorance is Bliss
- Pease Bay

Animal lover, Aileen Samuel, with the author's dog, Scooby

Aileen Samuel did not know what all the fuss was about when her friend who was staying with her during the storm was insisting that they move from room to room in the house. She quickly realized the reason, as seawater and rocks came rolling through the beautiful cottage by the sea. In her words, the following is Aileen's story:-

I was in Pease Bay in the house that Captain Stoll built in 1968. I understand it was the first stone house built in Cayman. I had been looking after this house for seven years.

Because he was a sea captain, Captain Stoll put this enormous seawall up, which was three feet thick by about two hundred yards long. We had a small gate, which was a good bit *up* from the beach. The house was a good bit *back* from the gate. The reef was a good mile out ... we thought.

On the house were tongue and groove shutters made to fit each window with nine-inch bolts, which went into the stonework. I thought this was quite secure. The house never took anything during Gilbert or Mitch. Neither did the seawall.

So I stayed put in the house with Gregory Rivers, a friend of mine, Kim, another friend, six dogs and a cat. We had books. We had dominoes. We had plenty of food and plenty of lights. The dogs had enough food to last for five days. I honestly thought I had done everything.

In the carport, there was a toilet and wash basin, a cupboard with the washer and dryer, and a cupboard with the water heater and tools. I had taken this rubber wheelbarrow and put it between the bumper of my CRV Honda and the doors of the cupboards, just in case this new car should get a knock and the chrome would get damaged. We had checked the coconut trees around the house and there were no coconuts that we could reach and take off with the pole.

Saturday afternoon, my friend, Greg, called and told me not to take this thing too lightly. He said, "I'm still on the road and I don't like the sky and I don't like what I'm seeing. I think you've got to be really careful." I said, "Well, we've done everything," and he said he would be there by about half past seven.

We were going to take the dogs for a walk across the grounds because it's got about eight acres of ground, full of palm trees and stuff. But, around half past seven, Greg called again and said, "I don't think you should take the dogs out. Just stay indoors." The wind was getting up but we often get a lot of wind up there. I just didn't expect anything until Sunday.

Then Greg got there. A Four Runner, which belongs to somebody off-island, sits on the grounds. Greg put it at the back of my CRV and drove his bus right along the back of those two vehicles to try to protect them in the L-shape of the building. Then he came inside.

I don't want to say he was agitated but he kept looking at his maps and going on the computer. I thought, God, he's a little bit over the top with this hurricane, isn't he? I still hadn't really given it much thought.

We were indoors and we were all in the lounge and I wanted to play Scrabble and things but the others weren't too keen on the idea. The six dogs and cat were with us. The lightest of the dogs is seventy-two pounds so they're not lap dogs. Greg had insisted that we were all in the one room at the one time and I kept thinking, What the damn is this for? But I never asked any questions.

I'm not a seafaring person. I nearly lost my life in 1970, with a brand new speedboat, in a river back home. From that day on, I have never let the water go above my knees. Every time I go into the water, I freeze. I go solid. I am petrified. That was a concern of Greg's but that never crossed my mind because I never thought the water was going to come up to my knees.

Anyway, the night went on and the wind got up and we could hear things bumping outside. I had taken everything that I could move and put it either in the carport, in the boat sheds, or wherever. It was all anchored down. I never thought that this big hundred and thirty year old sea grape tree, which I guess was about ten feet down from the house, could be moved.

The noise got worse and Greg decided that we should move from the lounge to one of the bedrooms. So we all - lock, stock and barrel - dogs, cat and us, went into this room and I said to Greg, "Why are you shoving us around the house like this? There are only a few boulders flapping around outside." He said, "Well, *just now* there are a few boulders …" and he never said anything more.

We were all in the bedroom and I was trying to be lighthearted and the power went out. I was flapping around, getting all my lanterns and things in place and lamps in every room and Greg said, "I don't think you should bother putting them in the back rooms. I think that's a waste of battery power." I said, "Well, I might want to go in there for something." He said, "I think you should stay at this end of the house." Nothing more was said and I didn't think to ask why.

We were completely encapsulated in this one room until about half past four on Sunday morning. That's when Greg said, "I think we should make our way to the kitchen."

Now we were in the farthest room of the house from the sea. It was a fabulous kitchen and I used to do a lot of my paperwork at the table in there. It was bright. You could see down the road and across the grounds. It had five windows but, on one window next to the back door, I didn't put any boards. I said that, if I boarded it up, we wouldn't be able to see anything. Greg said, "Well, it's in the L-shape of the building so it could be protected from the wind." Lucky I did leave that one off!

We were now in the kitchen and daylight was coming in and I wanted to make some breakfast on this wee burner that I had. Greg said, "I think the breakfast should wait," because it was getting quite rough outside. We heard a lot of banging. It was the seawall breaking up in chunks but it never crossed my mind that it was the seawall. I thought it was coming from somebody else's place along the sea line. The banging was semi-vibrating the building but it never crossed my mind that this was going to do major damage. I don't know what the heck I thought.

Now the dogs were a wee bit unsettled and started to wander about, which made me think, What do they know that I don't know? By this time, the cat was sitting on top of the microwave. Nothing was happening inside but the cat was on the microwave! She never sits up there! I kept passing remarks like, "Look at Shelley sitting on top of the microwave! What in the hell's wrong with her? She's afraid she's going to get her feet wet." *Ignorance is bliss!* About nine o'clock, Greg filled up a water jug and left it on the table. Now we were all around this table, the dogs were walking around, the cat was on the microwave, and the noises were getting quite fierce outside! So I said, "Greg, what the hell's all this banging?" He said, "I think it's some boulders or stones coming from somewhere." He never said it was the sea. I thought, That's grass out there so I don't know where these boulders are coming from. It never crossed my mind that boulders would come across the seawall.

At ten past nine, I looked at the double door between the shower, the toilet and the bedroom, from the kitchen, and saw that water was seeping under the door. I said, "Oh, my God, Shelley must've known something. There's water coming in."

Within thirty seconds of that, those two doors burst into streamers! I was gob-smacked! I just couldn't believe it!

They were blue doors. The house was painted in Caribbean colours and we didn't want to change Captain Stoll's idea. One room was green. One room was pink. One room was blue, and there was all this lovely gingerbread around the house.   It was a quaint wee cottage-type place.

Those doors broke into streamers and those blue streamers were flapping in this sea of water. Then these big rocks came in!   One rock hit me and I thought, Damn! That was sore! To this day, I don't have any feelings in my left leg between my hip and my knee.

Then, when I looked, the dogs were swimming in the kitchen! So we got the dogs up on the breakfast bar. In the meantime, Greg was saying, "Aileen, get up on the breakfast bar," and my adrenaline had kicked in so I was saying, "No, I'm going to get this water out of here," and I tried to open the back door.

Now, there was no way I could pull that door against four feet plus of water! It was up to my chest and I don't like water above my knees. I was thinking, This is serious. We could drown in this kitchen! Then I thought, I've never been beaten before and I'll be damned if I'm going to let this take me over!

Just then a piece of wood floated past with a handle on it and I thought, That's my knicker drawer. So I grabbed this drawer and I thought, Right, this is my last chance for survival here. Then I burst the six bottom panes of glass on the window but that didn't do much good. These windows have panels that turn out and they have Venetian blinds covering them. I pulled the blind up and thought, I've got to break out this metal frame. So I burst the four brackets – just with this piece of wood. I used to say to athletes, "When adrenaline's kicking, you use it!" Well, the adrenaline must've been kicking because there is no way, in a normal way of life, could I have broken those metal brackets!

I burst those things out and threw them! I'm a medical photographer by trade … always think ahead! I saw the glass and thought, Oh, my God, we might bleed to death and the hospital might be closed. So I swept the glass up and pitched it under the bin. The water hadn't been in that room but it was starting to seep in now.

At that point, I said to Greg and Kim, "Throw me the dogs and I'll put them in the CRV." The CRV never gets dirty feet in it but I opened the door and put the dogs in the back of it, in the carport. Now how could I carry a seventy-seven to eighty pound dog? I don't know because I can't even carry him on a normal day.

So the dogs were in the back of the car. Until we reached the point when I thought that we could all drown in the kitchen and I decided to have a go at the window, I never was afraid and I don't understand that. I guess it's like what happens in a road accident. My adrenaline was pumping and I had this extra energy. But Kim and Greg were fumbling. They were like snowflakes in a storm and I was standing, shouting, "Give me the dogs -

one by one!" They were collecting things that were floating and I was saying, "Never mind those. Just give me my dogs." I couldn't find the cat and I said, "Greg, you have to find Shelley!" Shelley had gone from the microwave to the top of the cupboards and, from there she had got on top of the gingerbread woodwork. She wasn't going to get her feet wet.

Greg got Shelley and brought her out. At about a quarter to ten, he got the car started because he thought that if the saltwater came in, it might damage the starter. Plus, we had a/c! The car ran for the whole twenty-four hours we were in it because I had filled the gas tank up. The surprising thing was that the dogs rotated in the car so everyone got a chance at the back to lie and stretch out. Before the storm, for some reason, when I took the cats that I look after to Prospect, I threw a half-gallon of water and some of the dry cat food in the back of the car. The dogs got a handful of the cat food. We shared the water amongst ourselves and with the dogs, over the twenty-four hour period. We were in the car from before ten on Sunday morning until about half past nine on Monday morning.

There was one oleander at the back of the carport on the grass side, the only shrub that was left when we got out to look, and it was like a barometer. It was kissing the ground on both sides. When it stopped, we thought, This is easing up a bit. I think the television mast helped to save our lives. It chipped two chunks of zinc off and they went flying about two hundred feet away. So this left us with an 'in and out' for the wind.

At about half past nine or a quarter to ten on Monday morning, this voice from out of nowhere shouted, "Is there anybody ALIVE in there?" Not knowing what was outside, I thought, What a stupid statement. I opened the window and said, "Of course, we're alive in here! There are three of us, and six dogs and a cat. You want to join us?" He said, "Oh, my God! I think you should come out and have a look." I said, "No, it's still windy out there. I'm quite safe in here and I have my a/c." He said, "No, I really think you should come out and have a look." I could see that this guy was dressed in black waterproof bags.

When I got out of the car, I went, "Oh, my God!" There was no seawall! The big sea grape tree was lifted and carried on top of the boat sheds. There had been about twenty-nine palm trees on the grounds and every one of them had gone! There had been seven big Australian pines, which must've been about fifty feet high. Four had gone and two spikes were left, about ten feet high. Somebody's deck was at the front of the house. I had no walls in the front of the house. The fence and the seawall were in chunks the size of coffee tables in the bedrooms, and no furniture! Everything else was down in front of the house. It was just a mass of rocks and sand. I have never seen so many boulders in my life!

Greg came out and looked around. Kim fell apart. She was just a wreck. So she got back into the car with the dogs. That sight will never leave me! That had been such a lush, green, protected area with its palm trees and all its shrubbery, and now nothing was standing. Absolutely nothing! The guy told us we weren't going to get out of there for some time

41

but I told him I had to get out because I had three cats down at Prospect Point that I had left in the house. I thought, If this has happened here, what on earth has happened on Old Prospect Road?

The guy said, "We've come from Bodden Town and we've got a road cleaner heading this way. We'll clear a track to let you out." Eventually, the truck came and led us out onto the main road. We took Greg's bus because it was the only vehicle that we could get out. It took quite some time for us to get from the house in Pease Bay to Bodden Town, because the road was blocked. We saw caskets that had come out of the graveyard.

We went through the back road to bypass Bodden Town to check on Milne in Savannah Meadows. He only had a little water in the house so he was okay. So I said, "I'm going to see how the cats are."

Never did I think, in my wildest dreams, Mariners Cove would be in the centre of the road! It took us two hours to get from Savannah to Old Prospect Road and I was not a happy person going up over the top of Mariners Cove so soon. I felt it was a wee bit risky to drive over those properties because there may have been some people trapped who had not wanted to leave [before the storm] and maybe we were driving over them.

The two oceans met down by Red Bay so we had to go down by Prospect. We had to enter Old Prospect Point from the back of Durty Reid's. When I got in there, what we saw was even more horrific! All the houses that were from the corner by the monument … the sea had just come into them and gone out the other side! I eventually got to the house where the cats were and the television was at the gate. The wall had been broken and you couldn't even see the gate for the trees. All the trees were in the driveway! We had to climb over the trees and furniture in the lawn to get to the house. When we went round the side of the house, there was no back! The six patio doors had gone. The pool was full of trees. There was no furniture in the house, and I thought, Oh, the cats!

I went to the end bedroom and crawled over boulders and sand in the corridors, and this poor cat was sitting in the windowsill behind the curtains, really traumatized. She was frozen to the spot. I went down the lawn to the cat shed, which houses two rooms; one is the cats' abode and the other houses the laundry. This shed did not have a scratch on it. The four kennels are on a wooden frame, the upper part of this end of the shed has mesh panels and the wind blew the large kennels over. The black cat and the white cat were sitting on top of them in all this mess. I managed to get the carriers out of the other shed and took all three cats to Savannah. I kept them in a small room there for ten days and pampered them back to as normal a life as I could.

That's the second time water has tried to take me but there won't be a third time! I owe my life to Greg Rivers. If it hadn't been for his knowledge of the sea, I wouldn't be here today! If another hurricane came, I would stay again because of my animals. I would stay put but not so close to the ocean! I'm a paper-Caymanian and proud of it. Cayman is my home so here I will remain!

Strong Shoulders
- Industrial Park

With the help of God and Martha Binns' strong shoulders, Martha and Desmond Binns' family survived Hurricane Ivan and lived to tell about it. They thought that for the duration of the storm, their family would be safe in their home behind their shop in Industrial Park but time would tell. The following is Martha's story in her own words:-

Desmond and Martha Binns, standing in front of their store in Industrial Park, four weeks after the storm.

We stayed right in our home on Seymour Drive Saturday night before the storm. We slept there okay. There was me, my husband, my daughter and her two children, ages three and five years old, and my niece, who is my daughter's helper.

It was on Sunday morning, when we wake up around six o'clock, that the rain and wind start coming and it continued all day. It was around nine o'clock when the heavy part came. We went into our grocery shop because we know the shop is very strong.

About nine o'clock, we see water coming in and it was up to our ankles. At this point, we thought it was fun but, in the next minute, the water reach to our waists. All of a sudden, it come to our bust-line and we say we couldn't stay there so we rushed from our shop to go inside the house in the back. The water reach up to our throats now. By the time we reach there, the water pick me up. It was bad because I had the baby at that time and I cried, "I'm drowning! I'm drowning!"

That's when I put the little baby up on the cupboard top, which is almost seven feet high. Then we put the other baby there too.

Around ten o'clock, the roof went and now the fridge is floating. The settee is floating. Cabinet is floating. Groceries is floating. Everything is floating, and even a big *snake* come inside! So we decide the only place to go is on the roof but it is ten feet up and we asked, "How we going to go up ten feet?" My husband take a stick and knock out a piece of the sheetrock and he climb up in there. But my daughter is three hundred pounds and I didn't know how to get her up there. My niece is three hundred pounds too. I decided they would have to use me to step on to get up.

When my husband go up, I passed the little children up to him and he keep them up there while I tried to put my niece up. She had to step up on some furniture but, when she step on my shoulders, she say she not going to make it because she's so heavy. But I say, "By the grace of God, you are going to make it." I tried to push her but the little hole between the rafters is only about a foot wide. I don't know how she got through, other than by the grace of God, but she pick up herself through. Then my daughter come and she's on my shoulders and the ceiling's ten feet up. I don't know how I did it with all that water. She was saying, "No, me can't," but I say, "Yes, you have to do it because it's the only how we can save ourselves," because the water was

Desmond, with Martha, pointing to the hole in which his family had to climb to safety

still rising. I keep pushing her up and my husband is pulling. She's so big that it take about ten minutes for her to wiggle, wiggle up through them little rafters and, by the time I get her up, I'm the last one and the water was really coming up now. Since there was nobody to push me up they grab both my hands and they pull, pull, pull. But, when I look, I see a bottle of rubbing alcohol and I say, "Hold on," and I strap the alcohol in my bosom quick and they can't believe it.

When I climb on one of the beams is where the miracle happened. One small ply board was holding us all up. My husband weighs two hundred pounds. I'm just under that. My niece weighs three hundred pounds. My daughter weighs three hundred pounds and then there's the children. We were all on this small piece of ply with a few little nails in it, with the water right under us. So we moved to another place where we could lean on the concrete.

Everybody was up there now and the children are screaming and crying, crying and screaming, and the rain is coming heavy. There was every sound that you could ever think about. We were so scared and didn't know what to do because we know there's no help in sight. The water down below and outside keep rising until it cover the car and it cover the truck. It cover everything in the yard. Our cars, them all, drowned.

We were wondering what we could do when suddenly we see a bright light coming. It was coming so quickly and we thought it was somebody coming with floodlight to rescue us and, lo and behold, it was the storm itself coming and all we could do was say the Twenty-Third Psalm because we know we are going to bury ourselves alive up there. The light come so quickly and it pass very quickly and I say, "Thank God!"

The roof was off and the rain still continued so hard. It rain and pour like it was sand beating in our face that we could hardly open our eyes. We didn't have anything to cover ourselves except one little piece of curtain to cover the children. My little granddaughter begin having fever. Her tongue begin to turn blue. My niece had bronchitis and she start shivering so it was a wonderful thing I take the alcohol because we keep rubbing them with it.

At about four-thirty in the afternoon, my husband said he couldn't take it no longer. It was starting to calm down so he went out. He went down the road in the water. He found some Filipinos and was telling them, "Mommy's on the roof." When they heard this, about eight of them come with ropes and they tie us with the ropes and take us down. Then they led us to shelter and there we stay two days with them in their house. After two days, we decided to go back and clean up our place and move back in. We got tarpaulin and we still live with it over our house and shop.

During the storm, in the afternoon, while we were there trying to save our lives, people was in the shop looting the goods, taking everything. When we came back two days later, there was nothing left – no water, no drinks. We had stock up a lot but now everything was gone. But we didn't mind because the people them didn't have anything to eat. They were so hungry and I was so glad for life. I didn't care what happened because I was alive!

We were in the rafters from about nine-thirty in the morning until about four-thirty that afternoon without food or water but we didn't think about it because it was like a nightmare up there. We were passing through 'the valley of the shadow of death'. There was no time to think about eating. Even the babies did not get hungry. All we could think about was life, life ... just life!

Now that it's over, I just simply try to see what I can get done every day and to love people. I realize and know that we are only here for a short time and don't know what is going to happen next. I questioned God and said, "There got to be something out of this thing," because, after the storm, some people get better and some people get worse. I said, "Lord, what should I do personal?" He said to me, "You can be better or you can be bitter." He say, "Choose one." I choose to be better!

A Letter to Friends
- West Bay

Brenda Bryce, a primary school teacher had been teaching in Cayman for several years until she had to return to her hometown in Canada after her home in West Bay was destroyed by Hurricane Ivan. She has since moved back to Cayman and is, once again, doing what she enjoys most – teaching and living in the land she has come to love so much. The following is a letter she wrote after her return to Canada just after the storm:-

Hello Everyone,

Just wanted you to know how much it meant to me that you were all so concerned about me this past week. Yes, I did survive Ivan. I am now back in Ontario at my parents' house in Waterloo and I am safe. It was an incredible experience but one that I

Brenda Bryce, getting her classroom in Cayman ready for classes, post-Hurricane Ivan

will never go through again. Next time there is a bit of a breeze I am out of there!!!

I was at Krista and Dave's townhouse with Jenn (my friend), Daniel (Jenn's boyfriend) and Godfrey (Dave's father). Krista, Dave and Sadie were already off of the island. It was a tough decision - should we go to a hurricane shelter or should we stay where we were. We decided to stay. Friday night and all day Saturday we waited for it to hit. They were long days with not much to do … little did we know the days were going to get longer. We cooked, showered and had light, telephone and water for the last time on Saturday. We were prepared (so we thought) as we had the bathtub full of water, big tubs of water on the floor and counter, drinking water, canned food, flashlights, battery powered radio and a barbecue.

We listened to the radio and the Governor came on and gave a speech. He said he had officially declared a "state of emergency" and that Ivan was coming straight for us and it was a Category Five. He said the results would be "catastrophic" and he ended his speech with "and God help us all!" This was even before the storm. After listening to this I was worried. Were we all going to die? Were some of us going to die? Would the entire island disappear underwater? Nobody slept Saturday night.

The wind started picking up and by Sunday morning Ivan had started. It got very windy and the rain came. It was sort of dark the entire time. We had Radio Cayman to listen to on Sunday morning, but the stories of people who were already in serious trouble were depressing. Then the radio cut out as well. It was very hot in the townhouse but we could not open any door or window. By eight o'clock a.m. we thought it must be close to three p.m. So we sat and when we looked at the time again (thinking it must be at least nine o'clock, it was only eight-thirteen). I don't remember the exact order of things but at some point we heard loud crashes that at first we thought was thunder but then realized it was the roof shingles blowing off the house. The trees that I could see were just bent over in the wind. A Category Five hurricane sounds loud and the winds are incredibly powerful, unlike anything I could have ever imagined. So we sat until we noticed that water was leaking in through the roof. We put down more buckets and moved everything downstairs. Then we noticed that a trickle of water was coming in through the glass sliding doors. About two minutes later the water was up to our hips inside the house. The bad news was that it tipped over all of our good water so we had no water anymore. It happened so fast. (It was the sea surge.) So we quickly moved everything back upstairs. Then more of the roof came off and we heard the most gigantic crash. Part of the ceiling had fallen off inside the house and crashed to the floor. So now we thought, Where do we go? The four of us sat in the kitchen on the counter. The water was the most disgusting colour of brown sewage and gunge, and it stunk. After a few hours the water receded and the storm was in a lull so we opened the doors and let the water out. Everything was covered in black sludge. You could sort of see outside and already we knew all of the trees were down and a lot of the tiles from the roof. The temperature in the house was very high, and everything was damp and smelled. We had to close up again as the tail of Ivan was coming. It was just so loud and it seemed to go on forever. We finally tried to sleep for a while but we were dripped on or things were just wet. Someone's car alarm kept going off and it lasted for hours until the battery finally gave out. The cars in one part of the car park were underwater to their roofs. Finally, on Monday morning we were able to open a window and get a breath of fresh air.

For so long we felt like we were the only people in the world, so isolated from everyone else. When we first stepped foot out on Monday and we saw another person, it was such a relief to know that we were alive. It was still blowing and raining but we looked out and inspected the damage. My car had an eight foot piece of wood on it from a construction site. It was dented, scraped and had a lot of water damage.

We walked to my house at Oceanside Plantation and we couldn't believe all of the sites along the way. Everything was different; there were no familiar landmarks. It is very difficult to describe. It sort of looked like a bomb had hit the island, with debris - pieces of houses, cars and trees everywhere. My house did not make it. Oceanside Plantation was still standing on three sides with no roof. The fronts were gone. We were afraid to go into my unit as we thought the building would collapse at any time. But I did go and get a few garbage bags full of stuff out.

Picture taken by Brenda Bryce

Inside Brenda's condominium at Oceanside Plantation after the storm.

The hardest part of the entire experience was knowing that physically we were all okay but we had no way of letting anyone else know we were fine. We knew family and friends at home would be so worried but we couldn't tell them we were alive. I thought often of the World Trade Center disaster.

Finally, I managed on Monday afternoon to get a thirty-second cell phone message to Mom and Dad to let them know I was all right. The message was garbled as I was in the car and stalled in a puddle of water. If I had stayed there we would have lost the car completely. My car (sort of running) was the best out of the six cars that we had before the hurricane. But I felt better just having made some contact with home.

The next few days took on a whole different way of life. I sort of felt at times like I was on '*Survivor*'. (The days you don't have an immunity challenge are the longest days of your life. I cooked and handed out our rations of rice.) We spent the days getting up when the sun got up, working on cleaning out the house (difficult with no water) and trying to get messages to people, eating a little bit when we could and then going to bed after dark, around eight o'clock p.m. The first time I drove down West Bay Road I didn't recognize a thing! Every power line was down. One condo after another had massive damage. We had to go through the sand by the Holiday Inn, dodge telephone poles, boats and other debris. I couldn't even recognize Governor's Beach (which I used to go to almost every day). I was so excited whenever I saw anyone I knew and saw that they were okay. Communication was very difficult. You either happened to see people when you were on the streets or you tried to find them at their house. Most people asked, "How did you do?" The typical answers were "I'm fine but my house is gone, or my car is gone, or my house and car are gone." So I was not the only one who was homeless.

It is hard to describe how hot it was afterwards and how smelly and dirty we all were. No water is a big deal (we still had our drinking water but it was precious and we didn't want to waste a drop). We tried to bathe in the sea one day but the waves were still too rough to go in. We slept in the house in puddles or under drips, or on the smelly, damp sofa, or wherever. We ate a couple of times a day, tried to clean, visit people and stay cool. I went to visit a friend in George Town to see if she was okay but when I got to her place she wasn't home. So I spoke to her next door neighbours to say, "Please pass along a message." They had water for an hour and they had just had showers. I must have looked disgusting and desperate because they asked if I wanted a shower. I said, "YES!" At that point I would have paid $1,000 for a shower. These strangers took me upstairs, gave me shampoo, and I had a beautiful cold shower. This is just one example of how people pulled together and the kindness of people.

The island was under Marshall Law; there was a curfew in place that you HAD to take seriously. Nobody was allowed out from six p.m. to six a.m. The looting was bad and some prisoners had escaped from the prison. The police all had rifles and semi-automatics, the British Navy had sent ships but the water was too rough so they couldn't anchor yet. The 'no water, electricity and sewage problem' was getting worse. No stores had opened, no gas, no money, etc. Very strange times. Big Hurley's at Grand Harbour was open and Foster's Food Fair opened as a food distribution centre where you could line up and get two bags of food (no choice).

People were being asked to leave the island unless they were essential because the island could not feed, clothe and house all of the people on it. There just weren't enough resources. So on Wednesday I decided it was time for me to get off of the island. I saw my immediate boss (by chance) and told her. She said, "Yes, go." I tried to find some of my friends to say good-bye but didn't see most of them.

On Thursday, I went to the airport right after curfew was lifted in the morning and got there by six-thirty a.m. There were already hundreds of people in line outside the airport trying to get off of the island. Nobody cared where they went; Miami, Jamaica, New York, Toronto, etc., just anywhere. Some of the big accounting and law companies had private charters coming in to take their employees off. It was so hot waiting outside all day. A water truck came and we got some drinking water. It was disorganized confusion at it's worst. I went from line to line to line, trying to put my name on lists to get Canadians off. I saw many of the families from our school. Everyone was trying to get off. I met one parent of a former student. She had two children (ages ten and eleven) and was desperate to get them off of the island. I told her I would take them with me to Toronto and then try and get them to their grandparents' home in Calgary. She was so grateful that she cried. She ran home and left a note for their father, packed one small bag for the kids and found $200 Canadian. She stood in one line with one child and I stood in another line, trying to find out accurate information about how to get off. I had my name on a list for a plane that was due to leave the next day for Toronto, but now there were three of us so I tried to get the children's names on the list as well. Their mother said I shouldn't give up my seat so that they could go but I said, "No, we will stay here until we can get them on the list." Besides what else did we have to do that day? So we stayed. I overheard someone say the Ritz had a plane so I ran over to where they were and got the three of us on a list (numbers 22, 23 & 24). There were only twenty-five extra seats on that plane!! So now we were in line to get on the Ritz plane to Miami. I would worry about how to get to Toronto later. It was a nightmare and everyone had such a sense of desperation to get off. Then I met up with another parent who said he knew someone at the accounting firm of KPMG who had a plane to Toronto. We ran over to this man and asked if we could get on the plane. He asked if I worked for KPMG. I said, "No." He asked if I knew anyone from KPMG and I said, "No," but I begged. I told him I was a schoolteacher and my school couldn't afford a plane and that I was taking two children with me and that we were all Canadian. Finally he agreed. So, because I did not give up, I knew someone who knew someone, and I was at the right place at the right time, we were on a plane that was chartered by KPMG accounting firm to Toronto. We finally left at five-thirty p.m. having been there from six-thirty a.m. Because there was no power, there were no night flights so we were one of the last flights to leave that day.

The KPMG people were so wonderful and it had never felt so good to be on a plane. There was a/c and cold drinks with ICE and the first person to use the loo came out and said, "It flushes!" On the plane, the KPMG people gave us care packages with a clean t-shirt, toothbrush, toothpaste and deodorant, and a pack of Smarties!! They had information for everyone and hotel reservations at the Fairmont Royal York.

When we landed, someone from Customs and Immigration got on the plane and helped us get through very quickly. Employees from KPMG Toronto were waiting as soon as we went through, to assist us further. I got a hotel near the airport and asked for a "reduced rate for compassionate reasons". The clerk at the desk listened to my tale and did give me a discount but said to speak to a manager in the morning to get a further discount. The next step was showers for us all and trying to get a flight out the next day for the children. Their grandparents in Calgary were so happy to hear from us and so grateful to me for getting the kids out. When I called Air Canada, I asked for a reduced fare for compassionate reasons. The agent asked, "Who died?" I thought, Well the island died! I explained the situation and she gave us a reduced fare. The next morning I went back to the airport and got the children on the plane. When we checked in at the gate I spoke to the Air Canada people. I said they were great children who were used to flying but, given what we had all just been through, they might be afraid. The lady said, "Well, we have two seats in business class. I think they will be more comfortable there."

I went back to the hotel to wait for Mom and Dad to come and get me. While I was waiting, I checked e-mail for the first time. I was so shocked to see twenty e-mails of love and concern from people. I started to cry for the first time. I just didn't know that it was such a big deal. Because I was living through it, I just was in survival mode and did what I had to do. I was speaking to the General Manager, telling him how kind his staff was and explaining my situation when up from behind me came Mom and Dad. They shouted, "You're alive!" and gave me a big hug. It couldn't have been scripted any better. The manager said, "Of course, we can give you the employee discount rate."

So I am back in Ontario and I could be here for the next three months, until the school needs me to come and do clean up. It will take Cayman a long time to restore the island but I do want to go back.

Sorry this is so long but I guess I had to get it out. There are so many more stories and so many stories of strangers helping strangers; it really makes you feel good that there are so many great people out there, not just the looters and people who take advantage. So I am homeless in Cayman but I will start over. Again, thank you for your e-mails of concern and remember now whenever there is a hint of a strong wind, I am OUT OF THERE!

Love,
Brenda.

Bailing Out
- Bodden Town

Annette Blunt had experienced Hurricane Gilbert in Jamaica and saw no reason why Ivan would be much worse than that. She stayed in her home in Bodden Town for the storm where she learned just how much worse Ivan would be:-

I told people that I had been through Gilbert in Jamaica but, trust me, it was nothing like Ivan. Ivan was so scary, and I mean scary!

I spoke with my brother Friday night in Jamaica and he told me they were preparing for the storm. I called him again later and he said that it was so windy and the storm was coming straight to them.

I live in Bodden Town. On Saturday night, the night of the storm, it started getting really windy there so I call him again and I say, "Tyrone, you couldn't tell me the storm was so dangerous?" And he said, "I tried to warn you to prepare yourself." It was no joke!

I tried to call him again and again but I got no further communication with him. It just cut off.

Annette Blunt, at work at Hurley's Marketplace, Grand Harbour.

Theresa from Hurley's called on the Saturday and told me she would come over and get me so I could stay with her family for the storm. I told her to give me five to ten minutes but ended up calling her back and said I could not leave because I would not be able to secure anything in my house. I was also scared for her to come because she might get caught in the storm. So I stayed.

The electricity went off late Saturday night. I was watching T.V. because they had the map of Jamaica placed on the T.V. and were playing gospel songs and songs like *'We don't need another hero'*. When the lights went, I started crying and crying because I knew this was it now. It was coming to us now! I tried to call Theresa to see if she was okay but I couldn't get through. I was so worried about her because her house was right on the beach.

About four or five of us was in one room. It got bad about three o'clock Sunday morning. My God, Sunday morning was the worst! We keep *bailing out* water, bailing water in order not to drown. We keep bailing it and keep it to about knee height. We were throwing it out the front door. We had to open the back door and the front door at the same time. It took two of us to open one door because the wind was so strong. We had to open the two doors so that the breeze, when it come through, don't break open the window. It just go right through the other door. We just throw the water out and then we start again. That's how we had to do it right through. We couldn't sleep.

The wind roared! It was screeching and part of the roof went. I heard something like crashing and I was like, "What was that?" It was a two-floor house so we run upstairs and saw that half of the upstairs had gone. So we had to come back down and lock the door to the stairs.

The worst of it was when I came out on the Monday morning and saw the damage that took place in the Cayman Islands. It was so devastating and I was so afraid. The trees were blocking the road and I was scared to come out. When I came out and saw the damage, I had to cry. I really cried. I realized that, in a blink of an eye, God could've just swept everybody away. We should give Him thanks everyday because He was so merciful to save us all.

After the storm, I went down to check on Theresa. She and her family were okay but their house was a mess. We just hugged each other and cried. We were so happy to see that each other was okay. The happiest thing for me was going back to work at Hurley's and helping my customers who I love so dearly. That's what kept me going – going back to work and seeing everybody come back. It made me so happy. I went and hugged Miss Mary and kissed her. Actually, I almost kissed everybody that I knew and saw. I was so happy to see them all, alive and well.

Hammer to the Ceiling
- South Sound

Bill McLeod has worked for the Michael Godfrey family for many years and lives on their property in South Sound. Unbeknownst to the Godfrey family who were struggling for survival in their own home, Bill was fighting for survival while the waters rose inside his. He lived and told his story several weeks later:-

Bill McLeod, at Jennifer and Michael Godfrey's home in South Sound

It was on the eleventh of September that I was in my room, which faces to the ocean, when Hurricane Ivan started. I saw what was happening with the hurricane and I said it was going to be very bad. Late that night around ten o'clock, water started coming into the room so I started to mop. Eventually though the water started to come in heavily and started to flood the place. So I just pulled the door open and took in a ladder and stand on it for a while. But, in the middle of the morning, I see that it was getting more serious and the water was about three to four feet. So I get down off the ladder and get a hammer and a machete that I had in my room and I said to myself, "All right, I'm going to have to make a serious move because I can't stay in this and I can't get outside." So I take the *hammer* and I start to lick the *ceiling* out.

After I licked the ceiling out, I realized that there was ply board on top and I said, "I have to get through this roof because I can't stay in here and die." So I take the hammer and hit the ply board out and get into the attic and that's where I stayed from early Sunday morning until Monday morning. It was a very long time.

During the storm, it sounded like heavy tugging on the roof as if it wanted to take it off. But, I could feel the solidness of the room and I said, "All right, I'm safe here because Mr. Godfrey always have his places well-built, you know."

While I was up there, I could look out through one little hole and see what was going on with the water. I was praying. I summoned the courage to pray and ask the Lord for his guidance and protection and I remember right away where the Bible tells us that, when Jesus went into a ship and his disciples followed Him, the sea became raging and water began to fill the boat. The disciples went to Him and woke Him up and asked Him to stop the storm and He did. So I asked Him to stop the water and the wind.

Eventually, I rested a little while and I realized that the water had started to drop down and I said, "Oh, God, I thank You that it's not me alone who prayed this prayer. I know that there are many more and I thank You." I watched the water go down inch-by-inch and I said, "Lord, I'm going to rest now," and I lay down and I rest for about an hour.

Then I heard voices calling me. At first, I did not recognize the voices then I realized that it was Dr. Marzouca and John Godfrey. They hugged me and I thanked God. Then I went inside the Godfrey's house and they were all in tears. That's where I stayed and I was very grateful to them. I just thank God that I'm alive and well in the Cayman Islands and that He cares. We are blessed. We are so blessed.

Trouble on The Avenue
- South Sound

Mike and Mary Bowerman felt secure in their South Sound home with their family and friends. Some even enjoyed a good night's sleep until trouble, in the name of Hurricane Ivan, showed up in the early morning hours of Sunday, 12th September 2004. Mike, Mary and their son, David, told of their ordeal a few months later:-

Mary and Mike Bowerman with their son, David, (centre) leaning on the unclaimed boat (now referred to as 'Ivan Gimme') in which they rescued their neighbours

Mike: There were ten of us in the house - Mary, David, Mary's mum, Miss Elizabeth, and myself. We also had my sister, Liz, Jonathan and Nickie Tibbetts and their two year old son, Isaac, and three week old baby, Caleb. There was also our helper, Jean. The Tibbetts family came fairly late on the Saturday, having only just decided they weren't going to stay in their home in North Sound Estates.

On the Friday, we had already put some of our family cars in the Piccadilly car park because we were told that that was a good place to keep them. We kept a couple of, what we called our 'better' cars in the garages, which was obviously a grave mistake.

My sister's Starlet was also in the yard and Jon and Nickie's two SUVs. All those cars, of course, were destroyed whilst all the old bangers down in Piccadilly were rescued later on!

Apart from the ten people, we had fifteen animals in the house with us.

Mary: We had ten cats and five dogs!

Mike: Saturday night, some of the members of our family slept quite well. Others didn't get much sleep. We won't say which ones slept and which ones didn't!

Sunday morning, when the storm was at its height, we began to recognize there were problems. For most of the morning, because of the pressure of the wind, we took turns holding the front door and Miss Elizabeth's door [whose house is attached], even though they both had shutters on them.

David: It was six o'clock in the morning when I realized it was going to be a long day holding that door! We took turns with at least two of us holding it because it was getting ready to blow in. We had shutters over it and everything but the wind was still blowing it. Inside, we had tables and furniture propped up in front of it but we still couldn't hold it. We finally just drilled screws all the way around the doors but the water started seeping in so we sent for all the towels, sheets and everything and used them all up. As the water came in the front door, I tasted it. I thought it was rain but it was the sea so I got extremely concerned. Then I noticed that the water was coming in the back door, as well as every other door. It was still dark inside even though we had some lanterns, but we could see the water rising.

Mike: We actually did lose two shutters that blew away. One was off a little round window facing north so we could see, through the mist and spray, down The Avenue towards town. We had an office upstairs which we were in for most of the day, either there or in one of the bedrooms. We never really got wet upstairs, although we had seepage through the windows and the vents.

At some point during the storm, one of the accordion shutters, which was facing east towards South Sound, blew out of the wall so we could see the level of the sea was very high - about six feet flowing down The Avenue.

It was daytime now but it was very difficult to see through the spray but, looking to the east, I could see a gap in the houses, which I had never noticed before and of course because of the spray and because it was difficult to see, I just thought it was my imagination that I could make out the actual main sea across the road.

David: That's when I got scared. My heart was just pounding because I saw that Mr. Lawrence Thompson's house was totally gone. I thought, if that was the case, I couldn't imagine what the rest of the island was like.

Mike: Not only that house was gone completely and later found in pieces across the road, along with Mr. Lawrence's Mercedes, but, facing west of our house, almost the same distance, about seventy-five yards up the road, Mr. Berkeley White's concrete house had totally and completely disappeared.

David: When we looked out the window to the north, we could see the waves going up The Avenue but from the allotment the other side, it was just like a river coming from that direction. It was baffling. We could see whitecaps going up The Avenue and whitecaps coming from the opposite direction. The waters were meeting and flowing like a river.

Mary: The water was so high that we could just make out the tops of the trees.

David: At eight o'clock in the morning, the water burst through the front door and the door just flapped in. It just folded from the bottom up and the water just gushed in and, all of a sudden, it was gushing in through every door. Jean, the helper, started screaming for everybody to get upstairs. She was scared because she couldn't swim. She ran upstairs and everybody ran behind her. It was so loud and everything was shaking.

Mary: The water gushing in was loud and the wind was howling.

David: While the water was rushing in, I called some good friends, Cecile and Malcolm Davies, who live up The Avenue, on the cell phone and said to them, "Watch out! The sea is coming!" They said, "Really? We're eating bacon and eggs!" I said, "Eating bacon and eggs?! Well, prepare yourselves, because this is it!" It was another hour before the water came into their house.

Mike: They ended up with about three feet of water and stayed in there throughout the storm, and they didn't have a second floor. We had about two feet in our house but David had the presence of mind to go down and rescue some valuable things, like photo albums and keys, which was wonderful.

The cars were almost completely underwater. One of the cars was a great big Lincoln Navigator, which floated and broke down the garage door on top of the other car that was inside. After the storm, we measured six to seven feet of sea had come flowing down The Avenue.

At one point, when we were upstairs in Deborah's bedroom, we all felt scared. We sang hymns and we had a time of prayer and different ones of us prayed and asked the Lord's hand upon us. We had this mum with her three week old baby and she was obviously very anxious. Going through this experience must have been pretty tough on her with a newborn baby.

Around about five o'clock in the evening, it was still daylight and David, Jonathan and I decided that the wind had subsided sufficiently and we wanted to go out and see what was happening.

The sea had gone down about three or four feet but was still probably about three feet deep down The Avenue and there were still marginally hurricane winds. But we decided to go out across the road onto the beach to see what was happening. We waded out down the driveway. We looked left and saw, coming down the road, Malcolm and his two sons, Brett and Christopher, and Denny Tomsu, who was staying with them. So we waited for them to join us and we all waded across the road.

One of the things that impressed me at that point was that, when we looked through one of the smashed windows of a house on the beach closest to us, the house was totally and completely cleaned out. There wasn't a stick of furniture or an appliance in it. It was just like the house had just been built. There was absolutely nothing in it! The sea had just totally cleaned it out!

When we first got outside, Jonathan noticed that his wife's SUV, a Ford Escape, wasn't where they had left it so they went to investigate and it had washed around to the back of the house. The interesting thing was that, where the Ford Escape had been in front of the house, instead there was a little ten foot white boat. We tied it so it wouldn't wash away.

David: When we went out, I heard a man calling. It was our neighbour. He was outside calling so I went to him and asked if he needed something. He said that his family was up in their attic and had been in there for about nine hours. So I asked him, "Do you need me to come over?" and he said, "Yes." So I went and untied the boat and Jonathan and I waded with it around to their house to the side door.

Mike: Our neighbours had three year old twins, a six year old daughter, a grandmother and an aunt. There were seven of them up in the rafters, just on the beams, balancing with these little ones.

Mary: One of the ladies had her legs bent for so long up there that she could hardly walk when she came down.

Mike: The boat was most useful because they put the children and the ladies in it and pulled the boat round to our house and we were able to give them somewhere for the night. We already had ten people but even with another seven we managed okay. Downstairs was wet so we all moved ourselves around upstairs and somehow made it work. We had some basic food and water to last us through the night.

After the storm, in the days that followed, when we would start to run out of something, somebody would come along and bring, for example, a case of water or some food. We just found that every day, we were provided for.

We still have that boat. We made some enquiries as to whom it belonged but nobody ever claimed it. I think it was my son-in-law, William, who gave it the name, *Ivan Gimme*. Three months later, he was able to use the boat to catch lobsters off South Sound!

Just Chillin'
- Ocean Club

In anticipation of Hurricane Ivan, Bradley McLean left his home in East End to 'chill out' and relax in his friend's condominium at Ocean Club. The relaxing ended when he woke up to find himself floating on an air mattress around the living room in the early morning hours of Sunday, 12th September. A few weeks later, he talked about his ordeal. In the words of Bradley McLean, the following is his fascinating story, which is short and to the point:-

Bradley McLean with his girlfriend, Tamika Solomon

I really didn't think the storm was going to be bad like that so I was *'just chillin'*.

I've lived in East End all my life but, for the storm, I decided to stay at Ocean Club with my friends, who live in the front building by the road. We thought we would just stay there and watch the storm, and just 'chill'.

At about five o'clock Sunday morning was when it started. The place wasn't really boarded up. It just had two-by-six boards, like an X, on the back door. It was me and my girlfriend, and a friend and his girlfriend. We were just relaxing, not really watching the storm from the first because we dropped asleep around ten or eleven on Saturday.

The electricity had gone off from about eight o'clock.

During the early morning, we were still sleeping when my friend's girlfriend came down and told us to wake up. When I woke up, I realized I was floating on the airbed. When we got up and looked, we see the seas coming through the building. From then, we were watching and it keep rising to about five and a half feet inside the house.

Then the front door facing the road blew off! I was so frightened. The pressure of the water blew it off so the furniture and the fridge and everything was in one spot in the corner at the back of the building. So we went upstairs then.

The roof was vibrating like it wanted to come off. Then the sheetrock around the side started cracking around the seal. We stayed there all day and were so scared. The wind sounded like people were crying. True!

It was like we were in the ocean and I was trying to figure out how I was going to reach my home in East End. I didn't think there was water up that way, though. I thought it was just kind of settling there where we were.

We were looking out and watching all the cars floating across, and the washers and dryers and televisions. We could see right out. The water was up to the windows and I would say about five to five and half feet up the sliding glass door.

The water started to go down on Monday. That's when we got outside - about six o'clock in the morning. When we left Ocean Club, we walked straight to East End. Along the way, we see all kind of debris all over the street, houses and everything. The whole place looked like people were dead.

When I reached East End, I didn't see too much people but the place was really destroyed and I seen one body lying in the road. It was a dead body that came out of the casket. It was a new one, still intact; head, foot and everything ... clothes on and everything. It was awful to see. Then I went by the church hall where people were sheltering.

My house was down in the buttonwood, on stilts. Even with the stilts, the whole thing was underwater and it was leaning. Eventually, the whole house dropped down and now it's gone. Next time there's a hurricane, I will go and look for safer ground!

Hoisting and Packing
- Prospect

Sister Catilda Wilson was determined not to let Ivan get the best of her. The following is her exciting tale of rescuing the neighbours and trying to save her employer's precious items - all the while never giving herself a second thought. Just five weeks after the storm, Sister Catilda told of the events that took place in her home that long weekend in September:-

Catilda Wilson, at the temporary tent of the New Testament Church of God

Thursday, I went to work and my boss told me not to come on Friday because everyone was preparing for the hurricane. So I did not go on Friday or on Saturday. My boss called and told me that I was supposed to come to his house in Spotts for the storm and stay. He said they would pick me up. I live with my boss's mother. During the storm, she was planning to stay with her son in Tropical Gardens. I was hearing what they were saying about the hurricane – how it was dangerous and thing like that.

Saturday, I phoned my son in Jamaica because they were supposed to get the hurricane before us. He said to me that it was terrible, even though they did not get the full blast of it. He is living in Portmore, in St. Catherine. Anyway, that was Saturday. We were preparing then. I went into town with my church sister, Sister Wilson, and she said that I must buy things that can keep. Coming back from town in the evening around five o'clock, I was telling her that I didn't feel like going anywhere. I told her, "You go, because I don't want anything to happen to you and then your children, them say it's because of me why you don't come to their house."

Her daughter-in-law came to take her to Tropical Gardens and, at the same time, my boss came for me. But in my heart, there was nothing telling me to go anywhere. I could feel nothing that would tell me to go so I said, "I don't ready yet." They say, "When you ready, call us."

Saturday night, about nine o'clock, they called and say, "Miss Catilda, you ready to come?" I said, "I don't ready, you know. If this storm not passing your way, I will come. But, if it passing your way, I'm not coming."

My home is in Prospect, Logwood Way. I lay down and prayed but no sleep could come to my eyes. Mrs. Wilson had left her granddaughter, Taesha, a young lady who was about twenty-four, with me so both of us were in the house. The tenants were at the other side in the apartment attached to the house.

I turn on the T.V. and watch it and I hear the same thing over and over about the storm. So I turn it off and turned on the radio and hear the same thing. So I thought this thing must be getting bad. Anyway, I did not sleep. The whole night, I was listening and talking to the Lord and asking him to have mercy on us. I could not sleep because the rain and breeze was coming. Each time it came, it was much stronger and it go on like that until about twelve o'clock Saturday night. I looked through the window and I saw the trees blowing and things like that.

About three-thirty, Taesha called from the other room and wanted a candle but I said that we wouldn't light any candles because we didn't know what can happen. It can turn over. I gave her a flashlight and she say I must come and look. When I went into her room, I saw water coming through the window from the air conditioning area and we begin to get some mats and things to caulk it up.

Around four o'clock, I made some coffee on the gas stove and Sister Wilson called from Tropical Gardens. I was telling her that water was coming into Taesha's room. We talked about things like the trees them shaking, and things like that.

When I went in Sister Wilson's room, the water was coming through her room air conditioner because it was in the window. I begin to get mats and everything that I could find to caulk the holes them.

Taesha then told me that I must come back into her room and look. When I went back, I saw the sheetrock begin to fall because the water was coming from the top now. We begin to move the things them from her room. I get plastic and give it to her to spread out on the bed, not knowing what was going to take place. We tried our best to pack up what we could in plastic bags.

Now, the breeze outside was blowing and sometime it whistled like when you blow into a bottle. When we got back into Sister Wilson's room, her sheetrock begin to come down so we begin to pack up her things them, trying to get everything together so that it do not wet up. Every minute, I would go and look outside and sometime the wind was white like foam and, at times, it come in like an octopus! To me, it looked like an octopus when it was swooping down. The trees were bowing down and coming back up, bowing down and coming back up! Sometime the wind come in with light. At times, it was clear, like it had a light in there, like it had a sense and knew directly what it was doing!

Even through that, Taesha and I were joking and laughing. I was so busy that I did not have any time to even fear. I was so busy, *packing* up the things them together and *hoisting* them up and looking at what was happening outside. Then I went back into the room and the tenant called to me and said that water from my part coming down into her room. So I get some floor mats and tell her to close that door where the water coming through and I barred the water with the mat. After that, when I went in my room, water begin to come up there and I begin to take up my things them and tried to put them in plastic bags and begin to hoist them up on what I could find.

I went from Taesha's room, to my room, to Sister Wilson's room, to the kitchen, to the hall, trying to see what I could hoist up.

At about five-thirty in the morning, the water was really coming up outside so I said to Taesha, "As soon as the wind settle down, let me hold the light and you see if you can go outside and put the car into the car porch," but when I try to open the door, the wind was going 'wh-ew-ew-ew-ew-ew'. I said to Taesha, "This wind is coming for us, you know? It's like he is waiting for us and, when we come out, he will grab we!"

Sometime, he was like somebody talking. Sometime, he was whistling! Sometime, he was playing music!

Taesha and I was very busy, packing things up and hoisting them as high as we could because the water was really coming in now. At this time, we didn't know that the tenants were in danger.

By then, all the sheetrock in the rooms had dropped down. One of the time, when I went to pack some of the things in Sister Wilson's room, Taesha come and say, "Water is coming up in the bath." So I get a piece of rug and stuffed it in the bathtub drain. The water was so dirty!

Going back into the living room, to go down to my part of the house, you have to take one step down. But, when I go to take a step down, I couldn't because there was so much water. I had to walk across the top of the chair there because I didn't want to step down into the dirty water. At the same time I was trying to save everything and watching outside too. But I had no time to fear because I have to be busy. Now water was coming in through the window at the front.

At one time, I said to Taesha, "Fly out, quick, and bring in the car, quick!" I hold the door for her to bring in her car but then, when we look, we see the water coming up on the sides of the car and the plants in the garage floating. The water begin to swim them.

After that, when I was going back down to my room again, the chair that I had walked on before to keep out of the water … I couldn't find it. It was covered in water. And, when I got to my room, my bed was covered in water. I took off the mattress and hoisted it up high on something but the frame of the bed and everything was covered. You could only see the back of the chair. The rest was covered in water.

When I come back into the living room, I see the T.V. stand begin to be covered with water. The water was near to covering the central table there so I took up all the pictures and things. At the same time, I hear knocking from the little window above the kitchen sink that is between the tenant and us. The tenant is a big, fat woman. She was knocking and I opened the window and, when me look over there, water had reached the tops of their windows and was coming over! When I look in, I could see their washing machine. Them have the type where the washer and dryer are together and it was floating on its side. I could see the zinc had blown from next door into their windows and break up the windows them and the water coming through higher than their window. The woman was standing on the table but the table was sinking.

The tenants them say, "We're going to drown over here so you have to mek we come in. There's no way we can get out." But there was no way we could open the door so she had to come through that little window. She was so big that I didn't know how she was going to come through. The young man come through first with bundles of clothes. When she come, one foot come through but she couldn't get the other one through. Me say to her, "No, you shouldn't come 'footway', you should come 'headway'." She fight and fight and fight, and she finally come through.

The water was up to my thighs now in the house and me holding the bottom of my dress because me don't wear pants. For the whole day, we stand up in the water because there was nowhere to sit ... water in the fridge, water in the stove, water over the cabinets, water everywhere.

Outside, Ivan was in a rage and, when we looked out, Logwood Way was a sea. It had waves. When we looked across the street, the house there, up to the fence, was surrounded by sea.

Now the hurricane sounded like he was talking and then he seemed to be singing. To me, it was like him come to kill and him come to tek. During the day, we were watching through the window and the water was mount and mount and mount, until it couldn't mount no further.

Then Taesha say I must look outside and the suitcase that I had packed some ornaments and things in was floating outside. The breeze had break off the board from the windows in my room. Then it break the windows and everything was floating outside. Even the drapes were outside. I mek an attempt to go out and tek up the suitcase but it was like him say, "If you come out here, I'm going to tear you up." When we open the door, everything that was inside was going out so we had to shut the door again. We had put plenty of things, like figurines, on the dining room table but they were on the ground now and some had break up. Another time, when we tried to open the door again, all them figurines went outside.

We were in the water until about four o'clock. When things settled down, we begin to try to sweep up. In the evening, the water was still high outside but, in the house, it was drying up. In the bathroom, it was a mess because the sewage came up through the toilets. Everything was in a mess so we did everything we could to clean it up for the rest of the evening. The tenant went round to her house that night and cooked on the gas stove and we eat. I even sleep that night! My mattress was dry because I had hoisted it up high. I disinfected the springs and put it on there. Taesha's bed was all gone and her room was in a mess. So I made a bed for her in the living room with chair cushions that we had hoisted up and didn't let get wet.

When we got up the next day, we still stepped in water but I say, "Thank God we're alive!" But I didn't know what was happening to the rest of the people them. So, early Monday morning at six o'clock, I mek a cup of coffee on the gas stove. Water was still outside to my waist and the street was still like a sea but I went outside. It was still dark and I saw a man at his house across the street with a light. He walked across to me in the water and he say he didn't even know anybody was in our house all that time. I told him I had never witnessed a flooding before even though I am Jamaican. I never experienced anything like this. I understand flooding now. Taesha's car is dead and the tenant's car is dead.

Then I decided I was going to walk past Spotts to see what had happened to my boss. It really struck me when I got to Old Prospect Road. Lord have mercy! When I look and see people's mattresses, fridges, T.V.s, mashed up cars, even a little boat … it seemed to me that everything that was on Old Prospect Road had come over. Lord, Jesus, I felt it in my heart.

Then I reached Ocean Club and saw the damage there. And, when I saw three other people walking, I had to raise my hand and say, "Thank you, Jesus. You is awesome. You is wonderful," knowing that I was alive and those people was alive.

But when my heart break was when I reach Mariners Cove. When I look across and see the height of the sea in the early morning and the breeze still coming in so heavy I had to balance myself not to fall but I was determined to find my boss. When I reach there, Mariners Cove was in the road and, when I see how the houses had come up off the foundation, my heart was break and I begin to think of them people that was there. I don't care how tough your heart is, it would break to see it. It was so devastating. My heart melt and I said to myself, "The devil meant it for evil but God meant it for good." God did not intend for Cayman to be destroyed. In the days of Noah, when he destroyed the earth with a flood, he made a covenant with Noah. He said that He would never destroy the earth again with flood. What helped me to believe this was that two days after the storm, I saw a rainbow. You see, God had said to Noah, "I'm going to give you a sign. When you see the rainbow, it means that I will not destroy the earth with water again."

My daddy's name was Ivan, but he was not terrible. Hurricane Ivan was terrible!

Memorial

Osley C. Ebanks

29th September 1930 - 12th September 2004

Thousands of people in Cayman survived Hurricane Ivan and lived to tell their stories but a couple of people were not so fortunate. In the days after the hurricane, two deaths were reported in Cayman. One of these was Cayman's very own Osley Ebanks who, being a seaman, had decided to ride out the storm on his twenty-seven foot boat in West Bay. Mr. Osley was reported missing by his family on Monday, 13th September 2004, and his body was found in the mangroves in West Bay on 15th October 2004. His family, together with the entire Cayman community, were saddened to hear of his passing. May his soul rest in peace.

Photos

Caribbean Paradise, South Sound, Monday, 13th September 2004

Picture taken by South Sound resident, Jennifer Godfrey

Ivan's Tears

Drowning in the tears
Of my broken heart.
Everyone and everything
So many miles apart.

Mother Nature showed
The true power of her name,
Hoping that soon
We would learn her game.

Memories of everything got washed away,
All in one very sad day!
Left Cayman bleeding and crying,
But our beautiful island won't be left dying.

Dreaming of a today
Without yesterday's pain,
But waking up tomorrow
And things are all the same.

Years of work,
But we hope and we pray
That we'll all be together again one day.

Drowning in the tears
Of my broken heart,
I know some day
We won't be apart!

Louisa Gibson (age 14),
South Sound resident,
at Caribbean Paradise

Merrendale Road and Arch's Square

Above: *George Town, Saturday, 11th September 2004, BEFORE Hurricane Ivan*
Below: *George Town, Sunday afternoon, 12th September 2004*

*Note: The old Printing Press (small building foreground in top picture)
was demolished by the hurricane.*

PHOTOS

Merrendale Road

Above: *George Town, Saturday evening, 11th September 2004, BEFORE Hurricane Ivan*
Below: *George Town, Sunday afternoon, 12th September 2004*

71

Above: *Debris blowing in George Town, around 10:00 a.m. Sunday, 12th September 2004*
Below: *Merrendale Road, George Town, Monday morning, 13th September 2004*
View from the Fifth Floor of the Citrus Grove Building

Theo R. Bodden Memorial Funeral Home, Walkers Road, Monday, 13th September 2004

Seaview Hotel, South Church Street, George Town, after Hurricane Ivan

Island Chiropractic
Walkers Road and Middle Road,
George Town,
Monday, 13th September 2004

Denham Thompson Way, George Town,
Monday, 13th September 2004

Pictures taken by South Sound resident, Dennis Mastry

The late Syl Coe's house,
South Church Street, George Town,
Monday, 13th September 2004

South Church Street, George Town,
Monday, 13th September 2004

Coconut Harbour, George Town,
Monday, 13th September 2004

Pictures taken by South Sound resident, Dennis Mastry

North Church Street

Inside Merren's Shopping Complex

Jasper Center, Eastern Avenue

Paddington Place, North Sound Way

Industrial Park, Monday, 13th September 2004

Pictures taken by former Ocean Club resident, Garry Bosley

Grand Harbour, Red Bay, one week after Hurricane Ivan.
Note the long line-up of people waiting to get into Hurley's Marketplace.

Picture taken by Shelley Leonard

Although their losses were great, having sustained major damage to their family home in Spotts and also to their stores throughout the island, the owners of Hurley's Marketplace and Cayman Imports opened the doors of their businesses on Tuesday, 14th September 2004, to the people of Cayman so that they could have the necessary food and supplies in order to survive during the storm's horrible aftermath.

During the storm, they rescued many, many people who were in dire straits from various locations throughout the island and sheltered them in their Grand Harbour location. As well, they offered them food and dry clothing. After the storm, they brought in container-loads of water, ice, charcoal and chicken, and distributed it island-wide free of charge. They also allowed popular restaurant, Castaways, use of their generator so that they could offer meals to the public, which was very much appreciated by the people, who were so busy trying to get their lives back in order, most of whom didn't have proper facilities (much less electricity or water) for cooking.

Shamrock Road/Spotts Straight, one week after the storm

PHOTOS

In Memory of Mariners Cove

Spotts, early Monday morning, 13th September 2004

Pictures taken by former Ocean Club resident, Garry Bosley

Warmest wishes to Bev, Stephen, Josh and Joel.

Mariners Cove, Spotts, Wednesday, 15th September 2004

Old Prospect Church (I.T.L.D. offices)

Smith Road Plaza
Monday, 13th September 2004

Smith Road,
Monday, 13th September 2004

Homes across the street from
Dr. Shirley Cridland's office on Smith Road,
Monday, 13th September 2004

Pictures taken by South Sound resident, Dennis Mastry

*Pasadora Place, Phase II, Smith Road,
Monday, 13th September 2004*

*Cayman Prep and High School,
Primary Department, Smith Road,
Monday,13th September 2004*

*Smith Road flooding,
Monday, 13th September 2004*

Pictures taken by South Sound resident, Dennis Mastry

Prospect Cemetery

Pictures taken by South Sound resident, Jennifer Godfrey

Prospect Cemetery

Pictures taken by South Sound resident, Jennifer Godfrey

"Trying to get home."
South Sound,
Monday, 13th September 2004

Condominiums in South Sound,
Monday, 13th September 2004

South Sound Road,
Monday, 13th September 2004

Pictures taken by South Sound resident, Dennis Mastry

By the Sea Condos, South Sound, one week after Hurricane Ivan

South Sound home

*Crow's Nest Restaurant,
South Sound,
Monday, 13th September 2004*

*Back of Crow's Nest Restaurant,
two weeks after the storm*

South Sound homes

Picture taken by South Sound resident, Jennifer Godfrey

South Sound Road, Monday, 13th September 2004
Note: Molly and (the late) Colin Whitelock's house on the right of picture. Due to the
devastation caused by the hurricane, this house has since been demolished.

Mary Read Crescent, South Sound, Monday, 13th September 2004.
Pictures taken by South Sound resident, Ed Powers

South Sound waves, Monday, 13th September 2004
Picture taken by South Sound resident, Dennis Mastry

South Sound mess
Picture taken by South Sound resident, Jennifer Godfrey

South Sound, Monday, 13th September 2004

Pictures taken by Ed Powers

South Sound windows

South Sound power pole

South Sound Road, one week after Hurricane Ivan

Cayman Islands Tennis Club, South Sound, one week after the storm

In memory of Pirates Lair, the way it was before Hurricane Ivan.
To Suzan ... much love.

Josh and Zachary Merren at what once was their favourite play spot, Pirates Lair (after Hurricane Ivan)

The remains of Pirates Lair's swimming pool

PHOTOS

Pirates Lair Condominiums

Suzan Merren's kitchen

Palm Springs Condominiums, South Sound, Monday, 13th September 2004

Pictures taken by South Sound resident, Dennis Mastry

*Sunrise Condominiums, South Sound,
September 2004*

Pictures taken by South Sound resident, Dennis Mastry

Sunrise Condominiums, South Sound, one week after the hurricane

Sunrise Condominiums Tennis Court, South Sound, two months after Hurricane Ivan

South Sound

"Unna see mi dish, mi satellite dish!"

ABOVE: *South Sound home*
BELOW: *George Town home*

"Ivan took my roof and my tree!"
More damaged homes in George Town

Pre-School on Walkers Road, Monday, 13th September 2004

Apartments on Walkers Road

*Cayman Imports, Walkers Road,
Monday, 13th September 2004*

*Walkers Road, Monday,
13th September 2004*

*Hurley's Entertainment, (far left) former home to
Z-99 and Rooster 101.9 on Walkers Road
Note: The building has since been demolished due
to extensive damage from the hurricane.*

Pictures taken by South Sound resident, Dennis Mastry

Picture provided by South Sound resident, Carole Kirkconnell

"Filling up the Tanks"

Debris from Walkers Road Texaco, Monday, 13th September 2004

Walkers Road Texaco, Monday, 13th September 2004

The Wight families' Walkers Road Texaco and many of the Wight family members' homes received extensive damage from Hurricane Ivan but that didn't stop them and their staff, who also suffered losses, from servicing the people in the immediate aftermath of the hurricane. Cars were lined up hundreds of yards for a fill-up but, thanks to the efficiency and organisation of the Wight brothers, the wait was not a long one considering the circumstances. Their efforts did not go unnoticed and were greatly appreciated by everyone during the desperate times that followed the storm.

Rubble on Palm Dale
A familiar sight across the island in the weeks and months following the storm

Cayman Prep and High School lunchroom, after the hurricane

North Church Street home

PHOTOS

Canal Point

Dock at Gene and Melisa Thompson's property

Overturned trailer at a luxury home

Kirk Home Centre, Eastern Avenue

Inside Kirk Supermarket, Eastern Avenue, after the storm

Family-owned business, Kirkconnell Brothers Limited, suffered heavy losses to their businesses on Eastern Avenue and in the Industrial Park area during the storm. However, in true Caymanian spirit, they do not dwell on their losses. Instead, after the hurricane, they continued to operate some of their businesses in less than ideal conditions.

With the assistance of their loyal staff, they are rebuilding, as they did in November of 1932 when their store in Cayman Brac was completely destroyed by the '32 Storm.

Many people have expressed their gratitude to the Kirkconnell family for their generosity in providing meals to their staff and families, and other people around them, in the days and weeks following Hurricane Ivan.

No House Leave
- East End

Before leaving for Boston on holiday in September, Cleo Conolly never imagined that she would return to Cayman to find not only her roof gone but, in fact, her entire house gone because of Hurricane Ivan. Not long after the storm, she told how she learned of the devastation and of her feelings afterwards:-

I didn't think we was going to have the storm that we had. I just think that they always pass to the south and miss us. I was in Boston during the storm and I called on Sunday morning and I got my nephew and he say, "Well, a piece of my housetop has gone and a part of yours has gone." So I was thinking that the storm had passed through and gone and I didn't hear any more.

Cleopatra Conolly, on the land where her house once stood

Then, Tuesday night, they called me and I was telling Ann, my brother, Frankie's daughter, what to tell Darcy to do to my housetop till I come. But she wouldn't tell me. She made Frankie come on the phone and he said, "Cleo, you don't have *no house leave!*" But, you know, I not cry yet. I don't know how I'm so tough. Sometimes, I feel myself getting upset. So many were promising to be there for me and nobody has come yet but I know I have to give them time. Beggars isn't any choosers, you know.

I'm living with my nephew now. I'm seventy-nine years old and I've lived in that house seventy-two years, since I was seven and a half. I was here for the '32 Storm and I remember it. Yes, I remember it. It wasn't as bad as this!

When Gilbert passed through, I wasn't at home neither. I was in Texas and I had insurance then but the insurance went so high after Gilbert passed through that I don't have insurance now. It was so high that I couldn't pay it.

I was there in Boston during the storm and I was praying that the Lord would still the winds and the waves as He had done in years gone by but He didn't mean to still it. That storm was for a purpose. I don't know what He was chastising us for but it was something.

When I got back to the island from Boston, my niece say, "Well, I can tell you one thing, you're not going back any other September," because she say that every time I go, a hurricane comes in. That's what Barrie Sue on the radio says too. She said that I go every September and then a storm comes!" So I don't think that next year I'll be going!

Massive Flooding
- South Sound

Hurlston brothers, Anthony and Stephen, standing next to the boat in which their family was rescued

Hurlston cousins, Anthony and Daniel, aged twelve and fifteen respectively, together with their uncle, Mr. Harry Hurlston, took refuge with other family members in Daniel's family home in South Sound just across the road from the Crow's Nest Restaurant. Anthony, Daniel and Mr. Harry told their story several weeks after Ivan struck:-

Mr. Harry: I was born in that house right there and have been living there for sixty-eight years but I boarded it up and took shelter in my cousin's son's house, there across the road. There were my cousin's son, Hank, his wife, my cousin's three grandsons and myself in that house.

On Saturday night, the eleventh, we were watching the news of the storm on T.V. The station was telling us about the hurricane, where it was and when it would be here. We were watching that until about eight o'clock when CUC cut out all the power. The wind was already picking up around that time. That must have been

119

when I went to sleep on the sofa.

Anthony: On Saturday night, at first, we didn't think much about the hurricane because we had such a good boarded up house. I didn't sleep much though because I was worried about my dad. He had stayed in our house in Prospect, in Bonnyview Estates, with my older brother, and had called to say the water was getting too high. He couldn't bail out anymore and they would soon have to go up into the attic." [Anthony's other brother, Stephen, was with his grandparents in his Aunt Judy's house next door.]

Daniel: We weren't scared really. We were anticipating the storm but we were playing video games. After awhile, we stopped and watched some T.V. After the electricity went off, we sat around the table with candles and then tried to get some sleep. I had my Bible under my arm the whole time. Anthony got about an hour's sleep, I got a lot, but Uncle Harry got the most!

Anthony: I didn't sleep much for worrying about my dad and brother but I really wasn't that scared until Daniel's brother shouted out this big old word – I don't know what it was – but he was scared because the door had started leaking.

Mr. Harry: We were all prepared for the lights to go out. We had our flashlights and everything. About ten o'clock in the morning, I woke up to the sound of one of the boy's voices, saying to his dad, "Dad, we're having a problem with water coming through that seal there." He had shined his flashlight at the door and could see the water coming in. It was blowing and raining so hard that I thought the wind was forcing the water in there so I said to the boys, "Why don't you get a towel and stuff it in there," so we done that.

Anthony: We got towels and shirts and put them in front of the door to try and dry everything up. A couple of hours later, Daniel's mom screamed and said that the water was coming in throughout the house. Then the sewage started coming up and the house started really flooding. I was worried that we would all get sick because of this.

Then my grandparents who were in my aunt's house next door called and scared us by saying the sheetrock had started falling and the place was flooding over there. They didn't know what they were going to do with my aunt, Julie-Mae, who can't walk. The water was knee-high and she was on the bed. They said that they would soon have to take her off and make her float on something. Then the line went dead. A couple hours later, my grandmother called again. She said we must try and get "help, help, help" and then the line went dead again. My uncle was pacing up and down the hallway. My grandparents called three times and, every time, there was more bad news.

Mr. Harry: After awhile, I thought to myself, Well, let me just go and check the door. I took my flashlight and, not only was the water gushing through the door now but it was also gushing through the window. So I said, "Guys, we got a serious problem here. We got a *flooding*."

What happened was that the water coming in really wasn't from the sea directly. It was just a *massive* rush of water that started anywhere from the cemetery right on up to above Lawrence Thompson's. They had seas coming in there from the southeast that just went over and crashed into everything on its way in. The water, which came down from over Lawrence Thompson's and all about there, got into these low-lying swamps and flooded them. Then we started having a *massive flooding*. We were in that water in the house for about four hours.

Harry Hurlston, with a friend, Bubbles

Anthony: Around four o'clock, we heard banging on the door. It was my uncle-in-law and we told him, "Don't bother with us – must go and check them next door." They found a boat, which had been banging against my Aunt Judy's house and my grandfather had tied to the window. They got the boat and were able to save everybody. They took us in the boat up to the road where my Uncle Ken's pickup truck was. Fourteen of us went in the back of the pickup truck. Julie-Mae went inside the truck.

The trip over to my aunt's house over by the Truman Bodden Field took forever because the water was killing us. The rain was stinging us, pelting us like rocks, and everyone was saying, "Aye, aye!" The wind was blowing ninety-three or ninety-five miles an hour – something like that! But we made it there safely and that's where we stayed.

Higgledy-Piggledy
- South Sound

Denham and Melva Hurlston had been living in their house in South Sound for forty-five years before Hurricane Ivan came to the island. They took shelter from

the hurricane with their daughter, Judy Hurlston, in her house across the road, together with their grandson, Stephen, their daughter, Julie-Mae, and their daughter-in-law, Natalia:-

Denham and Melva Hurlston, at home in South Sound

Mr. Denny: We were trying to save our little daughter, Julie-Mae, who suffers with Down's Syndrome and is now unable to walk.

On the Friday before the storm, we went to my other daughter's house, across the road there. It is a brand new house, the newest one built in South Sound. I know the sea and I knew Ivan was going to be a dangerous hurricane. We boarded our house up good. We had the shutters (which we had made when Andrew hit Homestead) on all the windows.

Miss Melva: We were doing fine at our daughter's house until Sunday morning around ten o'clock when the ceiling started to drop out. We had to take our little girl and run with her from one place to another. My grandson, Stephen, was a big help with her. We were up to our necks in water in the house. I prayed and prayed that a guardian angel would come and rescue us.

Stephen: From Saturday, I was in my aunt's house with my grandparents and Julie-Mae. I slept about two or three hours but was up most of the night. Things started getting bad when it started flooding. The water was up to about chest-high and we had no way to get out so everybody was up and about seeing what they could do. I was taking Julie-Mae off the bed and holding her until they could move the bed from spot to spot to set her on it to keep her from the water.

Mr. Denny: The house was full of water up to our necks. Sure, we were scared. We heard something hitting up against the house. At first we thought it was Ivan. My daughter-in-law saw it and said to me, "Papa, a boat is here." That's when I looked out and saw the boat. It was still on the trailer. The boat was called *'Which Craft'*. She had floated from over there [pointing south]. Now, the path that she took when she got away from there, I don't know, but this is where she ended up.

There were only two windows I wouldn't batten up and it's a good thing. I told my daughter-in-law, "I'm going to hold the boat and you go get me two sheets." So I took and tied those two sheets together. Then I took out the screens right from inside the house and put my hand through the window and tied the sheets around this mullion. You see, the separation between a double window is called a mullion.

Now, this was a big boat with a seventy-five horsepower engine and I had to push it off to keep it from hitting the house and crashing through the window. I had made a loop at the end of the sheet and tied it around the rail of the boat. She held there for about five hours until somebody finally came.

Miss Melva: We were in that house for hours listening to the wind and praying. Around four o'clock in the evening, we heard the knock on the door and somebody hollered "Marco!"

Mr. Denny: It was my grand-son-in-law, Marco, who had swum it down with two other men. One was my son-in-law and I think the other used to work with him at the submarine. They were big men but it took all of them to get the door open. The pressure of the water was shoving the door. They pulled the boat alongside the step and held the boat tight. When they finally tore open the door, my wife, Melva, was the first to get in the boat. Two of the men grabbed her and put her in. Then my son-in-law, Ken, got my little daughter, Julie-Mae, and put her in. Then they put the rest in. I was the last one – the captain is always the last. I know you heard that before! But, when I stepped out, I went right down and my hat floated away. That's how deep the water was. I was the only one who didn't make it into the boat. I held onto the side and they towed me.

Stephen: We had just bought two rare birds. We had a male and a female. We put one cage on top of the washer and one was on top of the dryer inside the house with us. While we were rescuing Julie-Mae, one of the cages floated off and, when we went back, one bird had drowned.

Mr. Denny: That was something about that boat. You know, when my son-in-law turned the key, the boat started right up. I tell you the water was so deep that we went right over the cistern top and never even knew it was there. When we got up by the road, my son-in-law tied the boat onto the thatch tree. Then we all had to get in the back of my son-in-law's pickup truck and went to my daughter's house over by the Truman Bodden Playing Field.

Miss Melva: Stephen took a chill after working so hard during the storm that he had a fever. He was cold and his chest was hurting. We had to rub him down with alcohol and, by the next morning, he was okay.

Mr. Denny: When we got back to my house, everything was *higgledy-piggledy!* The roof had come off during Ivan and all the radios, televisions and the furniture were floating all around. I managed to save my Bible, which my mother gave me. I lost all my land papers but that's okay since most of it has been archived. I lost most of my pictures except a framed picture of my parents. Let me show you. You can see how I look now. But you know I'm a good-looking man when you see this picture and what I came from!

Peril at Pet Paradise
- Newlands

Three months after the storm, Donna Baxter, owner of Cayman Pet Paradise, through endless tears, told of her agonizing experience of Ivan tearing through her lovely home and wreaking havoc on her safe haven for animals while she watched in disbelief from the refuge of her vehicle:-

Donna Baxter, next to her Ford Explorer in which she and her friends took shelter from Hurricane Ivan

I guess it started probably around six o'clock, Saturday night. It was getting pretty tough to walk around even then. It was windy and the rainsqualls were coming in. Between the squalls, I ran downstairs and checked the cattery and the dog kennels.

We were watching the weather channel. There were five of us: myself, my handyman, Adam, a friend, Lana, her son, Ian, and another friend of mine, Brenda, who is from Breakers.

Once we were upstairs, we cooked our last meal before the power and water went off. I guess the water went off around six or seven o'clock at night and the electricity went down before nine. We had decided to try and cook up what food we had and get that settled. So we did that and were doing fine. Between twelve and one o'clock in the morning, we heard the first of the AT&T tower go down. We had rolling shutters so we rolled them up and took a look.

Their generator was operating and they had strobe lights at different stages of the tower and it was twisting back and forth. The tower was on my property, which I lease to AT&T. It was approximately two hundred and eighty feet high.

So we were doing fine but nobody was sleeping, obviously. I had a huge bar with four stools upstairs and we were all sitting there with the hurricane lamps on. Tiles were blowing off the roof and we could hear them going but the plywood and tar paper were holding so we weren't taking any water in – not through the ceilings anyway.

About four o'clock in the morning, we heard what we thought was the second half of the tower go down. The wind was horrible to listen to. It sounded like a freight train coming through the house. Thankfully, the tower fell in the other direction. Within seconds of that, something huge hit the front of the house!

I had a big A-frame house. It was forty-two hundred square feet, with extended roofs on either end, and I had a huge screened-in patio at the back. The front wasn't screened in.

I don't know what it was but something hit the wall right up underneath the eave. Then the walls started waving in and out in the wind. I had huge double glass doors on the front of the house. We had two sheets of five-by-eight ply bolted right into the deck with three and a half inch stainless steel bolts. When the walls started swaying, the wind ripped the plywood off. It went flying and hit the corner of the house. Then it came up and hit the roof, and it flew off.

Then the glass doors flew and, I mean, FLEW into the house! They flew into the living room, about halfway across the room.

All of us ran downstairs then to the spare bedroom because the roof and walls just started peeling off. One whole section of a wall was still attached to the ceiling but was hanging over the side balcony and the wind was lifting it up and slamming it against the side of the house.

We decided to stay in the spare bedroom, although the sheetrock started coming down. I rolled up the shutters a bit and we could still see grass out there and, as long as there was grass, we weren't in any danger of flooding.

We were downstairs from about four-thirty until about ten-thirty or eleven o'clock on Sunday morning when we started seeing water coming in underneath the doors. At that point, I thought I had better take another look out. So I rolled up the shutters again, just a crack, and could see that all the trees were down and the water was high. The doors were the only thing keeping the water at bay.

After we talked about it, we decided we had better get the hell out. We had one door through the laundry room, which we didn't put anything on and left as an escape route. I know you're supposed to stay with your house and everything else but we had no choice but to go.

So we went out through the side and had to run out in between gusts of wind so we didn't get crushed to the ground with this wall that was slamming down on the ground. We got out through the gate and water was just underneath my bra line. I took my phone with me.

We made it across the yard. We had the truck parked over by the crematorium. We were all soaking wet and nobody had any spare clothes. We just ran out of the house and into the truck. We were all freezing to death!

Then I started making phone calls. Nobody else's phones were working. I was trying to get hold of the police or 911. I got hold of Graham, a good friend of mine who was staying at Citrus Grove with his two little dogs. He couldn't get through to the police but they actually showed up at Citrus Grove from what I understand and he told them about us. Then he called me back and said the police were going to try and get through to us in about an hour.

Of course, we were waiting and, every couple of hours, he would call back or I would call him (my battery was starting to run low and I was trying to conserve it) and I was trying to get hold of Adam's folks in Spotts/Newlands. We couldn't

Donna, standing on what was once her master bedroom floor

get anybody there and neither Lana or Brenda's phones were working. So Graham kept phoning us back saying, "They're on their way, they're on their way." We were in the truck for several hours until finally, just before the sun went down, he called us back and he was shouting at the police officer standing in front of him and trying to talk to me at the same time. He was saying, "You've got to get out there and get those people!"

We decided there was nothing much we could do but sit and wait and hope we didn't float away because, by that time, the water was so high the truck was floating. It was horrible. The water was coming in underneath the doors. The three women … we were sitting in the back with our feet up on the seats. The truck was bobbing up and down. We didn't think we would survive it.

After I got the last phone call from Graham, we heard another horrendous crash and I think it was the kennels down in the back had gone and, not long after that, four of my dogs were out swimming around in the water, trying to hang on. We couldn't get to them! One of the women in the car with me, as we sat and watched my house fall apart, said twice, "God teaches us not to value material things in this world."

Sometime during Sunday night – I have no idea what time it was - the water had gone down and Adam had opened up the truck door and said, "Oh, my God, the water is below the running board!" So I opened up my side and took a look down and, sure enough, we could actually see part of the cement.

When we got out of the truck Monday morning, everything including all the trees were down. The buildings were all ripped to pieces. My poor dogs were sitting in their smashed up kennels with water up to their chests. We had to get them settled back in and find some food and water for them. In the office, we had a huge storage container that had toppled over in the wind. That had all the dry dog food in it. We had to kick the door in because the container had come down and pushed the desk right up against the door. We couldn't get in around to the back side because a big filing cabinet had come down between the fridge and the work table. Once we got inside, we started opening cans of food.

In the office, there are three small kennels where we keep all the little dogs. There were four of them and they were soaking wet and had no roof or shelter from the kennel at all. So Brenda and I grabbed two of the cats out of one of the larger kennels in the back corner and mopped that out with as much water as we could and brought out the four dogs. One of them … I touched his eyes and he was alive but I wasn't going to move him then. I was going to take care of the ones I knew I could help. There was another Maltese dog in the kennel with him. They were siblings. We brought the three of them over and put them in the large cat kennel in the cattery and got them set up with some saltwater out of the swamp that was still in the yard. We gave them a little bit of food and then went to take care of the rest of the dogs and to feed them since Saturday morning was the last time they had been fed. I found a bottle of bleach and put a capful or two into each of their buckets of saltwater. When we went back to the office, I wrapped the little Maltese dog in a dry towel, which I somehow managed to find, and took him with us.

A big palm tree had come down right in front of the truck so we had to get over that. Thank God for the four-wheel drive. The water was so high, we couldn't tell where the road was. It drops off on both sides so we were inching along and hoping we didn't go off the edge. Trees were down all around so we had a hard time getting out.

We came around the corner and a telephone pole had come down across the road and was submerged in the water. We didn't see it and hit it with the truck. Three of us got out and picked up that telephone pole, with the lines still attached to it, and moved it to the side of the road so we could get out. It took us almost an hour and a half just to make it out to the main road.

By the time we got to Allison's house in Spotts/Newlands, there were seventeen other people there. That's where I stayed for the next few days until I went to Sunset House.

Brenda and I went over to Lana's house to see if her place was still intact and Adam went back to my house to see if he could find us some clothes because we had nothing, absolutely nothing. He did manage to find some things, although they were wet. I only had my sweatshirt and sweatpants that I had left the house in, and my Wellingtons.

Adrian and Bonnie Briggs are my partners. Adrian came around to check on things while Adam was still there getting my clothes. He told Adam that we should go down to Sunset House and stay there. He is such a sweet, generous person.

God bless my neighbours down the road, over at the fish farm: Benji Bodden, Frank Kahoun and David Alberga. They had gone down to check on the fish farm to see how it had made out. Then they went by my place. They thought the dogs had been abandoned so they opened up more cans of food of which I only had six cans left. It cut my supplies down even farther but they were only trying to help and I appreciated it so much.

The little Maltese dog didn't make it. When we got over to Allison's, we heated up and sealed warm water in plastic bags and put them around the little dog's body. His breathing had been very laboured so we gave him a good shot of Nutrical. He seemed to revive and started to breathe a little easier. He was trying to gasp air and, when I took a look at his gums, they were white. I think he died of hypothermia because he couldn't get warmed up. The same thing almost happened to Adam. Dr. Matthew lived directly across the street from them so Allison went across and got him and brought him over to look at Adam. He said that he never, ever thought he'd see, in the Caribbean, a case of hypothermia!

A skeleton of a building is what's left of my house. Out of all the buildings we have on the property, only the cattery is left standing. Everything else is pretty much destroyed but we're making it. Never in my wildest dreams though did I think I would lose absolutely everything!

Surfing Waters
- Crewe Road

Heather Panton sheltered with her mother in their home on Crewe Road during Hurricane Ivan. Heather recalled her frightening experience seven weeks later:-

I am fifty-five years old and I like a little storm but I don't like hurricanes. Every West Indian enjoys a little storm because of the breeze and it cools things off. But, when it comes to hurricanes, I don't want anything to do with them. I knew this was going to be bad and it was. I lost every tree in my yard. Our house took a direct hit. Some of my crepe myrtle plants wrapped around like a rubber band. That was a tornado that did that.

It was only my mother and I in the house, with three dogs, because my brothers, Dwight and Kennedy, had taken their families to Miami.

From the day it hit, Mama said, "Heather, this is not just a hurricane. This is a tornado, tidal wave and hurricane in one." I had

A bashful Heather in her garden, with the author's son (Zachary Merren)

four feet of water in my house. We lost televisions, chairs and sofas. Three bedrooms caved in because the gable end went. Part of our brand new roof went too. I was just numb. I'm going to tell you the truth, my darling child, I was just mesmerized! I couldn't panic though because of Mama's heart condition. I was back and forth from her room. We didn't sleep. We COULDN'T sleep!

I'm used to hurricanes but the only thing with this one that scared me was that wind! It sounded like a baby crying!

When I got up Sunday morning, I wouldn't look outside at first. I was scared because the little kitchen window wasn't covered with shutters. The wind was now blowing like ever but I had to get my mother breakfast and I had to fix her lunch. Luckily, I had cooked some food and had it up in the freezer and I had a good fridge. My food didn't spoil until Thursday.

You see, we had bought twenty pounds of turtle, lobster, shrimp and all kinds of stuff because my brother, Neely, was coming for a birthday party for Mama. She was eighty on the seventeenth of September. But, of course, everything had to be cancelled.

We had storm shutters up so there was hardly any breeze coming into the house but we didn't put boards up on the four big windows by the front door or the sliding door. That's where the mistake came. The water started to come in through the sliding door because it's low and because of the cistern overflowing …that's how so much water got into the house.

When I did look out that Sunday morning, I saw the wind! Geez, I could see all of my breadfruit trees and mango trees blowing! But I could hardly see through the wind and, the hurtful part was, where it was blowing so hard, the rain was horizontal. This is how it got into the house. When I looked out at that water, I said, "Well, anybody from California could come and *surf* in this!" Then, at two o'clock that afternoon, when I was washing dishes, I looked out and said, "Jesus, I can't live without You and now You've come to kill me! God, please make this stop," and, true to God, He answered my prayer. As I said that, it was like – 'whew!' – the wind just died down and you could just see the ripples fading.

My sister, K.K. had just put in a new kitchen for me and, when I looked, the brand new stove had started getting wet so I said, "Oh, yeah?" Then I ran to the utility door, because that is right onto the kitchen, and I forced that door open. That's got to be the strongest little door in the world and it slammed back! I still have cuts on my hand from it but, if I hadn't done it, I was going to lose the house.

Then I tried to get the front door open, which is a wooden door. That was jammed shut from swelling and I said, "Well, Nina" – that's Dwight's little puppy that the children left me to take care of. I grabbed Nina's leash and wrapped it around the doorknob and pulled that door open. Then I saw why the water was coming in as well.

The big arborvitae tree had fallen and was up against the door. This was at two-thirty in the afternoon. Darling, I got on my knees and, either I'm crazy or the bravest woman in the world – coconuts were zooming over my head but I took it. I said, "I've got to do this or Mama is going to die." I cut away limbs of that tree half the size of a van so the water could flow out on the little walkway. Then it started to go. When I looked, televisions that were thirty years old were scattered on the ground.

Daddy's garage went too. The whole top blew off where we had a lot of stuff stored. The glass exploded. My sister-in-law had her fifty thousand dollar Mercedes wagon in there. I had said to her, "Do not leave that there – those doors are not safe." When Dwight came back and got in that, the water that came out of there was brown and the waterline was up to the radio.

Eight days after the storm hit, my Aunt Catherine came to my house and said to me, "Heather, don't you realize Mama's door to the storeroom is kicked in?" That's down by Daddy's business. I said, "No." That had been like that since Monday, but I couldn't get down there because I don't have a car now. Ivan took my car, you see. Barefoot Man said Ivan put his motorcar up on the Sand Bar. Well, Ivan put mine on the lawn before dawn. I watched that car go out of the garage at two o'clock Sunday afternoon. It floated right out.

When I went down there to the shop, I had had a deadbolt lock at least three inches long on my door and I don't know what those sons of [guns] did to kick that door open but they did. Well, I just took a quick glance and left. I know I had eight boxes of English bone china and, whoever it was knew what they were taking. This English bone china starts from fourteen dollars up to ninety-five dollars. The only box they left me with was the miniature pieces and they went with all the big pieces and thousands of dollars of painted toys from Britain of the queen and all her soldiers and stuff. I don't know yet how much of that is gone. I haven't gone back since I don't have a car.

The first soul in my yard, after the storm, to see if my mother and I had survived was Dr. Denise Osterloh's husband, Andy. Dr. Osterloh sent him to see if we were okay, then a few Caymanians came. I'll never forget them for that and I'm very grateful to them for their thoughtfulness.

I'm on medication for my stomach and that medicine makes me sleep but, since that night, I take my medicine at nine p.m. and, at two/three in the morning, I'm still up. I can't sleep. I can't get that noise out of my head!

Hurricane in the House
- South Sound

Jennifer and Michael Godfrey had built and lived in their luxury home in South Sound for twenty years before Ivan blew through Cayman and demolished most of the homes in the South Sound area. Although they had evacuated their home for Hurricane Gilbert in 1988, the house sustained no damage so they thought they would be safe there while Ivan passed through.

Michael and Jennifer Godfrey, and their son, John (right)

Staying in the house, during Hurricane Ivan, were Michael and Jennifer, their daughter, Tina, her husband, David, and their two children, Ryan and Taylor, ages five and three respectively. Also, their son, John, was there, as well as his first cousin, Anna, and the housekeeper, Pat.

Months after the storm, Jennifer and her daughter, Tina, recalled how they thought they were all going to perish during the hurricane:-

Jennifer: Before Hurricane Gilbert back in '88, I had this vision of a wall of water. I could just see this wall of water and it was so real. I told Michael about it and he believed me. Gilbert was coming and so we evacuated our home. The funny thing was that, before Gilbert, the police went by with megaphones saying, "Everybody evacuate this area."

That didn't happen with Ivan. I don't know why that is.

So we evacuated for Gilbert, mainly because we had my elderly mother living with us. We came back the next day and our phones were working and, yes, the hedge was down but it was nothing. But I had got that vision and I had told many of my friends about it.

When Ivan was coming, I knew it was a very serious storm because it spawned off Africa and I realized how low it was in the Caribbean. We were very, very concerned but I did not see the wall of water! I don't know why but I just didn't see it. Our neighbour got a dream just before Ivan was approaching, about a wall of water and, when he saw that Ivan was coming, he insisted that his wife and children leave. I didn't know about this at the time.

Saturday afternoon around two or three o'clock, the hurricane had not yet hit Jamaica and, at that time, Grand Cayman was supposed to be getting the bottom end of the storm. So I quietly went upstairs to my office and had a good cry. I phoned my best friend in the whole wide world, Judy, in Jamaica, and said to her, "Juds, I feel like I'm on the Titanic and we're just going down." And she prayed with me and told me to be strong and to do all I had to do to prepare. I came back down with a smile and nobody knew I had made this call but I just had this horrible feeling.

Tina: My first cousin, Anna, who had been visiting, decided to stay with us instead of going to Jamaica, as she had planned to on the Thursday. Because Jamaica was getting a direct hit, she thought she would be safer with us. And I thought we'd all be safe, although I was kind of scared on Saturday night. The kids slept amazingly well that night, although Taylor woke up at one point with a nightmare that there were crabs crawling all over her and she started screaming. I think it was that Ryan's hand had touched her but she was obviously having night terror.

We were in the front room, on the east side of the house, and never, ever, in the twenty years since this house has been here has the wind ever howled like that. It was just howling and howling. The kids slept through it and I slept on and off. It started at about one a.m., Sunday morning. That's when the wind started getting pretty intense - and more on the east side of the house than anywhere else. But we were fine and under control at this point.

I think seven in the morning was when our phone rang for the last time. We could see the water starting to rise a little bit and the porch started to fill up. We did not realize, at that point, that it was the ocean. We thought it was rain.

Jennifer: So, around seven o'clock or seven-thirty, the phone rang. At this point, the wind was unbelievable, blowing from all directions and we were in our family room looking east through our huge screened-in patio. The screens and all the doors were tearing off in all directions. It was Judy's husband, Robert, on the phone and I said, "Robert, it's bad. It's really bad. We're not going to make it. Nobody can get through this," and Robert said, "Oh, come on. Your house is strong and you're well-boarded up." I said, "You don't know. I just don't see how we're going to live through this." Then John got on the phone and told him, "Uncle Robert, it's bad. It's really bad." We didn't speak to Robert again because the phones went down.

Tina: Around eight-thirty, David and John were sitting with their backs braced against the couch that they had put against the glass door, which eventually blew out. Anna was bailing water and mopping. She was amazing. For a while, we just sat there and watched the waves and watched the water sort of coming up inside. Then we saw the gutters and everything start to blow off outside from everywhere. All the doors were gone. All the screens were gone. Everything. Then we saw the water slowly rising. At some point, Mom told me to take the kids into the living room because she was afraid the door was going to blow. So we were in there for a while.

Jennifer: We were all in the living room. The kids were sitting at their little table calmly colouring and we're all thinking, Keep the children calm. So everyone was calm. Then Ryan wanted to go to the bathroom. I took him to the powder room with a flashlight. It was morning but it was dark because we were shuttered in. I shone the

Tina Kirkaldy with her children, Taylor and Ryan (right)

flashlight and Ryan gleefully said, "Mimi, it's bubbling," at which point I knew we had a problem but I said to myself, "Keep calm." So I said, "Yes, darling, it is," and then I said, "Michael, we have a problem!" Then Michael came and looked and, sure enough, the toilet was bubbling. He realized right away that we were in a lot of trouble. The septic tank was obviously coming up. He then peeked through the louvre window facing the crescent, on the land side of the house. We couldn't see out on the sea side because we were totally shuttered up. At this point, Michael gave the command, "Everybody upstairs!" Later, I asked him what he saw and he said, "Water, water, everywhere!" Now we only had ten minutes.

Tina: So I was now upstairs with the kids and everybody was trying to bring up the food supplies because it was all downstairs in the kitchen. We hadn't been thinking that this was going to happen. All our car keys and phone chargers were downstairs. Everything was downstairs.

Jennifer: But everything was organized! We were prepared.

Tina: … for a hurricane – not for a flood! I was with the kids upstairs and watched everybody bringing water upstairs and a box of Cheerios and the saltine crackers. I now understand that whole 'women and children first' thing because I felt so handicapped. I could not help anyone because my kids needed me. I couldn't assist in bringing things up the stairs. But I think the kids were a great calming factor in the house. Everybody kept calm for their sake and, because of that they were not scared.

Jennifer: And I grabbed the Lysol. Thank God, I grabbed the Lysol when I realized what was happening. And we took the dogs and their crates up. I had already put the cat in the carry bag. So that's all we had … a box of Cheerios and some saltine crackers. That's all we had time to get. There wasn't time to think.

My niece, Anna, was very clear-thinking and, when we moved from the family room into the living room, she said, "I am putting all the keys into this crystal bowl." Then she put this bowl with the keys on the buffet in the dining room. At the last minute, as the water was coming in the house, Anna shouted down to Michael, "Uncle Mike, get the keys," and he said, "I'll get them later." We had no clue. We just thought some water was coming in.

Tina: We thought we'd have a little flood and some damage and then it would be gone again. By now, we had been getting used to the sound of the wind but I think when it began to sound really intense was when the sliding door blew off and exploded. That was at about nine o'clock in the morning. The pressure of the water was so intense and we all jumped up and said, "What's that?" That's when we realized that *the hurricane was now inside the house*!

Now the water was rushing in and, when we looked over the balcony from upstairs with our flashlights, we could see it. Sometimes, it was running like a river down the passageway. Other times, it was swirling and it was just like a full hurricane inside our house. The men kept wanting to go down the stairs to look. So we had this buddy system where nobody could leave the bedroom without a buddy because, downstairs, the wind was so strong that we were worried that someone would get too far down the stairs and then get sucked into the madness.

We heard the sound of breaking wood when the furniture was breaking and the sound of crashing glass when the crystal was breaking. We could hear every crack and crash and then, at one point, we heard a big BANG and that's when the Boston Whaler from across the street came into the house. Then we started smelling the dead ocean.

Damaged furniture inside the Godfrey's home.

It was that smell and the sewage smell, and then we could smell gasoline mixed into that.

Jennifer: We knew now that it wasn't just a matter of water rising in the house. It was a ferocious river. I looked over the balcony and I was afraid I was going to see a dead body floating there. I thought, Oh, my God, how can I continue to live in this house if a body floats into here. Everything was just swirling like it was a washing machine - our big heavy dining table, our mahogany buffet full of Wedgewood China. Everything was just swirling and crashing and breaking.

Then Tina and I just looked at each other when we smelled the gasoline. I thought, Oh, Lord, how can we die by fire when we're in a flood?

Tina: I shouted, "Blow out all the candles! I smell gas!" So we did. Otherwise, if we survived the flood, we were going to die of fire. The smell was really, really strong and water was everywhere downstairs. We don't have an attic. We were upstairs and there was no attic so we had nowhere to go. Anna, at one point, looked at me and asked, "Where are the kids' life jackets?" They were in my car because we had been to the beach the day before. Then she looked at Pat and asked her if she could swim and Pat said, "No."

Anna had a T-mobile phone and her boyfriend, in California, had one too so, every three hours, she would turn on her phone and text him and ask for the coordinates of the storm and he would text them back. Ten o'clock was when we understood from his text message that the storm had changed course and it was coming due north, towards us. That's when many of us resigned ourselves to the fact that there was a good possibility we weren't going to live. We didn't want to believe his text.

Inside the Godfrey's home on Sunday night, 12th September 2004
Note the water line on the walls around the room.
Pictures taken by Jennifer Godfrey

The only station on the radio that we could get was a Cuban station and Anna speaks Spanish. So we listened to that and confirmed that the coordinates were correct. At this point, we really thought that might be it for us.

Jennifer: That was a very defining moment for us. Anna was texting and getting the messages and John was plotting it. So, when Anna got that text showing it had changed course, John said to her, "Check it." So Anna text-messaged her boyfriend back, "Confirm please." Then he text-messaged back, "Confirmed. Correct." John still wouldn't mark it on the map because he realized this was a northern turn - towards us. So, when Anna got the coordinates from the Cuban station and she said, "Confirmed," John didn't want to show us the map. He put that dot on the map, his eyes filled with tears and he hugged me.

Tina: I don't know if it was before or after that that we felt that pressure in our ears. The pressure was so intense that I thought that my head was going to explode. I had never felt anything quite like that. It was like if you had gone on a really deep scuba dive and you hadn't equalized your pressure and you kept going down. That's all I can relate it to – going down deeper and not equalizing the pressure.

All through the storm, we prayed. We prayed and prayed and prayed. We prayed for our neighbours; the Stone and Aquart families in their single storey house, Patricia Priestley, her husband and their eight month old baby in a single storey house, Bill, who lives on our property and was by himself, and Dr. Marzouca, who was in the house across the street. I just felt like our family, if we made it, would be the only survivors. On Monday, every time one of our neighbours came over, I cried. I just cried because I couldn't believe that there were other people who survived it.

About eleven or eleven-thirty, we heard the tiles and the gutter ripping off. It really hit a peak of intensity then. The roof stayed during that, which was just mind-boggling to me. I tell you what … I'm having Dad build my house because the fact that this roof held is amazing.

Then, at about twelve-thirty, I looked at Mom and said, "Do you hear that? It's moving away. It's not as intense." We didn't get the eye. The eye did not pass over. We had had no break in the storm. That's when I started to breathe again. That's when I realized and thought, We are not going to die. We are going to live.

Jennifer: We knew that, if the eye hit us, we would get the worst part after that. Michael had been very quietly saying to me, "Jen, the house can't take much more. It just can't take much more." For Michael, as a builder and knowing how this house was built, to say that was saying a lot.

After the hurricane, it was written in the newspaper by someone that Ivan was only a Category Four. It went on to state that people, after a storm of this magnitude, tend to exaggerate. There was no exaggeration here. No exaggeration! None!

Little did we know at the time but, after Robert phoned Sunday morning from Jamaica and the phone cut off, he and my sister, against all odds, arranged a charter plane that could fly from Jamaica to Cayman, and back to Jamaica, without re-fueling to come and take the mothers and children who would be in our house.

On Tuesday, I cried when I saw Robert, when he arrived on the front-end loader. He came with all the necessary things like Cipro, antibiotics for the children and baby bottles. Our neighbour's baby hadn't had a meal in two days because they were stuck up in their attic. When Robert got off the plane, he walked from the plane to the roundabout with two heavy bags. He got a drive somewhere down by Old Crewe Road. Then he started walking again and saw a front-end loader. He asked the driver to take him to the Godfrey's in South Sound. He offered him money but the driver said he didn't want anything. He just said, "Get on." Robert had his camera but didn't take pictures because what he saw was so awful it just devastated him. Although he had been to our house hundreds of times, the front-end loader passed our house and, when he got as far as what he recognized to be the tennis club, he realized he had passed us so they turned around. At this point, we heard machinery and we thought, Wow, there's life out there.

So we looked out and Pat, my housekeeper, shouted, "That's Mr. Levy." There he was standing up in the loader with his hands over his head looking for our house. Well, he passed it again and we shouted, "Robert!" So he jumped off this loader with two heavy bags and we started crying. I cried. I wept. I sobbed. It was the kind of sobbing that comes from your belly. Michael, Robert and I just stood there in the middle of fallen trees, sand a foot thick on my patio, sewage everywhere, a dock that had come across from the road, and we just stood there and sobbed. Then we said, "Okay, work to do, people to take care of, house to clean," and I never cried again. We had to keep going.

By now, we had twenty people in our house. The plane took Tina and her children, my niece, Anna, my neighbour, Patricia, and her eight-month old baby, and our neighbour, Googie, and her two children to Jamaica.

Robert stayed and slept on the floor that night. We had people sleeping everywhere. Every piece of bedding, towels that were special and sheets that were my very best sheets, mattered not at all. Everything was used for mopping, cleaning and bedding. None of these possessions were important anymore. The only thing that mattered was that we were alive.

My big, heavy, mahogany buffet, which had inside it a full twelve-piece setting of Wedgewood China, was on its side. On top of it used to be crystal decanters and bowls, including a beautiful Waterford punchbowl, which my mother had given me years ago, and that famous bowl that had the keys in it. During the storm, I watched the buffet as the water rose and it just tipped over and then we heard crashing, crashing, crashing and the buffet ended up in the middle of the living/dining room. It completely swirled around the room and ended up on its side there. Well, I didn't touch it so, on the Wednesday, when we started cleaning in there, I said, "Don't try and right it. Just leave it where it is and, one day, I'll get to it," because I was sure everything was completely smashed to smithereens.

About a week after the storm, a friend came over and asked what she could do to help me so I said, "I don't even want to open that buffet. Would you have a look inside there?" When she opened it, it was full of mud and mess, but we took out plate, by plate, by plate and not one thing in that buffet was broken. None of the Wedgewood place settings, my coffee pot, cream and sugar, side plates … the whole set – not a thing broken!

On top of the buffet, all the decanters, Lalique vases and everything broke and that's fine but the crystal punchbowl, which had been on the other end of the buffet, just sort of floated into the water and submerged. Then, after the water went down, it ended up on the tile floor exactly as it was on the buffet, without a scratch. The keys were okay too but, of course, we didn't need them anymore because we lost every car in our yard – Michael's, mine, John's, Tina's, Pat's, Bill's, every single car in our family flooded. Our next door neighbour's Hummer was parked there on the road by our house and it too was totally submerged.

On the Thursday before the storm, Tina's father-in-law said to me, "You're not staying in South Sound. There's going to be a wall of water." But I didn't feel it strongly. I had not seen the vision again. But, as we all know, there WAS a wall of water. Several days after the storm had passed, I was walking along South Sound Road and talking to the Lord and I said, "Why, Lord? Why didn't you give me this vision again? Why?" He spoke to me and it was so clear. It may sound airy-fairy to some people but it was very real to me. He said, "I only have to speak once."

Compared to Ivan, Gilbert was but a puff!

Through the Eyes of Little Children
- South Sound

Taylor and Ryan Kirkaldy, having breakfast at Mimi and Bampa's house in South Sound

Ryan Kirkaldy and his sister, Taylor, together with their parents, were at their grandparents' house in South Sound during the storm. They shared their recollections of Ivan several weeks later:-

Ryan: I remember Hurricane Ivan. He sounded like animals screaming really loud and he *broke the road* too. Outside, the hurricane looked foggy and the water was coming into our house from the porch. I wasn't scared because it wasn't a tornado. I was only scared when the lights went out. My mommy was not scared.

Taylor: I was scared when the lights went out too. I was looking for Mimi because I was scared. It was really dark and I couldn't see anything but darkness.

Ryan: I was upstairs when the water came in the house because I would drown because the water was up to those fishies on the wall. The only thing we could eat was Cheerios.

Taylor: Our dogs were upstairs too. One dog's name is Kelsey and one's name is DeDe.

Ryan: There was a cat too but I didn't know where it was. I thought it was downstairs.

Taylor: After the storm, Max and Madeleine came. Before we went to bed, we read some books. And we sleeped in Mimi's bed.

Ryan: Max and Madeleine came over from their house to our door [on the men's shoulders] in the water. When I was leaving the island, there was no water anymore. We were just trying to clean the house because it was really dirty and all of the glass was broken. Then we went on a plane and it was hard because it was still windy. We had to get off the plane and then back on it. It was hard to walk. My mommy went on the plane too. Daddy couldn't come because he had to stay to do some work.

Ryan: During the storm, people stayed in Daddy's work place.

Taylor: I bought this costume from the Disney store. It was upstairs when the hurricane was here so I still have it.

Ryan: And I still have *this* costume too because it was upstairs. If it was downstairs during the storm, it would've been gone.

After the hurricane, my playroom looked like it was broken apart from the house and it was in the middle of nowhere. But my Bampa fixed it back. He's the one that built this house. I know he built it because it's really strong!

Fleeing Refugees
- George Town

Pam Needham and her family could have waited out Ivan in their own home but instead chose to spend the evening of the storm with their good friends who lived close by - never imagining, in their wildest dreams, what Ivan had in store for them. The following is Pam's story:-

Saturday afternoon, 11th September, we left our house and went around to our friends, Kathy and Adrian Barnett's house. They've got two small children, ages four and six, and we had our teenage son, Mark, with us. Kathy and Adrian live not far from where we live on Fairview Road. They have a bungalow.

Saturday, everything was normal but, in the early morning, it all started.

Pam Needham

The first sign of things going wrong was when one of the walls cracked in the den and the water started trickling in. From then, the water was rising outside and it got to the door. As we could see the water was going to come in the house, we made the necessary provisions for getting up into the attic. The men had gone up in there, got the ladder down and taken a few cushions up, as well as pillows, food, water and things like that because that was the only escape route we had. So we all climbed up into the attic. There were seven adults, two children, four cats and a dog up in there.

Then the water really started coming under the door. It eventually pushed the door open and THROUGH IT CAME!

We were in the attic watching the water rising down below, thinking, If it gets higher and higher, how will we get out? That was just the scariest thing – wondering how high the water would rise. The men had an ax ready up in the roof just in case we had to hack our way out.

All of the corrugated roof from the low cost housing nearby was hitting up against the house. That, combined with the sound of the wind, was very noisy and scary. It was really awful up in that attic! The worst of it was watching the water rise not knowing how high up it would come up. My husband, Mike, who is the Superintendent of the Financial Crime Unit at the Police Department, was still in communication with other police. He was told that there was going to be a high tide and that was very scary.

We were up in that attic listening to the wind for about eight hours, from about ten o'clock in the morning until a fire truck came around six in the evening. But the fire truck couldn't get to us because there was so much water. So we had to wade through to the road up to this huge dump truck that was waiting there for us all to climb into. It was just like what you'd imagine during a war, when all these *refugees* are *fleeing* and are being piled up in these trucks and being taken away. It felt very much like that. Everybody was climbing into the back of this dump truck, trying to find a space to sit amongst all the other people (there must have been twenty already piled in there) with all the garbage in the bottom of the bed of the truck. It was very scary being hoisted up into the truck by these men I didn't know – one pushing me up out of the water and another pulling from the top. It was really quite an experience. Once we were all in, we were taken to the Agape Church where we spent the night.

After the storm, I took my son, Mark, to the U.K., since it was a critical time for him, as he was doing his GCSEs. He enjoyed it there and made some nice new friends but he wanted to come back home to Cayman. So did I. I just wanted to be back home and, now, I'm so glad to be here. It's where we want to be no matter what happens.

Walking Houses
- East End

Donnova McLaughlin-Christian stayed in her home in East End for the storm with her cousin, while her neighbour, Charron Whittaker, watched from the nearby church hall as Donnova's roof blew off. On a beautiful Saturday morning in East End, over two months later, Donnova and Charron told of the events that took place that dreadful Sunday when Hurricane Ivan passed through. The following is their story in their own words:-

Donnova McLaughlin-Christian at home in East End

Donnova: I never thought in my wildest dreams that Ivan was going to be that bad. Me and my cousin were up and down until about ten that Saturday night driving down around the back roads. When we got home, we made some porridge and were watching T.V. until the electricity went off. Then we were just talking and laughing. After that, I told my cousin I was going to clean up my room. I cleaned the wall unit and I swept up the house. Everything was in order but, after Ivan, it didn't even look like the same place.

Charron: I started out staying in a house because my cousin's wife, who was pregnant, didn't want to go to the shelter. We decided we wasn't going to leave my cousin by himself with her because he couldn't cook. So we stayed. Later, when we went over to the church hall, I remembered that Donnova was over in her house and we kept shouting for them to come over to where we were. We were shouting and shouting but they didn't come out so we thought they had went to the shelter.

Her roof had start coming off early in the storm. Hers was one of the first roofs I see start movement. This was early, like eleven or twelve on Saturday night. That was some drama, you know! It looked just like a river out there and we could see this dog going around and around in circles in it. The wind was just taking him around in circles. It was unbelievable, man.

Donnova: I went into my room and went to sleep sometime after ten. What wakened me was water dripping on me. I'm really not sure about the time because I had went to sleep. I got up and came out in the hall. My cousin, Sophia, was lying down on the sofa. I said, "The top leaking!" When we looked, everywhere we look, we could see drip, drip and I said, "That's sheetrock. We're going to have to get out of here." We decided to go by my grandmother's. But before that, I look out the window and I could actually see the sea going down between the buildings and houses. When I shined the flashlight, it looked like the sea was breaking way down in the back and I said, "Boy, we got to get out of this house because it's wooden." My grandmother's house is cement so we would be safer there. My grandmother had already evacuated and went over to the Civic Centre.

We decided to go outside then. I had my father's parrot and I said, "I'm going to take him with me because, if anything happened to him, my father would kill me." We stepped out through the back door. The storm had already torn it off. The breeze had tear it off and throw it right across my car!

When we stepped out, the breeze dragged us way down in the back. I then crawled back to my house, pulling the parrot cage. I put the cage back into the house because I didn't want anything to happen to him. I put him in my closet and put some bags over him. Then we decide we were goin' make a run for it again to my grandmother's house. We had to kneel down on the ground, and crawl and fight our way there. We crawled all the way over in water about knee deep. On the other side of my house, over by the church, it was real deep but, by God's will, it wasn't as deep where we had to crawl.

The wind was blowing hard and the sand felt like someone was picking up big rocks and licking us with them. I washed my hair three days straight and couldn't get the sand out of it. I really don't know how long it took us to get over to my grandmother's but that was the hardest moving I ever had to do in my life!

Charron: When I looked, the house across the road was coming our way. Then, when I looked again, the house up by Miss Cony … that *house* moved and *walked* down here and *walked* back up the road again!

My grandmother had a shed across the road with a deep freeze, which they use when my uncle and them go fishing. When I looked, that little shack had moved and was actually right in front of the church hall where we were. Then I remembered we had some turtle meat inside the freezer and I said, "Now, we can't make this turtle meat go to waste, you know!" We went out into the storm, about eleven or twelve o'clock on Sunday, and get that turtle meat and season it up and cooked it up in the church hall. We had a feast, trust me!

Donnova: When I got on my grandmother's porch, I looked back at my house and the top had already gone. We got into the house through the front door but the two of us had to fight to get the door locked again because of the wind.

My uncle didn't batten up the front window at my grandmother's and, after we got in, the hammock was blowing so hard that it broke the glass and the wind started coming in there. It was so frightening! I have high blood pressure, which made things even worse. I was so glad Sophia was there with me. She said that if I wasn't leaving, she wasn't leaving. She had left her kids home with her parents but she decided to stay with me. We just didn't know it was going to be so bad. I was worried and I didn't know what was happening with my baby because he had went up to the Civic Centre with his father because my grandmother was there.

Then my grandmother's ceiling in the hall started to lift up. The breeze up in there sounded like a tornado or something. That had to have been a tornado that crossed through here. When the top piece in the hall started to tear out, we run into the west room and had to put the chest of drawers against the door. We stood against that door and pushed the bed. Then we pushed up the bureau so that the door couldn't open. That roof was going 'WOOF, WOOF, WOOF' and it has been on that house since 1952!

After we came out of that room, we went into the back room and slept for about three and a half hours. We came out then when it calmed down. We were looking for everybody and couldn't find them because they were in the church hall so that's where we went.

Once we reached there, the food started cooking! I had turtle meat in the church hall for breakfast the next morning and, through the day, we had fried fish. In the night, for supper, we had curried chicken …

Charron: … because we were salvaging stuff out of that freezer and not making it waste. We cook everything.

Donnova: I didn't thought life would come back after the hurricane, to tell the truth. When I came out and saw the devastation … the sand was high up all about the place. My car … she was buried in sand way up to the door. There was so much sand that you couldn't even see the road. I wanted to bathe and I couldn't bathe. I wanted to go to the bathroom and I couldn't.

Charron: In the next few days, I did a lot of shopping at Little Hurley's without any money. One little guy told me he had been down by Cayman Imports and one lady in Hurley's family, I think it was Miss Leonie, overheard him say that the wall had cave in at Little Hurley's and she had told him, "When you go back up there to East End, you tell them to take whatever they want." That's what she say.

Donnova: Them were the roughest days I ever went through in my life and I don't ever want to go through anything like that again!

Rescue Heroes
- Tropical Gardens

Frank Kahoun and Chip Whitney, in Tropical Gardens

Frank Kahoun took refuge from Hurricane Ivan with his friend, Chip Whitney, and his family, in Tropical Gardens, realizing that his own home in Savannah/Newlands wouldn't be as secure but not knowing that, by the end of the storm, they would be heroes for saving the lives of total strangers who lived down the road. Three months after the storm wrecked their homes, they told of their experience:-

Chip: On the Saturday, my wife and I, together with my parents and friend, Frank, started the night out in my house. We felt confident there because it's a very solid cement house.
Frank: I have a fish farm near Savannah, Aquaponics, and my house there isn't as strong as Chip's in Tropical Gardens so I stayed with them. During the night, I fell asleep and Chip woke me up sometime later because we were moving from his house to his parents' across the street, as water was seeping under the door.
Chip: We noticed water coming into the house underneath the front door sometime Saturday night. So my father and I waded over to his house to get some silicone

sealant. The wind had picked up and the road was completely flooded. We got some tubes of silicone sealant and started waterproofing the doorjambs, which at the time seemed like a good idea. I didn't realize how futile that effort would be.

When the water was a couple of inches deep in my house, we decided it was time to leave to go to my parents' since their house is built up higher and has a second floor. So we put everything of value up high on the kitchen counters or on the beds because we thought that would be safe enough. We figured we would have some flooding in the house but nothing too bad. We secured everything and left through the back of the house because we had sealed the front door ... or so we thought.

I have a motorcycle and some helmets so I put on one helmet and Frank put on the other. That way, with the wind blowing the rain, our faces were protected. I carried one dog, my wife carried another and Frank carried his Siberian husky.

Frank: I carried him over my shoulders. There was quite a heavy current in the water and, if we had dropped the dogs, they would've floated away.

Chip: We just kind of formed a chain with everybody holding onto each other and, since Frank and I had on the helmets, we were the only ones who could see clearly, so we guided everybody across.

We got over to my parents' house and watched as the water kept getting higher and higher. Eventually, it started flooding into my parents' house as well. We grabbed everything that we could try and save. We moved the T.V. up onto a table and whatever else we could. Then we just watched as the water kept rising until, finally, it was about waist-deep in my parents' house. Of course, at that point, I knew that everything in my house was completely ruined.

My wife had some notes and photographs of her mother, which she had put on top of the bed. She kept asking, "Do you think the photographs of my mom are okay?" I said, "Yeah, I'm sure they're fine." But I knew they weren't.

At one point, we watched the ceiling fan on the second storey shaking. You could almost hear the wind hit the house and the fan would shake. The house was boarded up but my parents have big, glass French doors at the front, which weren't boarded, so we could see out. The wind looked gray. When it was really kicking up, we could see maybe ten feet in front of us but, when it would settle down, you could almost see across the street to my house. Everything just looked gray. We could see the wind just sucking the water almost out of the waves and taking it downwind.

Frank: And we saw fish swimming in the house in the morning, which was interesting.

Chip: We had been awake for so long and were so exhausted that we went to sleep. The storm went on into Sunday morning and, when we got up, my parents' house was still very flooded so we had to open the doors to let the water equalize. This must be when the fish came in. We had some large doors at the back. The water outside the house was much higher than on the inside so there was quite a lot of pressure.

The French doors in the front buckled. When I unlocked the lock, they just opened and our ice chest and a bunch of stuff inside the house floated out. So we just tried to keep them closed and worked with them to let the pressure equalize.

At one point, I watched my full-size SUV get washed down the road. I saw something red in the middle of the road and I thought, What is that? Later, I realized that it was my Mustang. You just don't expect to see full-size vehicles drifting down the road in front of your house – especially not your own!

Frank: My truck was fine because I had parked it at the Piccadilly car park.

Chip: Frank's truck, my parents' Explorer and my friend's SUV, which was at my house, are two-wheel drive vehicles. We thought it would be difficult to get them out after the storm with all the debris so we decided to put them all at Piccadilly car park. It turned out to be the best decision because all of the vehicles left at our house got ruined.

During the storm, we could smell gas. We had some gas cans for a generator inside the porch by the front door. We had put them there to keep them safe but, during the storm, we forgot about them. When the water got to its highest point was when we smelled the gas inside the house. We were wondering what it was so I looked out and saw about ten five gallon containers of gas floating upside down right by our front door. My first thought was, Are there any candles lit? I figured it wouldn't be good to survive the hurricane only to catch ourselves on fire. But there were no candles lit so we just waited for the gas to wash out.

Just when the wind finally changed direction, the water level dropped almost instantly. Within five minutes of the wind changing, the house completely drained out.

But it was still storming. Easily, there were about seventy to eighty mile an hour winds but Frank and I put on our helmets and went back over to my house to check it out and to check out my wife's mother's pictures. A brand new laptop computer that we had put on the kitchen counter, since we assumed there was no way the water was going to get that high, was ruined. Everything was ruined. Everything that we thought would've been safe at that height was gone. We found out the importance of Tupperware containers. All the things that weren't important, like wrapping paper and other things of no significance, were in containers, which just floated up and sat back down again, completely unharmed.

On the way back from my house, I looked down the street and could see that the roof off the neighbour's house was completely gone! Once I got inside, I told my mom that I hoped nobody was in there. She knew the people and had spoken to them before the storm so she told me they indeed were staying there for the storm. When I found that out, Frank and I put the helmets back on and waded over in the storm to check it out.

There's a little porch that goes around the entire house and we were just going from one window to another looking inside the house. I was looking for whichever room looked like it had shelter over it but, as we got to the back of the house, we realized that none of the rooms had any shelter over them anymore.

I stuck my head in the window a little bit and I saw a man come out from behind the head of a bed which was up against the wall and my immediate thought was, I hope this guy doesn't think I'm looting and I hope he doesn't shoot me! That too would be ironic ... to survive the storm and then get shot while I was trying to help somebody. So I asked him if he was okay and made sure he KNEW that I was there to help him.

There was his wife, his sister and him. They were behind the head of the bed trying to get some form of protection. There was no shelter above at all and the rain was coming in on them. We told them that our house was okay and that we would help them over if they wanted, at which point, they went around collecting things of value, like some warm clothes because they were so cold and wet.

Meanwhile, Frank and I went around to the front door and were outside on the porch, waiting for them. The front door was locked so we couldn't get it opened. We were looking directly upwind of us and could see the neighbour's zinc roof was coming off. Half the zinc had ripped off and it was wobbling and shaking back and forth. We knew that, if it blew off, it was heading directly for us.

Frank: At one point, one of the steel cables from the light pole whipped across my face so it was a good thing I had the helmet and facemask on. We were hiding behind the big pillars of the house, watching this roof flapping and coming off.

Chip: I told Frank, "If you hear me yell DUCK, don't look around to see why I'm saying it, just duck!" That was the scariest part of the storm for me. It seemed like we were there for an hour or more but it was only just a few minutes. It took the two ladies and the gentleman a little while to climb over the debris that was inside their house to get to the front door.

Frank: But they still couldn't even get out that door. We had to pull them out of the window. When I held the gentleman's hand, his skin was just flaking off because he had been wet for so many hours. His hands were blue. When I tried to pull him out the window, I just got a handful of skin.

Chip: It's like when you've been in the tub for too long. I think they had been wet for about twelve hours. His hands were completely pruned and his sister's hands were very blue.

We helped them out of the window. I was helping the man's wife along. At first, I was just holding her arm but then I had to actually get my arm behind her and push her forwards because the wind was just blowing so strong, and we were going against it. Every now and then, a good gust would come and stop me in my tracks and blow me backwards and I had to just keep pushing her forwards. I got her and her husband, who was making it on his own, over to my parents' house and then I went back.

At that point, I saw Frank was actually carrying the other lady.

Frank: She just couldn't make it. She couldn't stand. She couldn't walk. The wind was blowing her down so I had to put her over my shoulder and carried her down the street.

Chip: She was kind of out of it, like in shock. Right at the last minute, when we got her to our house, we had to fit between some trees, which had fallen, to get onto the front porch. Frank couldn't carry her through there because it was so narrow so he had to put her on her feet but she was just standing there. I was in front of her, gesturing for her to come to me but she just couldn't move. She wasn't really going forward on her own so we had to nudge her through.

Then we got them all inside and got them all dry. I was told the lady was diabetic and didn't have any of her medication so we got her an apple and some other fruit to eat. They stayed with us for the rest of the storm and for a week or so later because they weren't able to stay in their houses.

Two days before the storm, we had purchased a generator from Reflections at a pretty decent price but it didn't work when we first got it home. The engine worked but it couldn't produce electricity. So we called Reflections and they sent somebody that night but the person wasn't able to fix it. They said they would send somebody else out the next day, which was Saturday, the day it started getting really windy. Around sundown, some people from Reflections showed up, pulled the generator apart, fixed the wires in it and it started right up. The fact that Reflections went that extra mile made such a huge difference for us after the storm because, although most everything was floating at my parents' house, the refrigerator did not. We had a generator that worked and were able to use our fridge. It made me very happy and Reflections deserves a lot of credit for that!

Frank: After the storm, Mariners Cove was in the road so I couldn't get to my fish farm for three days. We lost tens of thousands of fish at the fish farm and my house had a lot of damage and my furniture was destroyed but thankfully the structure of the house was okay.

Chip: Everything was a real mess after the storm. I was pretty much in shock looking at what had happened all around. I figure Ivan was about as bad as we can expect to get so I think we would be okay if another hurricane came our way.

Going Out in Full Colour
- Windsor Park

Errol Nisbeth was warned of the dangers of Hurricane Ivan but decided to ride out the storm in the comforts of his own home and lived to tell his tale a few weeks later. In his own words, the following is Errol's story of survival:-

I live on Smith Road, right at the entrance of Windsor Park, by the plaza. I figured we would have heavy rain and plenty wind with the storm but didn't expect anything more serious than that.

Errol Nisbeth, enjoying life after Hurricane Ivan

Prior to the storm, we were doing the precautionary procedures like battening down. I was one of those helping my employer, Mr. Merren, to batten down his work premises.

It was Friday night, at closing time around eight p.m. when we finished and he said there was going to be a bunch of people staying at his home for the storm. He said I could come over and stay with his family there. Unfortunately, Saturday morning he called me first thing and said, "Boy, this thing seems to be serious so I'm taking my family to a shelter and you'd better do the same thing." He was thoughtful because he say he had some knick-knacks that he could give me. I'm talking about knick-knacks as in food – stuff to really tide you over. But I didn't go by and get them and, in the end, I'm happy I didn't.

Saturday night, the electricity went off somewhere between eight and nine o'clock. I went to bed early to make sure I get my full sleep so I would be awake from one o'clock in the morning because I understand that, at two a.m., the storm would be starting. That's when it was really howling but the thing that really scared me the most was the noise on the roof over my section, and all the pounding. I was getting worried.

Later in the morning, we hear all different kind of whistling at various pitch and sound, like "whew, WHEW, whew."

My roof went off in the early morning but there was plywood there in the ceiling so I bored some holes in it to let the water seep out so it wouldn't get heavy and come down.

The rough part of the weather start on Saturday but somewhere around nine o'clock on Sunday morning was when it REALLY got rough. At first I had everything under control as far as possible. I got my claw hammer, some nails, a piece of binding wire, pliers, screwdriver and some biscuits to munch on but all that was washed out. That's the reason why I say I'm happy I didn't take that stuff from Mr. Merren. It would've been ruined but I eventually got it from him after the storm.

So I had everything under control at that time but, then I really get panicked. I was standing up on one dresser, maybe five feet tall, because the water was now four feet high in my house. I had a five gallon igloo cooler full of water and I poured it out because I say, "If the worst should come, I might as well *go out in full colour,*" as it was a bright orange-coloured cooler!

It was beginning to look real bad at that point. There were five other people in the building and my section of the building was the only area we could get out onto the roof, because my roof had blown off completely.

About nine o'clock in the morning, I was in the neighbour's section. Water was coming into mine through the roof. Then water started seeping under their door and we were in water up to four feet. It was like we were in a tank. But, when the next door neighbours cried out that they are going to perish, that's when I kind of get shook up. We were planning to go out through the roof, in case … well … you know. At the same time, I was trying to keep them calm, saying, "We are not going to drown," even though I'm not a good swimmer. But I had my igloo cooler to hold onto!

I say, "You people are not in a better position than I am because water is leaking from your roof and water is coming in under your door so I'm going back into my section." That's the time that everybody panicked and I hear them screaming. I say, "Now, wait," because I have a little emergency kit - a hammer and nails. The water keep rising and their refrigerator was floating so we went over my section. That's when I saw my refrigerator floating and the food being washed out. My furniture was not floating because it was underwater. The water was up to my chest now so I had to climb on top of the dresser with the other tenants and we had access to my ceiling, in case we need to go up on the roof. We were on that dresser from eleven o'clock until five-thirty.

That's when the worst part of the storm was over - at five-thirty in the evening. That's the time we pulled out into the water, which was still waist high. The wind was still blowing hard and it was pushing us but we made it to the George Town Hospital and that's where we spent the night.

The next day, Mr. Merren called and said, "Come on over and get some food." From that time, instead of saying 'Grand Cayman', probably I should say, 'THE GRAND PEOPLE OF THE CAYMAN ISLANDS'! That would be more like it! People that make sure their employees are okay and, even after a storm, that they are taken care of in just the same way. Because of them, I am a survivor of Hurricane Ivan. I am really a survivor!

Only One Foot
- East End

Frank and Alma Conolly, standing at the back of their home in East End

Frank and Alma Conolly had been living in their home by the sea for most of their lives and had seen many hurricanes ... but nothing compared to Ivan. During the storm, from across the street, they watched the hurricane tear the roof off their son's home, devastate their home and demolish Mr. Frank's sister's home, which had been there for over one hundred years. With a smile and a few tears, they recalled that weekend in September when Hurricane Ivan visited their quaint little district of East End and turned their lives upside down:-

Mr. Frank: Saturday afternoon, eleventh of September, my wife, my helper and I moved from our house by the sea. Next to us is my son and they all moved up with us, across the road, to my daughter, Ann's house. My sister, Cleo ... she was in Boston ... but we battened up her house and put on all her storm shutters. Then we came and lodged up here.
Miss Alma: We moved from our house because the Government said that if you were living on a low-lying area, you should move. So we did but still it didn't come to me that it was going to be this kind of storm. I didn't take anything with me. I left all of my shoes and all of my clothes. My grandson's wife came to me and said, "Alma, you got your

156

passport?" I said, "Yes." She said, "Bring it and let me see it." I did that and she said, "Oh, no, this one has gone for years. Go back and see if you've got another one." So I bring her a bag that I used to use up and down George Town and she searched it and she say, "Yes, this is what I want." Still, with that, I am not thinking that the storm would be as furious as it was. I never took nothing with me. I had a big box in my house with nothing in the world but shoes – different shoes that I wear with different dresses … but I took nothing!

Mr. Frank: I would say it was around five or six o'clock Saturday afternoon when it started blowing hard but early into Sunday morning was when it got bad! Where we were, we had the house battened up and we were looking through the door but we couldn't really see anything. It was just like fog outside. All we could see was a mass of white. So we couldn't really see when the sea was coming up but we know that it went right over our houses because part of our house ended up on the roof. The chest of drawers out of my bedroom was up on top of the roof too. Therefore, we know the seas was coming over. It came as far as into the bush on the lee side of the road.

The wind had sounded terrible! It sounded like Heaven and Earth were coming together! The front window was coming in so we barred that from the inside with a mattress and some bookshelves. Then the next window started to come in. They was all boarded up but the wind got in between the boards and the windows.

I was sitting across the hall and one of the windowpanes exploded. It was a big noise and a piece of the glass came from there and licked me right on my eye! It cut it but it didn't go in. I was scared. I was really scared then!

Miss Alma: When all of this wind was blowing and going on, I was crying. I said, "God, you made this wind and you can stop it." That was all I cried that night - for God to stop the wind because it was so terrible. It seemed like the whole place was blowing up. We never did went to sleep. We was up all night.

Mr. Frank: When it come day, we could definitely see then that my sister, Cleo's house was gone. Then we could see that the top went off my son, Mac's house. The sea came through the house and wiped out inside. It came right through our house too and wiped out our bedroom and took the toilet out of the bathroom. All of my wife's clothes and a lot of mine was in there but we saved some of them. The sea came right through and into the kitchen where I had my water heater, stove, deep freeze, washer and dryer and a lot of songbooks into boxes. That really hurt me … that all my songbooks are gone. I was a musician and we sang a lot. I look like I can't, but I can sing!

Me and my wife used to go out singing in different districts of the island. So I had a lot of books but they're all gone now. I had two tanks and pumps over the cistern and they're gone too! Our loss was a lot.

Miss Alma: After the storm, the children went to the house and started searching and, of all the shoes in the world that I had, they bring me *one foot*! I said, "*Only one foot*? Go so put that one back in the sea and tell him to carry that one too! He might need it!" It was bad for me to say that because I realize, you know, that God was in the midst.

Mr. Frank: We lost two vehicles to the hurricane. One was downtown in the garage and a container fell on it. The other one was with my driver up by his house and the seawater came up over the cars there. I used to be in the taxi business and I ran tours from the airport to Tortuga Club, and from Tortuga Club back to the airport, and to the Kaibo, Rum Point, and all those places. Therefore, I'm not working now! I looking a job from you, maybe!

It is hard though. I used to make five or six trips to George Town in a day and I'm down now to zero. It's hard for me. Yes, it is.

But we had too much. That's why we lost so much. This hurricane was the worst that I have seen and I witnessed the '32 Storm! I was born in 'twenty-seven so I was about five years old and I remember it. The sea came up to where we were living up in Colliers so we moved and came down to where you call Uncle Fuddy's, where the Honychurch family is now. When the sea came up there, we moved down to where Cleo's house was. Then, when the sea came there, we moved a little ways down the road and that's where we weathered the '32 Storm! Therefore, this was much, much worse!

In 1932, in East End, they had a lot of homes that the roofs went off – quite a lot of them. But this time, the roofs didn't just go off … the houses just went down!

Mr. Frank, holding Tortuga Club's first guestbook (which was damaged by Hurricane Ivan). The first entry in the book was made by Mr. Eric Bergstrom's mother in 1964.

Miss Alma: Every paper that come out that I read makes me feel bad. I was just reading a story in the paper and they was giving the whole thing of the storm. I cry just to hear what they was saying and to know what we went through. Still, God saved us to be here!

Mr. Frank: My sister, Cleo's house was a hundred and seventeen years old and Hurricane Ivan took it down. It was there for the '32 Storm and it was there for 1903. Apparently, there was something like Ivan in 1903 but Ivan was the worst one! I witnessed Gilbert. I was up Tortuga Club and I witnessed that from the beginning to the ending. This hurricane was much, much worse than that!

Sunday morning, during the storm, I called the family together and we prayed, asking the Lord to speak to the winds and the waves. I know that He had the power to do it and He did. He spoke to the winds and the waves and He saved our lives. Even though we lost all that we might have had, none of us was taken away, because of Him!

Time Well Spent
- Prospect

Godfrey Harrison, at work in Industrial Park, October 2004

Godfrey Harrison owes his life to God and the Prospect Shelter where he is grateful to have been able to stay while Ivan's seas were rising all around and across the island. A few weeks after Ivan had passed through, Godfrey talked about life in the shelter:-

I was at work on the Friday and I understood that the storm was heading for Jamaica at a Category Four and they say that by the time it reach Cayman it would be a Category Five. I was really scared because I've never been in Cayman in a hurricane. My friends had told me that Hurricane Mitch had damaged most of the condos in West Bay. They were talking about this Ivan and that the sea would come up over the land, so I was pretty scared. They were telling me where the water would come but I just could not understand. I didn't really believe the water could come up as far as where I live in Windsor Park. I just didn't believe it.

On Saturday, we all know that it's heading straight for Cayman and I did not take it for a joke. All my friends were talking about whether to leave the house and go for shelter. Some of them say that they would stay. Then we decided to get the house battened up. It was somewhere around four-thirty in the afternoon. I was in the bathroom and saw the lights flickering and going off. I was wondering what was really going on. We had some heavy rain at that time and some breeze. I was thinking it was a normal power cut but then I realized that maybe CUC was cutting out the lights. I was trying to fill some containers with water. The place was getting very dark because it was battened up. Then the lights went out completely. There were probably about eight of us inside the house and everybody was saying, "We're going to the shelter. We're not going to stay." So I say I was not going to stay there either.

We left after five or six o'clock in the evening. Five of us from our home went to the Prospect Shelter. Sometime after eight at night was when we start getting heavy winds. The winds and rain started coming on strong. I had to go outside to call my wife in Jamaica. I had to go back into the building, so I tell her that I would talk to her the following day. After I went inside, the pounding really start. The wind and rain start! Everything start now – excitement!

Inside there were a lot of people. I understand that there was over six hundred people inside that shelter. The rain come in the evening and the pounding was so loud! That was around ten o'clock Saturday night. So it go on and on, and we went up to where the clear glass was to look outside. We could see the water like the sea out there all around, and some guttering was shaking and going "CHT-CHT-CHT-CHT." On two occasions, the shutters had blown open and one man had to go outside and lock it back. I heard they tied a rope on him. Then the wind blew him and he went and buck up on the wall. Anyway, they got it closed up.

I was inside the library. People were all around inside the building. People were in the passage. People were in the hall. People were in different sections of the building.

Around four o'clock on Sunday morning, when you went inside the passage, you hear something like "wh-ew-ew-ew-ew-ew-ew-ew, wh-ew-ew-ew-ew-ew-ew." It sounded like several people crying - like a multitude just crying. You could hear that crying sound just go on and on like "wh-ew-ew-ew-ew-ew-ew-ew." It go up and come down like when the wind blow through willows and the willows weep.

People were so worried about their families who was not there. People were trying to make contact with others but could not get through. People had left friends in West Bay and some in Windsor Park but nowhere on the island could you make contact to see if they were all right. Some people didn't know to charge up their cell phones before time. People expected the storm to come very quick and to pass quick but it really last a long time. The centres could get some information, though. They had communication with each other so they could hear things and sometimes they say that some people on Crewe Road and Randyke Gardens, and also Marina Drive, were trapped in their houses and they were asking for help, but during the storm the rescuers couldn't make any move. It was terrible, mon. It was just terrible! I tried to get my people them from Sunday but I never got a phone call through until Thursday.

They fed us well in the shelter and we were well taken care of. Some nice people cooked food and brought it to us. When I leave the shelter on Wednesday to go to Windsor Park to look at my place, I come outside and looked. I could not believe what I saw, mon! The seawater had come up around the building. None of us had ever seen anything like that before. We saw small dead fishes out on the landing and we knew the fishes had come out from the sea. The seawater had come up so high! There were vehicles, which catch fire out there because the seawater come up into them and ignite them.

When you look at the trees, it was like when you are preparing to build a house and you get a bulldozer and bulldoze down the thick bushes and trees. That was what it looked like – just like a bulldozer had went through. We saw wood boards, zinc and everything like that, and containers were all 'bout the place! I never believe water could move containers like that!

When I went by my home and saw the front of the building, the whole of the front of the house roof was gone. I saw that the water on my side in the back had gone into the building about two and half feet high.

I don't think this storm was something simple. I think this thing was a sign from God. But He is not a God of destruction. I don't think He really sent this thing. I think it was sent by Satan but God stop it before it reached any more damage. I think that He step in and say, "Okay, you've gone too far now. It's time to stop." He is wonderful because, if He had wanted this thing to continue and wipe the place out, it would have happened. I think He is a merciful God and He stepped in and had mercy on Cayman.

Terror Inside the Kitchen Cupboard
- North Sound Road

Horace Williams and his friend, Beatrice, rode out much of the storm in his apartment on Wren Road by CUC. Weeks later, Horace recounted their morning of horror. The following is Horace's survival story, in his own words:-

Horace Williams, in Tropical Gardens

I spent the week before Ivan helping my employers batten up. On Saturday morning, I went by my employer, Greg's house to get some tools to help my other employer, Tony, in Newlands, to batten up. Greg talked to me about going to a shelter and I thought about it.

I was at Tony's until about twelve o'clock. After that, I went back home and we moved our things – like furniture and personal things that might get wet – into the middle of the house, away from the front door. It had been raining all day but, in the evening, it started to rain heavily.

My place looked safe to us so we decided to just stay home and stick it out. Then in the evening, the wind start and that's when we got a little scared and I say, "Boy, I wonder if this roof will hold out." We listened to the radio all night. We hear a couple of people calling in, talking about a roof that had gone by Ryan Road off Crewe Road. At that time, I think it was just after seven o'clock, because they say the wind was already heavy on that side. Then, Joel, on Radio Cayman, was telling a lady, "All you need to do is get under a mattress or get into a cupboard."

Then the power must've gone about eleven o'clock that night. We were scared because the place was dark and the wind really start now. Our radio had battery so we listened to it up until about twelve o'clock. We were listening to the people calling in. Because the wind sounded so bad we didn't want to sleep.

Then the serious part started. It was about three o'clock in the morning. I was finally having a nap and I hear the wind and we jump back up! The things them keep rattling so we didn't sleep again. We sit up, listening, trying to take a peep out through the window. The wind sounded awful. One time, we hear like somebody was in the back of the house whistling, whistling. We hear this whistling sound and we talking to each other and we say, "Boy, you know, we can't move now. We going to have to stay." Then we hear some other guys next door to us so we felt much better because we realize that it's not we alone. At one time, they were over in their apartment and they climb up and were talking to us.

In the morning about six o'clock, from my side of the apartment, we heard (from the other end) the zinc start lifting off. We could hear it banging, banging down in there. Now we were frightened and I was wondering if the zinc was going to tear off above us. The section on apartment number three went first and then we were watching the zinc flying off next door. About seven in the morning, mon, that's when the roof on our part start tear up and zinc start flying out! I have a trap door in the ceiling. So I climb up and peep through the trap door and realized I was looking up at the sky. All the zinc was gone!

Then we see the sheetrock start to swell so we say, "It's time now." We had some clothes there. I looked under the *kitchen cupboard* and I say, "Bebe, me and you can fit under there." Then I cleared it out and put everything in a plastic bag. I throw some clothes under the cupboard because it looked to me that it was the safest place. At first, I found I couldn't go in so me have to turn at a different angle. After I got in, I kind of felt comfortable.

When we squeeze under there it was just about eight o'clock on Sunday morning. That's when the water start coming down now. Then everything start coming down. All the sheetrock start coming down and we could see right out through the ceiling. At about eight-thirty, I said, "Wait now," because all the water keep coming down through the cupboard and I was getting wet! Shortly after that, Beatrice's employer called and asked her if she was all right and she told her, "No," and that we were under the cupboard and she must pray. A while later, my employer's wife called and told us to get to a secure part of the house and to go underneath one of the mattresses and stay there. But we stayed under the cupboard until twelve o'clock. That's when we looked through the peephole and we could see the front of the house. There was a car parked just out front and we could see the water halfway up the car door so we say, "Boy, we're getting the flooding here now."

When we peep outside and look next door, we realize the house there was still intact so I said, "That look like the safest place around here," because, at that time, the wind was still blowing hard. So we kind of open the door. It was very hard to get the door open and it keep coming back at us but we get it open and we peep next door and we say to each other, "What are we going to do?" We couldn't go straight ahead – we have to go to the side because zinc was flying all over. At one time there, I see zinc from off our roof hurl into the next apartment building and cut the board that was blocking the window. It chop it off completely. So me say, "Boy, that was dangerous! We can't go that way," so we ran sideways to the next house to our right.

We had to jump a fence. I put Beatrice over the fence, then I jumped over and we run. The water was about knee-height and then we make it over to next door. Our neighbours next to us came running behind us. About eight of us end up next door and that's where we spent the rest of the night, and Monday. When we got there, we were so wet and cold because we were in that cupboard from roughly about eight in the morning until twelve o'clock noon. When I reach over there, that's when I realize that my arm was all bruised but I didn't feel the bruises until I got there. They gave us dry clothes. They have a little stove so they made some tea and cooked some food for us.

On Tuesday, I went by my employer's house and saw there were trees all over the road, mon. We could barely drive through because there were so many trees and wires and zinc all over the place. Boy, things just looked so awful everywhere!

But, at this time, I was just giving thanks that I was still alive because, under that cupboard, I was saying, "Bebe, this is the last of us, you know." I know the place was devastated - so mashed up - but I had not heard of any loss of life at this time and I was so thankful.

Sheer Terror
- Red Bay

Freeps Ridley, with one of her Montessori students, Jade

Rosanna Ridley, better known to most people as 'Freeps' (and at the school where she teaches as 'Miss Rosie'), was raised in her family's beautiful home in South Sound. Although her parents, Tim and Liz, and siblings, Pips and Michael, were already off-island before Hurricane Ivan's approach to Cayman, Freeps planned to stay in the family home in South Sound during the storm. She had second thoughts after speaking with her parents, just hours before the winds started picking up on the afternoon of Saturday, 11ᵗʰ September 2004. The following is Freeps' remarkable story of survival:-

On the Saturday, I was going to stay at my house in South Sound. I had some people come to help put the hurricane shutters up and all the big pot plants away. I moved the cars around and took a few important things upstairs. I wasn't really expecting everything to come through the house so I didn't really move too many things around inside. Since I had initially planned to stay there, I thought, Well, if the water comes in, then I can just move things up as it happens.

At about two o'clock in the afternoon, I got a phone call from my parents who were away in Canada. They said to me, "Whatever you do, don't stay in the house!" I said, "Well, that's where I was going to stay. I don't know where else to go." They told me to just go to an office building and that I would be safer there.

My boyfriend was there with me and we packed up what we could. I thought I would just need one pair of jeans and a top because I would be back the next day. The Bullmores are close friends of ours so we went to their house [on the sea, in front of Grand Harbour] but they decided they weren't going to the office. So we stayed there with them and had snacks and wine. We played card games and dominoes.

There were seven of us there - my boyfriend, Neil, Theo and Judy Bullmore, their son, Ali, his girlfriend, Philippa, their helper, Marisa, and myself. At first, it all seemed like fun and I thought, Oh, this is great!

I had left the school rabbit at my parents' house because I thought it was going to be safer there. I already had my dog at the Bullmore's so I felt bad to ask if I could have a rabbit as well. But, sometime in the afternoon, we noticed that in South Sound the waves were starting to break where this floating pontoon would normally be. I said to Neil, "I've got to get the rabbit," so we got in the car to go and get it. Already, the sea and rubble were coming over the road in South Sound so I started to get a little nervous. But we got the rabbit and went back to the Bullmore's. I soon forgot about my nervousness and carried on playing games.

The house didn't have any boarding or hurricane shutters on the windows at all. They had hurricane-proof windows and doors specially installed but they were only guaranteed for up to one hundred and ten mile an hour winds.

Late in the evening, the power went out and the storm really started. Theo went downstairs and saw that, for some reason, a handle on one of the glass doors on the sea side of the house had broken. Now the wind was blowing the door and it couldn't stay shut. It was banging around so we went downstairs and were trying to hold it. We fed ropes through, trying to somehow make a knot for the handle on the other side so we would be able to close it and lock it again. There were four of us holding this rope, which was tied to the handle on the outside.

The Bullmores had recently built this lovely wooden bar downstairs but we smashed that up and used the wood to board up the door from the inside. At that point, it wasn't safe to go out and we thought that, if the eye of the hurricane went over later it would be calm then and we could whip outside and board up the other side of the door. It was still only Saturday night and the sea was coming up but we thought we would be okay.

Then the sea started getting really rough and the water smashed through the big glass doors! Frames and all just burst right through and now the sea was in the house! So I had the dog and grabbed the rabbit, and everybody ran upstairs with all our food which, not thinking that this was going to happen, we had put downstairs.

The water was smashing through the house but the doors on the road side of the house didn't break through. There was like four feet of really rough sea inside the house. Judy had about six of these really nice, very heavy, wine barrels, which were banging against the walls downstairs. It felt like they were going to break the walls down. We thought at that point that the house might go.

Where we were on the second floor, the floorboards were warping and we could feel them. We could see them warping as the winds and water came through downstairs and that was really scary. We also didn't know if the roof was going to go.

The house had these huge double glass doors upstairs. I was thinking that the ones like it downstairs had just burst through and these could burst through as well. I thought that either we were going to get killed by glass or by getting swept out the window. So we had to make a decision on whether to go back downstairs or hide in the marble bathroom upstairs. The marble in the master bathroom was very thick and, had those glass doors broken and things started flying in, maybe the marble would break up and then we would be killed by marble-stone. If we had gone downstairs, we wouldn't have known how high the water level would eventually get and we might have got stuck there and drowned, or might have had to swim and then drown later.

The house was being renovated but the renovations weren't complete, so downstairs where the door on the road side hadn't yet been installed, there was just a board nailed on, covering the opening. Well, sometime into Sunday morning, the wind just blew that board out and relieved a lot of the pressure on the house.

Judy and Theo had just ordered this beautiful wood flooring which had yet to be installed. We spent a lot of time moving this flooring up from downstairs to try and save it.

All of this was happening before the hurricane really intensified. I was thinking before that board blew out, Okay, this has to nearly be over now, and Judy said, "No, it hasn't even started yet."

When it got really bad, I was petrified. I kept thinking, I can't go now. It isn't my time to go. There are still things that I haven't done yet that I need to do. So, at this point, when we were trying to decide whether to go downstairs or to stay upstairs, Judy said that we had to tie ourselves to a partner because we might have to swim for it. I thought, I can't swim for it. I can't. I'm not strong enough to fight the currents or the winds. I thought, I can't hang on to a tree for another eight hours or whatever. I have my dog and a rabbit! My boyfriend told me that I would have to leave the rabbit if we had to swim and I was so upset.

So we tied a harness-type rope to my dog. I tied myself to Neil. Judy and Theo tied themselves together. Alley and Pips tied themselves together, and Marisa tied herself onto Theo, as well. We stayed tied like that for a long time, just in case.

There was a cement block by the house, where the a/c units were. The water just broke that whole cement block off the house. With these barrels banging downstairs, at one point Judy said, "The house is going to go." All I kept saying to myself was, "My parents are going to kill me because I should've gone to an office building!" That was really what concerned me the most.

Water did start to come through the windows upstairs eventually. It was partly rain and partly the sea spray coming in. We could see everything outside and could see the Bullmore's lovely, wooden deck as the water took one bit of wood at a time. Bit by bit, it just flew away. It was still dark outside but we could see everything.

The sea was between a gray and blackish colour. I have never seen a sea so angry! I can't describe it. It just looked evil. If I had to describe what death looked like, that's what it looked like. The wind was a different story. It was very gray and we could actually see it. The wind was awful and scary but, in some ways, perhaps inside, it had a little bit of forgiveness to it. The sea had no forgiveness! It was like it was saying, "You human beings think you know everything. You think you own everything but you don't own me and I will take control of you." That's what the sea looked like. Now I have more respect for it than I ever had before. I don't trust it but I very much respect it.

Early Sunday morning, the wind was picking up more and more. It wasn't dying down. The sea was already so fierce and huge but the wind started to get scarier. It started to get louder. It sounded like screams - like witches' cackles. It was just *sheer terror*. We didn't talk much. It was so intense. I've never been a big pray-er but I prayed and prayed. I said, "Please, stop, because my nerves are so raw. I am so exhausted. My fear is beyond control. Please, stop!"

We could see the sea from the North Sound on the road by Grand Harbour, as well. So the seas were meeting. We watched cars just sail by. I didn't know what to think. I couldn't believe it! It was like something you would see on the news … only I was IN the news. I thought, My parents are going to be so upset if something happens to me. When the seas were meeting, that was really quite scary because the winds came from one side and, as the hurricane moved around, the winds came then from the south. We had the bad seas on one side and then the bad seas AND winds on the other.

It still wasn't daylight so, every few minutes, we would try and get some sleep. We never really slept though because we were waiting for that last moment when we had to get out or we had to do something quick.

It seemed like there were about four hours when it was really bad and none of us spoke to each other at all. There was not even any sweet talk like, "I love you. You've always been a good friend." There wasn't any of that. In a way, it's quite sad but I suppose, in a time like that, you just turn so into yourself and contemplate so many things. A lot of what happened during this period is a blur to me because we were just in survival mode then.

When we still could receive phone calls, we did receive a few from people out of the country. They would say things like, "Oh, don't worry. You've only got another 'so many hours' left," and "it's swinging around to the south now." Eventually, I think, Judy reached a point where she said to somebody, "Don't call now. Just don't call." It's better to just get taken by surprise in a time like that and have to deal with it, rather than anticipating something and wasting all your energies worrying about something that's about to happen, which may not actually happen at all.

A long time before we reached this point, I realized this wasn't fun anymore. We stayed in the master bedroom upstairs for most of the storm but eventually moved into the marble bathroom because in there we couldn't hear the storm as much. The noise was just terrifying.

During the storm, the fear was so intense. It is indescribable. Although I wanted to, I didn't cry. But, after the storm, when I walked down to my parents' house and saw it, I completely broke down and cried. That was my home where all my memories are ... my growing up ... my whole family life was in that one house. But I was more sad for my dad because I realized that all the years of work ... thirty years of working and not being able to spend time with your children and not getting to do the family thing - thirty years' work ... in eighteen hours ... just washed across the road with no respect at all. It was just pure destruction. If just one little something special had stayed there for him, at least we could say that nature was saying, "I'm sorry I had to do this but I thank you for your work in life and here you go," but there was nothing. That upset me the most. Nature is very cruel and harsh. I didn't care about what I lost because I hadn't put in thirty years' work. When my parents came back, I don't even know what my dad's reaction was. I didn't look to see what it was because I couldn't have coped with it. It was a huge emotional turmoil.

A couple of days after the storm, I was actually able to speak with my mum and dad. Dad said they would be flying home to Cayman on the first plane they could catch. He asked me, "So, what do we need to bring?" I said, "Well, I don't know ... everything. You need everything." When I told him he needed clothes, he said, "Well, there are clothes in my closet. Are you saying there are no clothes in the closets?" I said, "Dad, you don't have any clothes and you don't have any closets," and he said,

"Ah, well, that's ridiculous. What about the cars? The cars must work." "Dad," I said, "the cars are under so much sand and rubble. The water went right over them in the garage." He even asked if I had a phone charger and I had to tell him 'no'.

In the days after the storm, when I was going through the rubble in our house, I said to Neil, "I can't find the post office key." He asked me why it was so important that I found this key and I said to him, "My dad really cares about this post office key." I couldn't find it and I was going through all this sand and … there was no way I COULD'VE found it. So my dad said to me on the phone, "Have you got the post office key?" Everything that he asked if we still had I had to say, "No, we don't have it." I had to tell him, "We don't have a phone charger. We don't have a car. We don't have any closets. We don't actually have a house."

In the days before the hurricane hit and so many people left the island, I thought, Huh, so much for sinking with your ship. But, you know, if another hurricane was coming, I don't think I could do it again. I'm glad that those people did go. If it can save people that bit of energy and that bit of suffering, it's better to go.

On the Sunday evening when the storm died down a bit, we went out. It was still very windy and there was still a lot of water in the house and on the roads, but there were people walking around and saying, "Is everybody okay?" It was so lovely. We had the Jamaicans. We had the Caymanians. We had the expats. We had all the nationalities in the streets coming together asking each other, "Are you okay? Are you okay?" It was just so lovely and that was so wonderful to see. People were so caring. All prejudices and any preconceived ideas of people changed that day, and I think that is so lovely!

Photos

Dead fish in the North Sound six days after the storm

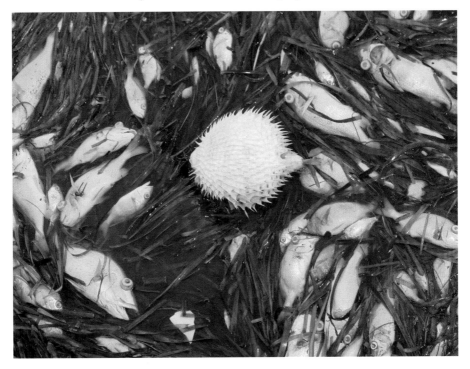

There was serious damage to boats, vehicles and homes in Canal Point

Canal Point, off West Bay Road

Atlantis Submarine's Seaworld Explorer I, was 'high and dry' in Governor's Harbour for weeks and the business suffered other losses, as did many boat operators in the tourism industry. But they were back up and running within two months of the storm.

Governor's Harbour, Lime Tree Bay

Governor's Harbour

Picture taken by South Sound resident, Jennifer Godfrey

Governor's Harbour

Picture taken by South Sound resident, Jennifer Godfrey

Governor's Harbour

Governor's Harbour

Above: *Luxury cabin cruisers in the bush in Governor's Harbour*
Below: *Foster Bay Villas in Governor's Harbour*

Old Danube, Cayman Kai

A drive through Bodden Town in the months following the storm brought tears to the eyes of many people.

The people of Bodden Town suffered heavy losses.

Damage in Bodden Town

... and more Bodden Town damage

The sea which brought in the sand caused much of the damage as in the picture shown above, but the wind tore off many a roof, as shown below!

Sea and wind damage in Bodden Town

The damage seems endless in Bodden Town ...

... but the courage of its people is not.
Men cleaning up Bodden Town

Before Hurricane Ivan, Palm Beach Restaurant was a popular eating spot for locals and tourists alike.

Bodden Town, 17th September 2004

Gary and Angel Rutty's luxury home in Frank Sound

Above: *Seaside Cottages in Frank Sound*
Below: *One of the best views on the island (looking from Gary and Angel Rutty's porch in Frank Sound, after Ivan wrecked their home)*

It was reported in the days and weeks following the storm that ten thousand cars were lost, damaged or destroyed by Hurricane Ivan. These two were destroyed in South Sound.

Above: *South Sound*
Below: *Spotts Straight*

Picture taken by South Sound resident, Dennis Mastry

Above: *South Sound*
Below: *George Town, Shedden Road/Printers Way*

Bel Air Gardens, South Sound

"Overturned"

Cayman Islands Yacht Club

Bodden Town
Picture taken by South Sound resident, Jennifer Godfrey

Businesses on West Bay Road were heavily damaged by Hurricane Ivan but were soon up and running. In particular, the Lone Star Bar and Grill (shown below) opened its doors to the public within three weeks of the storm's passing.

PHOTOS

Galleria Plaza, West Bay Road

"Poor Santa"

Sports Supply

200

Oceanside Plantation, West Bay

Picture taken by Oceanside Plantation resident, Brenda Bryce

Oceanside Plantation, West Bay, BEFORE Hurricane Ivan
Picture taken by Oceanside Plantation resident, Brenda Bryce

Oceanside Plantation, West Bay, AFTER Hurricane Ivan

Damage to West Bay homes

West Bay Road, two months after Hurricane Ivan

"Sheetrock Rubble"

PHOTOS

Foster's Food Fair, Produce Department, after Ivan

Picture taken by Robert Joseph

Hurricane Ivan dealt a severe blow to the chain of Foster's Food Fair stores, all of which received extensive damage. Foster's store at the airport location was flooded and lost its roof, resulting in complete destruction and stranding members of the Foster family who had chosen to shelter there.

Despite all of this, on Tuesday, 14th September 2004, Foster's opened its warehouse and gave away supplies to thousands of people lined up outside the store. All of their stores were flooded with seawater and sewage. In the weeks following the hurricane, the Foster family continued to feed their employees and their families. They also donated thousands of dollars to Cayman's National Recovery Fund, which were applied to building schoolrooms on the island.

Cayman Islands Yacht Club, off West Bay Road

Commercial boats on the dock at the Cayman Islands Yacht Club

Privately owned boats on land at the Cayman Islands Yacht Club

Cayman Islands Yacht Club

"Pile Up"

East End Cemetery

East End

Josephine Jackson's home crossed the road during the storm.

Ivan did not spare this home (above) or business (below) in East End.

Seaside home in East End

... another home on the seaside - East End
(front and side views)

... and yet another East End seaside residence

An Ocean Club unit after Hurricane Ivan

PHOTOS

LEFT: *Ocean Club BEFORE the storm*

RIGHT AND BELOW:
*Ocean Club on Monday,
13th September 2004*

Pictures taken by former Ocean Club resident, Garry Bosley

217

LEFT: *Ocean Club,
Monday, 13th September 2004*

Picture taken by former Ocean Club resident, Garry Bosley

BELOW: *Ocean Club courtyard*

Condo Units at Ocean Club

Lower Valley

Private residence

South Sound Road

The Cayman Rugby Football Club

Ivan the Terrible

September eleventh, two thousand and four,
Hurricane Ivan came knocking at our door.
Memorials and tributes were being held in the States,
While we were battening down hatches and locking the gates.

At seven a.m., the storm came rolling in,
You couldn't hear a pin drop, only prayers and silent hymns.
The waves came crashing through our door,
Knocking down tables and cabinets to the floor.

The water, the water, it started to rise,
The wind was howling, the tide was so high!
It rocketed, it roared. It knocked off the boards,
It brought down the timbers. It flooded our floors!

The storm kept on coming throughout the day,
Then finally it started to move away.
The water receded, the muck left behind,
The roof to the sheetrock was left filled with brine.

Our house was still standing, our boat just next door,
When Gary saw that, oh how he ROARED!
Coconuts in my kitchen, grass on my plates,
Mud on the windows, what a terrible state!

Clean and clean till the day is done,
Then in the back of the pickup for a shower and family fun.
We'd steal up to the marina for water to soap
Our bodies full of dirt, I don't know how we could cope.

Then fuel and water ... next food to survive,
After that we then began to surmise.
How best to fix this? Where to start?
Insurance adjusters came out of the dark.

IVAN THE TERRIBLE

Measures and matches not always a part,
You're underinsured, and it's all your fault!
Oh Ivan the Terrible, what have you done?
You destroyed our island, our home in the sun.

We will rebuild, that is a fact,
Regardless of storm, earthquake or attack.
Our spirit will not falter, our strength has grown,
We've learned no man's better because of a home.

We are the people of Grand Cayman,
Make no mistake, God is our Man.
He has guided us through the worst time of our lives,
To be champions and heroes to our neighbors and allies.

Once the dust has settled and all is restored,
We'll count our blessings and be sure to record
The day our small island was nearly washed away,
By IVAN the TERRIBLE one haunting September day.

Theresa Foster,
Cayman Islands Yacht Club resident

Explosions on South Church Street
- George Town

Although Zoe Bodden was encouraged by friends and relatives to go to a hurricane shelter for the storm, she felt it was too risky taking her ninety-year old mother, Miss Queenie, out of the comforts of their home on South Church Street. So they stayed home, together with the helper, Esther, and Zoe's sister, Kay Coe. Four months to the day after Hurricane

Kay Coe (left) and Zoe Bodden with their mother, Queenie Bodden (centre)

Ivan tore through a portion of their house, causing serious injury to Miss Queenie, Zoe told of their frightening ordeal:-

A couple of people tried to get us to go to Citrus Grove or one of the other buildings for the storm, but Mom couldn't have done it. She would have been entirely out of her element and I didn't know how she would've been with that, or what I would've done with her. Plus, she would've needed to lie down. It was too risky taking her out so I felt we should just stay at home. We knew the current was going off at eight o'clock Saturday night.

My nephew, Andrew, came by and was trying to get our garage door down before he left but unfortunately he couldn't so I had to call my brother, Ernie, and my other nephew, who had to manually try and do it. It broke, so it took them two hours to get it pulled down.

That night, Mom and I slept upstairs. My sister, Kay (who lives next door), and my helper, Esther, stayed downstairs. We have accordion shutters, which make the wind sound even ten times worse! It sounded like *explosions* all through the night.

About six-thirty on Sunday morning, Mom wasn't awake yet, when something crashed through the gable end of the house. All the wood and everything above us fell on top of her and she screamed! I had been sleeping practically right next to her in the room when this happened and I was lying there awake. I got to her as quickly as I could but I could not lift the stuff off her. In the meantime, Kay and Esther had heard all this and thought that the whole roof had gone. I don't know how Esther got up the stairs as quickly as she did but she managed to get all the stuff off Mom.

When everything was off her, we could see that one side of her face was covered in blood. Esther just grabbed her up and got her downstairs as quickly as she could. Then we locked her bedroom door and the door to the passageway downstairs. We never went back up there until the Tuesday after the storm. When we got Mom downstairs and cleaned her face up, she kept saying that her leg was hurting but it didn't look all that bad. It was dark inside the house and, by this time, all the blood had covered up the wound so we couldn't see that the cut was very deep.

Once we got downstairs, the water started coming in down there. The ceilings started coming down all over the house – in the downstairs bedrooms and the kitchen. Water was just pouring into the kitchen. If we hadn't got that garage door down on Saturday, I hate to think what else would've happened! We were all in the family room and I prayed and prayed, "Lord, please preserve this little area for us," so all we got in there were drips of water through the fans, which we could cope with okay.

All day Sunday, we sat in the family room. We had been told that by six o'clock Sunday evening the storm would have subsided but I kept saying, "It's not subsiding at all. It's just as bad!" It lasted all through Sunday night. All we could do was sit there. None of us could eat. There was so much water in the house and it was so difficult with Mom. She wasn't frightened because she had all of us around her. She was just quiet, which helped, but being out of her environment and being so uncomfortable made it hard. Kay and I were very, very frightened but both of us have such a deep faith in the Lord that we knew we were going to be all right. We knew it was going to be very difficult ... so we just prayed and prayed.

The accordion shutters just made the wind sound so terrible! It was like explosion after explosion and this went on all Saturday night, through Sunday and until Monday morning. Monday morning, when things calmed down, some of Esther's family came and helped us to get some of the water out.

Mom had to sleep on the couch and I slept in the chair for two weeks. Kay's entire roof next door had blown off so she lost everything. She slept with us after the storm and she's still with us.

It was awfully hot in the days after the storm, and dark. It was really bad. Tuesday, the bedroom upstairs was one big mound and one of the ceiling beams was lying across Mom's bed. Her eye was black and blue and swollen. It looked terrible but my brother, Churchill, came and we managed to get her to Dr. Tomlinson, who said that we shouldn't worry too much about the eye but that her leg was very bad. He had to put her on antibiotics but she still got infections and had to go into the hospital for one night.

Every night, Mom wants to go to her bedroom and we have to stop her from going up the stairs. Thankfully … she doesn't remember anything about Hurricane Ivan!

Mr. Ivan Pounds Down
- Palm Dale

Kathleen Oliver has had many regrets over not heeding the warnings and going to a hurricane shelter before Ivan hit Grand Cayman and ripped her home's roof off, piece by piece, during the morning of Sunday, 12th September 2004. She told of her horrifying experience three weeks after the storm. The following is her story in her own words:-

There had been much talk about Hurricane Ivan in the news every day on television. They would say, "This storm is very serious and it's getting more powerful." They said it was heading for Jamaica and would be coming to Cayman where I was. After a few days, on the Friday, it reach there. We were watching it on the television at my employer's place. I

Kathleen Oliver, inside the home in which she lived when Ivan 'came to town'

called my friend, Judith, in Jamaica, and asked her what was happening there. She said there was some flooding and they were evacuating people on the Olympic Way, and that sort of thing.

It was raining all this time in Cayman. The whole week, it seemed like we'd never stop getting rain, and the wind was beginning to blow. On Friday night, it was pouring and it looked like it was going to get here before Sunday, when it was predicted to get here.

When we got up on Saturday morning, it was raining so much. My employers called and said I should come by the house in Tropical Gardens. I went by to check with them and they were packing to go to a shelter and they insist that I go to some shelter too and I said I would. But, when I got back home, my housemates and I all decided to stay and bond together. We thought that since we were on a slight rise we wouldn't have any flooding as such. The water went off from about four p.m. and the lights went off before time too. So we were in darkness from early Saturday evening. After we went to bed on Saturday night … it keep pouring and blowing as we went to sleep.

Then around three o'clock in the morning, we were awakened by a phone call and got out of bed! Someone we know at a shelter called to say, "The storm is here now. The eye is almost over Cayman." By this time, we only have cell phones to keep in touch with people. After this phone call, we tried to go back to bed but the wind and rain was so heavy and loud. We tried to stay calm. The house in which I lived had four bedrooms. We keep going back and forth and checking on each other. At about eight o'clock the rain is pouring and the wind is blowing. We keep watching through the windows going back and forth from room to room. About this time, one fellow's ceiling cave in right by his window in the house so he shift his bed. After some time pass, one of the tenants, Angie, said her bath was fulling up with water.

About quarter to ten, we could see the yard start to gather water but we thought it was not going to get any worse. About ten o'clock, we could see the water really flooding. It seemed like it came up SUDDENLY and we see it come up over the door about twelve inches. We could see it because we had a glass door. We started getting serious now because we know we would be having water in the house, but not thinking that the roof would be going off too. When that started happening, we hear pounding. The wind was pounding off the zinc as if there was somebody up there tearing it off.

Then we see on the west side of the house, one of the lady tenants running around inside saying that her roof is tearing off. We keep listening to the wind pounding on the zinc. We keep looking through the window and we see the trees bowing and bowing back and forth. We see two trees at the front of the yard blowing over and then another tree went down. We keep going back and forth, looking in amazement from one place to the other.

Around that time, the roof was tearing off like someone was up there ripping it off, pounding, pounding. It sound like somebody singing at the same time. The sound of that wind was awful and I was so terrified. I wasn't feeling so well but I still was trying to keep calm. Then I saw the wind change direction. It's like it spin around like a ball. It spin around globe-like and I could see the coconut tree at the front going around and around and I say "Oh God, it's going to kill us in here now." I thought, With all this wind, we are not going to be able to stand in here much longer. Then the sheetrock underneath the car porch went "RRRRRCHH" and it gone! I was so frightened, I look around and I said, "Oh God, we're done now because the wind take away the ceiling from under the car porch and it's going to lif' off the roof," not realizing at this time that the roof round the other side had already went. It didn't leave anything. It's like somebody just lif' all the roof off completely and went with it. So we run into the next room and saw the sheetrock in there went down. We ran to another corner and somebody say, "Oh, the whole roof going down now!" I ran into my room and onto my bed. I squeeze my stomach because I was nervous, nervous and thinking I was going to die!

At this time, the water was about eighteen inches deep in the room. Then I look up in the roof and see the fan in the ceiling vibrating, vibrating and hear the pounding still on the roof like a hammer. Then I hear "GRRRRRRCCHH!" and the roof in my room was gone. I'm so nervous and somebody yell, "The roof gone, let's get next door!" It was so dark and we have to be using flashlights going back and forth in the rooms. We run to the back door where there's another house and those people are shining their flashlights over to us, beckoning like we should come because they realize our roof had gone. So we grabbed our two pieces that we were told to pack but we couldn't open the back door because the wind was so strong. I thought we would drown in that high water that was around there. It reached to our waists and I'm five-foot-two. So we decided we would form a chain link to go across but there was a force in the water taking us back and forth, back and forth. We were screaming and holding onto each other. As we were going over, we saw Capture, the neighbourhood dog, swimming and I feared he would be drowned.

Then the men over at the next house pulled the door and had to hold each other like a chain link to keep it open. Then, when one person slip in, they pull it again and then the next one slip in, and that's how we all went over to that house.

It was about ten-fifteen a.m. when our roof went and now *Mr. Ivan* was *pounding* on these people's house but they were more fortunate than us because they have plywood in their ceiling. There we stay for many hours, from ten-fifteen until after four o'clock in the evening. We stay there and get hungry, hungry, hungry so one fellow decide he would go back over to our house but, when he tried to open the door, the wind take it and fly out all the glass from the door. He went in anyway and got some ripe bananas and bread that we had put down on top of the fridge which we thought was a safe place. It was safe from the flooding but not from the water because all of the roof went as well as all of the furniture.

In one of the rooms, you would have thought that somebody went in there and demolish all the furniture – even the shelves in the cupboard. Everything looked like a bulldozer went in and tear those things apart. Since the water kept dripping in, we decided we couldn't stay there so the people next door took us in and gave us some clothes, as we were soaking wet. There we spend about four nights and sleep. We couldn't receive any phone calls because our cell phones went dead. For four days then, we had to charge them in a car. Then my employers called and they give us shelter. We have been living at their house since that day.

But I tell you, I would never want to go through that experience I've been through with Ivan because he take away so much – not from me especially, but from so many people. It's devastating – make you have a pain in your stomach when you walk around and see and hear some people's experiences. Cayman really got a slapping from this hurricane but I am praying and trusting that God will help us and, as a people, we will bond together and keep helping each other.

Oh, I am happy to say that the neighbourhood dog, Capture, is still alive because he could swim and he made it to some safe place!

A Long Stay on Astral Way
- Savannah

Wendy Lauer and her daughter, Ann Margaret

For Wendy Lauer and her young daughter, Annie, it turned out to be a long stay at Wendy's sister's house on Astral Way in Savannah. What they thought would be a pleasant night's stay with family ended up being a long weekend inside the cab of a pickup truck. A few weeks after the storm had passed, they recalled their memories of those twenty-four hours in the truck 'riding' out the storm:-

Annie: On Saturday afternoon, the eleventh, around four o'clock, we were sitting in our house at Sunset Retreat and were worried about Uncle Graham because we didn't know how secure he was going to be. We phoned him and decided we would go and pick him up. Then we would all go to Auntie Shirley's house in Savannah so that we would all be together.

So we drove up to Uncle Graham's and picked him up but ended up dropping him off at our house and left our car with him. We now know that was the wrong thing to do but we did it just in case he needed to get out of the house.

Wendy: It was six o'clock when the skies started to really, really get dark and the wind was brewing up. My brother, Graham, had decided to stay at my house to keep it secure. I just wish we had all stayed together but it didn't happen that way.

As we were driving up Bobby Thompson Way, where the roundabout is, I saw all the garbage trucks there and all these cars lined up and I thought, What on earth are they doing up there? They were on high land. That's really what I should've asked Graham to do – to put my car up there and walk down to Sunset Retreat. Well, we didn't think.

So Ann Margaret and I went to Shirley's house. We couldn't sleep through the night with the noise of the wind and wondering if the roof was going to blow off. Besides that, Sandy Wallin called around eleven that night from the States and said, "How ya'll doin' down there? Have the freight trains come through yet?" In fact, for three nights, we didn't sleep – Saturday, Sunday or Monday. We were too terribly hot by Monday night to sleep.

We got through Saturday night not sleeping much and every sound that was made, I was up and praying desperately.

At a quarter to nine on Sunday morning, Ann Margaret was having breakfast. The wind was now howling like a freight train!

Annie: I was sitting eating some pretzels for breakfast and then we heard a POW!

Wendy: Shirley was standing in the utility room and I was next to her in the kitchen about a foot away and, at nine o'clock, there was this 'POW' and, several seconds later, the utility room ceiling, right where Shirley was standing, just went 'WOOF'!

Annie: When I heard the 'POW', I was just so shocked because I thought the screen porch had blown away so I ran over to the front door to look and then heard this huge 'WOOF' and the roof came off. Auntie Shirley's hair was flying up because she was standing right underneath the roof where it blew off.

Wendy: All of a sudden, there was light!

Annie: It was so bright. I was so scared that the door had blown open and I was afraid Fudge, my dog, would run out.

Wendy: When we realized part of the roof in Shirley's bedroom had come off, we knew we had to find a secure room within the house. Ann Margaret went into the dining room and shouted, "Oh, my gosh!"

Annie: When I got into the dining room, the room was shaking. I could see it moving really rapidly. I had gone in there to find Fudge because I was so scared for him. I grabbed him assuming that my other dog, Toto, was with Auntie Shirl.

Then I saw water leaking from the light and it felt like we were in one of those horror movies like 'The Ring' when the T.V. starts leaking. It was so scary and I was really freaked out. I had worn socks the night before because my mom had said, "Just in case we have to run, we can quickly get on some trainers." Auntie Shirley had everything ready at the door so I threw on my trainers and grabbed my teddies and my pink bag that had my Game Boy inside it.

Then my mum said, "Go for the truck!" We kept looking up because we thought the garage ceiling was going to fall down on us.

Wendy: We went into the truck from nine o'clock on Sunday morning until Monday morning. It might've been an hour after we got in, when there was a little lull in the wind, that we did go back in quickly for one or two little things like passports and that sort of thing. It was scary going back into the house – kind of eerie. We didn't know when something was going to fall on our heads. It was really frightening in that sense. When we went in, we kept calling "Chewey, Chewey, Chewey" because, although we had our dogs, we couldn't find our Persian cat, Chewey.

At eleven o'clock, when the wind started getting really strong, I started to videotape and the water was rising up to the tires and the front of the house steps. We were getting worried that the truck would start to float and then what would we do? We couldn't drive out because the road was like a river and large trees had fallen across the driveway.

After a while, the water started to recede and we started to feel a little secure again.

Annie: There was a time when the water came all the way up to the fence and there was this little cat that kept jumping up on it, then falling into the water and then jumping back up onto the fence again. He was so shocked and scared. He finally jumped on a tree and climbed up to the roof.

Wendy: When I saw him the next morning, he was walking like a little drunk cat. He was so traumatized and we felt so sorry for him.

Annie: When there was a lull, my mum and auntie ran inside to see what else they could salvage before the water came back up again. My mum was standing by the door and that's when a panel blew out. It was so frightening.

Wendy: On Monday morning, when we got out of the truck, I walked into the bedroom and that's when I found Chewey lying on the bed. Then Ned Miller and some neighbours came and chopped the trees so that we could get out. We went to George Ebanks' house to stay with his wife, Carol, because Shirley's house was just too wet. We just couldn't stay there.

We couldn't get through from Savannah to call family and friends until the next day.

Annie: On Monday afternoon, we saw this figure walking down the road and I was like, "Hey, hey, Mum! That's Uncle Graham!" He looked like Jesus walking down the road.

Wendy: My car had flooded so he had to walk. Bless his heart. I had stored Annie's arts and crafts, some paintings, photographs and records that date back thirty years under the stairway in my apartment and there was four feet of saltwater and sewage in there. He salvaged a lot for us but, although he had duct taped the front door, the seawater had seeped through and the downstairs bathroom backed up.

Looking back, I just feel this has been a slowing down period for everyone. My good friends, Keith and Claire Norman, contacted Irvin and Diane Naylor in the U.S., who offered us their apartment on the beach at Casa Caribe for which we are so grateful. It was so lovely to stay there. So few people were walking the beach.

One afternoon, as I was sitting on the patio, I saw a bare rusty casuarina tree which stood firmly rooted in the sand on the beach. For me, it symbolized God's power and strength and I fondly termed it 'the tree of life'. Like that tree, we've got the will to go on and we WILL go on.

Family Time in the Family Van
- George Town

Eighty-seven year old, Hebe McKenzie of Breakers, spent an entire day, Sunday, 12th September 2004, and much of the night braving the storm in a van in the garage of her daughter's home. She shared her experience a few months after the storm. In her own words, the following is Miss Hebe's story:-

Hebe McKenzie, at her home in Breakers

I'm eighty-seven years old and I can't see very well, you know. During the storm, I was going to stay here in my house in Breakers but my daughter, Sandra, came and got me on the Saturday evening and I went to her house. She's my daughter that lives down at South Cayman Palms in George Town. She had called and said, "At six o'clock, I'm coming for you." When I left, I picked up a couple of little things, which wasn't much. We went and it started to rain and blow kind of early. I really didn't look to see what time it was.

Then we were in the house with my daughter's husband, Kennedy, just the two of us and him, and he said, "This housetop is coming off! We can't stay in this!" A part of their housetop went and we had to go into the garage. That's where the van was. My daughter's husband said, "We're going to have to go into this," and I say to myself, "That's not a safe place, either," but we went in and that's where we spent Saturday night and all day Sunday, without eating. We could see everything flying around, like trees and things. It was a kind of an open garage so we could see out. I was just bewildered. We stayed in the van all day until Sunday night when the wind stopped. Then we stepped back into my daughter's house and realized we were stepping in water. She had a lot of water in the house and one of the mattresses was just soaked and the house was a real mess.

My zinc roof came off too at my house and that's not easy when you're poor. All the roof came off, and was all down in the bush and, because of that happening, all the sheetrock came down. Some nice people came and put the sheetrock back up for me but it's going to take something to replace everything I lost. I used to have a thing here where I kept my little ornaments and things but that fall right down and mash up. My children came in and rinsed and hung up all my clothes because they had got wet.

On Monday after the storm, my other daughter came and took me up to her house. My son, Clinton, came up to my house in Breakers and put the zinc back on the roof. They wouldn't bring me back until they had it fixed. They didn't want me to see it like that.

I'm more than thankful I still have what I have. I could've been gone. Somebody brought me a dining room table and they put some of my furniture in the yard to dry, but I know it's not what it used to be. I lost most of my things and some pictures but there's one picture left which is fine. I think it was there before the storm so I don't know how it's still here – maybe it's because it's a picture of Jesus.

Run for Your Life
- Palm Dale

Maxine Harriott could not swim but she could run – only she had to do it in four feet of water during the height of the storm on Sunday morning, 12th September 2004. Six weeks after Ivan wreaked havoc in her George Town neighbourhood, Maxine recalled fleeing her home on Palm Dale to the safety of her next door neighbours' house:-

Maxine Harriott, in front of her former home

On 6th September 2004, it was broadcast on the television that a hurricane alert was out for Hurricane Ivan. It was predicted to be a Category Five and it would be a direct threat to the Cayman Islands.

By Thursday and Friday, the grocery stores and lumber stores was like 'carnival'. It was so crowded, you hardly find a space to pass the next person. Everyone was buying up the necessary food items and lumber to batten up their houses.

On Friday, it was windy with lots of rain all night, continuing until Saturday morning. I went to the gas station to buy ice and garbage bags … late, eh … but better later than never! On the street, there was just a few cars and persons doing last minute shopping. It was raining a lot and the road was so foggy. When I reached home on Palm Dale and started to put my stuff in garbage bags, my brother-in-law battened the windows and glass door, leaving my front door and the window under the garage unbattened. It rain all night

Saturday with heavy winds. Sometimes, it sound as if the roof was going to come off and the windowpane was about to fell in.

I was just between sleep and wake at three a.m. Sunday morning when I received a phone call from one Pauline Ffrench asking if everything was okay where I was. She said she was watching the weather channel and, by seven a.m., Ivan would pass Cayman. Then came another call from one Ronald Smith who had left his house at Wren Road to shelter at the New Testament Church because his roof had gone. He said, "Now the roof is gone off the church too and the water is gushing inside."

Then I heard "knock, knock, knock" in one room of my house. When I went to investigate, the windows in that room was breaking in and water was coming in, although it was battened down with the two inch thick ply board. Everybody was up from then with flashlights and candles and looking around. Around seven a.m., the wind turned east. The yard was covered in water. It reached up to the door and started coming into the house. Water was coming out of one of the tenant's toilets and tub. The sheetrock in my brother-in-law's room started falling off.

Ivan was pounding on the zinc on the roof as if he was nailing down nails. Then it sounded as if he pull them out and have the zinc flapping. The sheetrock in the garage started falling off one-by-one. By this time, at least seventeen inches of water was in the house. I ran into my room and looked outside the door. The wind was like fog. The light and fan in my room started to dance. Then the sheetrock started coming off into my room. My brother-in-law shouted, "Maxine, move! It's coming down over your head!" We all gathered in the dining hall when the roof in one of the tenant's room came down. The furniture started falling and that room was turn upside down. Then it started in the kitchen. It sounded like "ku-ku-ku-ku." Some of the tenant ran into the washroom. As they reach there, the washroom roof went.

My brother-in-law suggested we went next door and he point his flashlight onto the window. The neighbour saw us and open the door. The wind was so strong they have to be pulling on the door to keep it from blowing off. We all *ran* across through the water, which was waist-high. I was so scared because most of us could not swim and it was like sea waves coming in at us. When we got in the house, we looked for shelter in corners that was not leaking. But now, the zinc started coming off from that house. A guy that was living there was saying, "Ivan, Ivan, lef da wan deh nu mon. Mi God, Ivan, yu ca tek everything mon, Ivan." After four p.m., the water subsided but the wind was still strong. I ran over to my house to get some food. They were saying to me, "Be careful, Maxine, of nail and zinc."

I looked into my room. Everything that was up was down. I gathered some food and went back next door. Around six p.m., the other next door neighbour came out looking for us wondering where we were. They had been saying, "Dem people over deh must be dead. The housetop gone." So we went over to their house – everybody heading for the toilet. I guess you know what I mean. So we had somewhere dry to sleep that night. The twelfth of September, to me, lasted seventy-two hours. That was the longest day of my life!

Losing Everything
- George Town

Merlene and Keith Morrison

Keith Morrison had been living in Cayman for forty-eight years before Ivan hit and never had he seen anything like it. Three months after the storm, he and his wife Merlene told of that Sunday morning of horror, inside their home on Printers Way. Here is their story in their words:-

Mr. Keith: We knew this hurricane was going to come but I am accustomed to hurricanes, as I am a seaman. It happens out there all the time. With this one, I didn't expect any flooding. I've been living in Cayman over forty-eight years and I know hurricanes is rough but I didn't have any idea Ivan would be like that.

When it come down into Sunday morning – that was when it really started to get rough! It was still dark. When I looked out through the windows, I see my two dogs swimming in the car porch. We had storm shutters in the front but, since the car porch is enclosed, we didn't put any shutters on those windows. My stepson, Orville, pulled the dogs in through the window and the water keep rising and rising until it came over the top of the window.

The water came in and everything started to float. Everything flooded and the fridge fall down. We had to push things out of the way to go anywhere in the house.

Then I heard a loud sound outside and I shined the light through the top of the glass and saw this big container sitting on top of my wall. Before the storm, there were all these containers across the road on the other side of the fence. The two blue containers … one of them crossed the fence and the other one came behind it, and slammed into it!

The red container went down in my neighbour's yard. Just like you would drive a car or a truck on the road … it just went down there like that.

Miss Merlene: My son, Orville, lives on Marina Drive but he came and stay with us because we are his family. Thank God he did because, if not … I don't know!

I was so frightened because I never experienced anything like this. All I did was just fold my hands, frightened. I just stand up, looking, until the water rise above my waist. Then I sat up on the kitchen cupboard and hang my feet in the water. I called out to Orville and I say, "Look! The water is coming in like the sea!" If it hadn't been for him, we would not have saved anything, because he get down in the water and start to pick things up.

He helped us so much and he saved our two dogs. They were swimming and the water was so high. It was bursting through the creases of the window. Orville forced the window up and a gush of water just blew in. Then he drew the dogs in. They are sensitive so they just came to him.

The water was so high in the house that we had to put a piece of board on top of the washtub and one of the dogs stand on it. They were aware of what was going on. One of them stay beside me until we put something up for him in the kitchen. He stand on it and hold his head up. They stood there for a long time. I didn't check the hours but it was a very long time.

The dogs were frightened and we were frightened.

Mr. Keith: The wind was coming through the vent and it get under the ceiling. Then the wind blew out the whole vent and it blew out the motion lights. The wind sounded like it was whistling! It was howling! I heard every sound there is to hear!

Miss Merlene: I hear groaning, groaning. I hear whistling. I hear like somebody talking. I hear all kind of things and it sounded like somebody walking on the housetop.

Mr. Keith: Outside was white. You couldn't see much of anything.

Miss Merlene: The wind looked like snow and all you could see was pure sea!

Mr. Keith: It was the sea. Yes, it was! The airport runway is right across from my house and the sea came right across it. I was walking around inside the house in the water, listening to the pounding on the roof. When the vent blew out in the bedroom, the storm start coming in there and the ceiling start to come down. It crash down on top of everything!

Miss Merlene: We have a deep cistern and, after the storm, I said, "Thank God, we can get some water!" But, when I went to take up the water from the cistern, it was so salty! And fish was all in the road there. Some little children swim and get the fishes them. There were grunts and a big Snapper in the bush because the sea just take them out and leave them there. I saw it myself.

The fridge had fallen over on its side, so when the water started to go down, Orville got two comforters and pillows and made me a bed on top of the fridge and I slept there Sunday night.

It was really hard. We lost most everything inside our house and we lost our tenants' duplexes. We lost three ways: we lost our rent houses here and everything was washed out at the one we have at Windsor Park! We lost our car, our washing machine, stove and fridge. We *lost* most *everything*! We worked at the Hyatt and the Hyatt was washed out so we lost our jobs too.

We had worked hard and put together a little savings, so that when we retired, we would have some little something if we get sick and things like that … it's all we have to use to see what we can buy now. We doesn't have help elsewhere.

We in Cayman are so materialistic. Some of us don't remember where we came from. We came from afar, and out of nowhere the Lord has blessed us, and then we turn away from Him. I believe that He needed some attention and want the people to call to Him and serve Him.

In the Bible days, He did something to wake up Israel to make them remember that He is God. I believe that He had a hand in this because if He didn't, so many more lives would have been lost. He was there through the storm to shield and protect us and to say, "My child, don't worry, you will not be lost. I will keep you safe. Just watch and see my handiwork and know that I am God."

Miss Mary Sees a 'Monister'
- East End

A few weeks after the storm, on a drive from George Town to East End with Mary Bodden, who has worked many years in the bakery at Hurley's Supermarket, she talked about her experience with Hurricane Ivan. The following is Miss Mary's story as only SHE could tell it:-

Mary Bodden, in the bakery at Hurley's Marketplace, Grand Harbour, where she works

This hurricane was a warning from God because you could not say Cayman did not had time to prepare for it. From Tuesday, Mr. Sambula was on the radio. He say, "Everybody in the Cayman Islands, get ready because this hurricane is a serious one. Do not wait until Friday or Saturday." The man couldn't do no more than that and, still, some people say we never had enough warning. What more warning could we want? You see, what happened was that, when Hurricane Charley was coming, people rushed. They bought up their pile of stuff and, the next morning when I went to work at Hurley's, several people came inside the store and say, "Where is the hurricane?" And I say, "What do you mean, where is the hurricane? Remember, there's another one out there and this might be the one that going to get ya, and unna won't be able to come inside the store and say, "Where is the hurricane?"

Sure enough, on Tuesday morning after Ivan, I went back to the store and saw the same sad people who said that and I went to them and I say, "Good morning, everybody. I'm glad to see you all is alive but, tell me something today. Is unna still saying, 'Where is the hurricane?'" They say, "No, Miss Mary, we can't say that." I say, "You know what unna should be doing? Giving God thanks that any of us is here alive today!"

All week, we come to work and hear about this hurricane. Thursday, they been sending out memos saying where the hurricane was heading. Our manager was talking to one of the other managers and he remarked to him, "Well, we should get some excitement by Friday." I say, "Excitement? You better mind that you don't get TOO much excitement!"

On Friday, they bring the newspapers and that bring down a 'full house'! Everybody had started shopping from Tuesday. They never really wait till Friday. But, now Thursday and Friday, were our deadline. PEOPLE, PEOPLE, PEOPLE!

Then Saturday evening, because we were closed, I went home and we could see the sea was rough, but the part that got me was when we went down there High Rock. First in history that we had see white sand floating on top the water in all of this 'gull feed', and different people say, "You know, this not a good sign. This going to be a terrible hurricane!" The '32 Storm was something like that.

On Saturday evening, we went up to Colliers to see how the sea was. The seas were coming in then. At the new building that Mr. Norberg Thompson was putting there, the seas had already come down to there. That had done make gully and the storm didn't come yet.

It must've been around twelve or one o'clock in the morning when he really start! The power had went off quite early because I remember talking to my daughter, Carilee. The last words she said to me were, "Mommy, move, and move now, because this hurricane is headed straight for unna." I replied back to her, "Wherever God goin' be in this hurricane, I goin' be," and that was it. The phone went dead and we never had no more connection. That was Saturday night.

It must've been three or four o'clock on Sunday morning that I was in the chair in the sitting room that it start to really rain and blow. It sounded like tiger cats! It sound like tigers were at the back. It sound like tigers were at the front. We had two little spaces inside the window that weren't board up and we could look out. I had stood up with my little grandson, and every one of them waves that come in – God have mercy! I never saw nothing like that! THEM WAVES, THEM WAVES, THEM WAVES! They were all shape and form. They turn and they twist and when they broke, they come right over the road. They would broke and they would come up. They came right up to my gate but the other house down there below mine ... the sea went to the front window and the a/c was covered.

It must've been about four o'clock in the morning when my front door start to 'shake, shake, shake' and I said to my husband, "Go so see if you can find a piece of twine inside the back and come because, if the door goin' blow off, too sad for us – we not got no house!" My little grandson and I hold onto the door, because this time the door seemed like it was going out with me and him holding onto it. Outside our window, everything was flying around and bouncing off the house - sheetrock, zinc, shingles, all kinds of things. You could see it flying and licking up against the windows.

Around five o'clock at Donton's house next door, a big puff of wind just licked that pole that held the telephone and the lights up against the east side of his house. When we looked, the whole housetop went flying and my husband had say, "Oh God, Mary, Nancy Lee and them is dead, dead." And I say, 'No, don't say that!' We couldn't get to them and they couldn't get to us. Later, I learned that my son and the rescue team had went down and rescued them.

And then she start, she really start! I never slept. No sir! All through Saturday, I never slept. All through Sunday, I never slept. I was still awake up till Monday morning because we still had it bad then in East End. Ya, but I tell you, you would had to have seen them waves because this wasn't an ordinary hurricane. It was not! It was a 'monister' because we had the 'monister' with the sea and we had the 'monister' with the waves. *Monister*, I call it, you know, by the roaring, the roaring, and the sea. THE SEA, you would had to see the sea! It was all colours in the world. It looked like it had diamonds in it. All I could see was the sea and hear the wind. Oh, the wind were awful! Yes sir! It were awful, awful! If that hurricane had stay about another half an hour or more, Cayman would've been swept away because, when he come around that point, he start to beat us!

The next day, the road in front of my house was a little trail. It were terrible. Everything you could think about was blocking the road - pieces of trees, pieces of zinc, conch shells, rocks, sand, you name it. The point of it is that I didn't thought there was that much sand in the sea until I seen it in the road!

Another thing was that we had a lot of dead people from the cemetery in the road and up in people's places up there. I saw a lot of people's bones. Sunday gone, me and my daughter walked the bay and I see bones and I even see somebody's false teeth from the cemetery, on the west side where the diving lodge is. The false teeth had two teeth on this side, two on this one and the front one was a big gold teeth!

Around Colliers, in two places, it was like the pond and the sea had met. The road was cut off at two places. I heard rumours that people were on their rooftops.

My son like to got killed saving people that couldn't come out of their houses. He's in heavy equipment and the Government had him on standby. On Monday, all of the road was blocked off after the storm, with sand, rocks, trees and so forth. He had to walk most of the way to get to me to see if I was okay, because we had no phone. I was glad to see all my children!

God had mercy on us. He didn't send the hurricane but he controlled it. If He had made him stay there another half an hour, Cayman would be gone but He told him, "No, that is enough!" He not ready to sweep us yet. He give us another chance.

I've been on this island sixty-five years and I had never in my life seen the sea as angry as it was that Sunday morning. When the last wave broke, that was a powerful one, and he stop by my gate. Then I came out of my chair and I hold my hands up and I say, "Thank you, Jesus! Thank you, Jesus." That was all I could say.

This Old House
- South Sound

Along with her nephew, Mona Bush braved the storm in her home in South Sound. She spoke of Hurricane Ivan just five weeks after he passed through and flooded her house, as well as those belonging to loved ones dear to her heart:-

During the storm there were just my nephew, Dale, and me in the house. I was scared but I knew I was going to get through it. I've been in this house during storms. I was in this house in 'eighty-eight for Hurricane Gilbert but it was nothing like this, no.

The water came up about three feet in my house. My sister-in-law, Enora, was up to her breasts. She is married to

Mona Bush (centre) with her cousin, Denham Hurlston and his wife, Melva

my brother, the one who has the leg off. He's my oldest brother and I love him so much. They live next to me in the little white house with the blue trim. The pink house down behind them is where his granddaughter that he raised lives. During the hurricane, my nephew, Dale, was swimming back and forth, checking on them and checking on my brother for me.

During the storm, an electrical cord had fallen and was hanging. That's what I had to hold on to because the water was up to my waist. The wind and water was coming through the bathroom. It took the door off and it was streaming right through the house. One … two … three windows gone! I lost all my land papers but Government has those saved. I also lost my pictures but was able to save one of my younger brother, who had died.

Between my brother's house and mine was the old house that I was born in. Now, it's gone. A lot of people took pictures of it. Mrs. Janet Walker was always painting it. After Hurricane Ivan, you would never know it had been there. Oh, it had a lovely garden! I had lots of flowers … I don't have any now because of the storm but we're starting to get some back. The storm took the house and I was in here watching it go down. It was old. I was born in it. My mother died there and my father died there.

I've not done anything to my house yet. Somebody from Government came here to look and they said they were going to help fix me back up. At least I hope so but, if not … so what! I am so grateful to people like Mr. and Mrs. Ernest Foster and their son, Michael, who fed hot meals to the people in the community for weeks after the storm, and Mr. and Mrs. Ron Moser for their kindness to me. I lost all my furniture and all my little trinkets. But people are good and are bringing me things. Everything I had has just turned to rust. My niece brought me a little bed and somebody gave me a couch. I've got a table too so I'm all right. I don't miss the T.V. I just miss my work because I love to work. I've been at Lobster Pot for sixteen years. That's my job. That's what I do. Since the storm, the manager there has been good to me. He stayed in line for hours to buy things for me like groceries. He is a real angel.

So I have no worries. I've got one stove and it has one burner and it works perfectly. Now I sit out there at night and look at the stars and I think, This is like what it used to be, and thank God. This hurricane has made everybody know that we're all equal in His eyes. You know, I never had a book to read all through this except the Bible.

Like Old Times
- Tropical Gardens

Not knowing what was to come, Goldie Panton and her family rode out most of Hurricane Ivan inside her home in Tropical Gardens. She shared her experience several weeks later:-

I spent the days before the storm preparing, cooking some food in case the electricity went out.

Miss Goldie, at home

I had my son, Prentice, my daughter-in-law, my grandson, my helper, Miss Paulette, her daughter and her husband - also my son, Chris, and Lester and Lyndon. Everyone was in the house on Saturday and then the electricity went off early during the night. We went to bed early, just in case, so we would be prepared in the morning. I woke up to heavy wind at one o'clock in the morning and looked outside, through the window. I didn't have any boards. Everything was so misty and it looked like the old man from the clouds – it was almost like a figure howling out at the front. I kept asking, "When is this going to end?" and my son said, "Mommy, it's not going to end now – it's just starting."

By listening to the weather channel on Saturday, I thought the storm was just going across Cuba. I was listening to the American weather during the day and, later in the evening they had said it was going across Cuba and across the Gulf of Mexico. When I was watching, they weren't talking about Cayman at all.

In the morning, I saw things outside start flying all over the place. It was so scary. A lot of tin was hitting our windows. Then the shingles started coming off our roof. The wind was so noisy. It was such a heavy wind and so frightening. It sounded like things were knocking and pounding in the ceilings. All the ceilings in the house started coming down. The sheetrock in every room came down, except one. That was in the living room and it was the only safe place we could go. We were all bundled up there together. Thank God, that room has concrete walls. That's where we were until the storm was almost over.

We couldn't really see much outside because the wind was so thick which I think was a good thing in a way, because if we could've seen, it would've been even more scary. We just didn't know what to do but I had cooked on Saturday so we heated it up on my two-burner stove and that's how we ate.

The wind sounded like somebody was hollering into it. Sometimes, it went on like somebody was screaming. Ivan was making a horrible sound. I never will forget him.

At six-thirty in the evening, we decided we couldn't stay at my house any longer so we all went over to Prentice's place next door. That was difficult because it was getting dark and it was so windy. His place was okay, although a piece of plywood from our neighbour's roof flew into his back window and broke the glass. Prentice didn't have any water in his place but I had three feet of water in my basement, which came in through the electrical outlets. Before the storm, I had thought about using that as a shelter from the hurricane.

Monday, after the storm when I ventured out and looked around, I couldn't believe what I saw in the yard. Everything was a terrible mess and I wondered how I would ever get it cleaned up. I lost coconut trees, avocado trees, breadfruit trees and a few others. I salvaged a few trees and they're now blooming seven weeks later. Yesterday I went out and started trimming, and my crepe myrtles which usually bloom in May or early June, are blooming in my yard now.

Before the storm, we had taken everything for granted. Then, in the days after that, we had to stand in line outside the grocery store for an hour and a half to get in. Fortunately, I had filled my car up with gas before the storm. I didn't hardly go anywhere anyway. I tried to stay off the road.

Cleaning up the yard was tough. I had to borrow my son's thick shoes to get through all the nails from the shingles. But it had to be done, so I did it. We cooked our meals using propane and, some days, we made a fire out of firewood out at the back and cooked in a pot out there. They used to call this the caboose! We didn't have a gas grill so we built the fire outside and cooked things like salt beef and beans and things that took a lot of time. We also cooked on the little gas stove inside the house. It was just *like old times.*

We washed our clothes by hand after the storm too. The only thing missing was the washboard. If we had had that, it would've been easier.

A couple of days after the storm, my daughter-in-law said, "Let's go for a drive." At this time, I had only seen around my house. When I left the entrance of Tropical Gardens and saw all the destruction, I started to cry. I cried until I went all the way down to the Cinema where I work. I had bought a lot of water and put it there so I wanted to pick some up. I couldn't believe it was the same place. I cried all the way, going and coming back. I was crying for everybody because all the people in Cayman had lost their homes.

But I'm very thankful that I didn't get as much damage as I could have. I got a lot of damage but I feel a lot sorrier for the others that got so much more. I'm just thankful to be alive and that my family and friends didn't get hurt. It's just such a miracle!

Just Another Day in the Classroom
- George Town

Nicola Sowerby, a teacher at a private school in Cayman, spent two and a half days in the school with fellow teachers and their families making sure that their friend, while in the early stages of childbirth, was comfortable while Hurricane Ivan wreaked havoc all around them. Several weeks after Ivan left Cayman in ruins, Miss Sowerby told of her experience:-

Nicola Sowerby, at her new house in George Town

I, together with five other adults, two kids and two dogs stayed inside my classroom for Ivan.

On the Saturday, my friend, Leanne, who was due to give birth to her first child, phoned up about three or four o'clock and asked if she could stay with us at the school. She and her husband came along with their three Huskies. Leanne said she had to remain horizontal because she was in the beginnings of labour so we got the sofa from the staff room and put it in Mrs. Wheaton's classroom. Leanne just stayed there, lying down on the sofa.

Saturday night was fine but it got worse early on the Sunday morning. The water started coming in through the roof and down into the classrooms, and the ceiling tiles were dropping down. It was really uncomfortable and we were worried that Leanne would get wet so we moved the sofa, with her on it, into the corridor. Meanwhile, the water was coming in up to about mid-calf. In the end, we had to move to the other side of the corridor, to Graham Scott's classroom, because the corridor itself was getting wet and the ceiling tiles were coming off.

We were in that classroom sleeping and Janine Stabler was following the ceiling tiles with the torch, in case they should fall.

The worst thing I saw was on that Sunday morning. We were all in the bottom corridor and the doors started flapping open. The men put electrical wiring across the doors and fastened them to each other to try and anchor them in. While we were looking out the back window of the computer room, we watched the canteen roof and the art room roof peel off. Then we watched the sports hall roof just peel back like a tin. It was just like somebody had a can opener peeling it back. We could see all the roof tiles flying around. Looking out from the front doorway, we really couldn't see more than eight to ten feet away because the wind was just swirling around … just a white swirl. It sounded like a steam engine just going constantly around the school for about twenty-four hours.

Mr. Livery, the school maintenance guy came in the middle of the storm because he didn't have anywhere else to go. We couldn't open the doors, because of the wind, so he went into the sports hall with his family but the roof was coming off and the doors blew out. So he and his family ended up under the stage for the whole of the time.

The scariest moment for me though was when my cell phone was still working and my dad called from the U.K. at about five o'clock in the morning and asked, "What's it like?" And I said, "Well, we're getting a bit scared. The winds are now swirling around." The shutters had come off my room and the shutters went through the window in the computer room. We heard all that and just locked the door and never went in. But I told my dad, "Everything seems to be okay." Then he said, "It isn't that close to you yet. It's going to come closer to you than that, Nicola." At that point I got scared and thought, Well, how close is it going to get and where are we going to go? That was the scariest thing.

But the worst part of Sunday morning was when most of us were in the bottom corridor with our crash mats. We had shut all the doors to the classrooms. Because the corridor is cement, we thought we'd all be safe there, although we were in three inches of water.

The dogs and the children were unbelievable. It was good having them there because we just played with them and talked to them, pretending everything was perfectly fine and that it was perfectly normal to be sleeping in the school corridor on crash mats. The only thing was we didn't have any dry clothes, which was certainly uncomfortable.

Early on Monday morning, the first person we saw was Mel Hydes' husband,

251

David. Two policemen came with him to the school and they were the first people we had seen since Saturday lunchtime. They said, "It's really bad. Don't go out." We didn't go out of the school until about nine o'clock and, when we went out, the sea was up to the end of Denham Thompson Way, just coming onto Walkers Road. People were swimming down Denham Thompson Way and the waves were breaking onto Walkers Road. Then we walked down as far as the Citrus Grove Building and just couldn't believe what we saw everywhere. I saw two or three of my friends on the road who didn't have homes anymore. They had gone back to find their houses had been destroyed. One lived on Walkers Road and one lived down Denham Thompson Way. Their roofs had caved in and the water had just gone straight through. I just cried my eyes out. I think everybody cried that day.

I had just bought my house. I had a container full of brand new stuff to go in my house and during the storm all I was thinking was, I hope all my things are okay. I hope nothing gets too damaged. Then I came out of the school and saw what had happened and I thought, I don't really care. I have to admit, I had a brand new T.V. and a brand new VCR, neither of which ever got out of the boxes. It all went straight from the container into the dustbin and I just didn't care. I really didn't because I appreciated that we were all alive and still had each other. As long as we have that and a safe place to sleep, I don't think all the other things matter. All you need is a safe place and people you love around you and everything's okay.

As soon as Leanne got out of the school, her husband's company got an air ambulance and she was flown off on Tuesday morning. When they got her to the hospital, the doctors stopped the labour with medication and the baby was born on Friday in Ft. Lauderdale. It was a baby boy who weighed four pounds and they named him 'Finn Nicholas'. She said she's never using the name 'Ivan' for any of her children!

Time Stands Still
- West Bay

Max Consolini, Manager of the Grape Vine Wine Bar at Harbour Place, like many others, underestimated the hurricane and decided to stay in his home on Marsh Road to ride out the storm. He told of his frightening experience several weeks later. The following is Max's story of survival, in his own words:-

I live on Marsh Road, along Seven Mile Beach, West Bay Road. My house is there. All of my belongings are there so that's where I decided to stay for the storm. But I think that I underestimated the hurricane, like many people did. I was thinking we would get like maybe two or three feet of water, but it was much worse than that. It was a very scary experience.

Max Consolini

I had prepared my place by boarding it up and I had put sandbags everywhere. At one certain point during the storm, the water outside was really, really high. It was the sea. I looked out and it was so high that it was covering my jeep – the Bimini top and everything. I couldn't see my car anymore at all. At this point, inside the house, the water was up to my knees and coming up. I was getting very scared and knew I had to get everything upstairs.

I was very prepared with bottled water, food in cans and everything. I had put it all downstairs but, once the water started rising, I had to be very quick, taking up the things I needed. As it turned out, I moved everything in the whole apartment up to the second floor like in about an hour all by myself. I haven't a clue what time that was. I lost all concept of day and night. Hours were passing like days … it was like the *time was standing still*. Two days after the storm, I went out of the house and I didn't know which day it was. It was the first day I saw the ray of light because it had been pitch black in my house for almost three days.

And the wind … like one of my friends said to me after the storm … it sounded like a seven-forty-seven jet was parked in the front yard with the engine going constantly. It seemed like it went on like that for two days – for forty-eight hours. During all that time, I was in all this water and I knew that, at any minute, my roof can blow away. It was very scary. The storm lasted for so long and it was so terrible. It was like it was never finishing. I was thinking, When is this hurricane going to stop?

I was by myself in the house with my cat, which I couldn't find. I just could not find him. I looked everywhere in the dark for him. I knew he was in the house hiding somewhere but I didn't know where for a couple of days. Two days after Hurricane Ivan, the first time I lie down on the bed, the cat just popped out from somewhere.

In the days after the storm, I was looking at myself in the mirror and it was like, with the long beard and everything, I looked like Jesus Christ or maybe the guy in *'Castaway'* so I had to cut my hair off. It was long down my back but I had no water or time for shampoo and conditioner. It was very long and it had taken me a very long time to grow it that way but I shaved it all off. Now my friends don't recognize me.

I could not get in contact with my family back home for about two weeks after Hurricane Ivan. My friends were calling me here and I was keeping in contact with them for a while but then, all of the sudden, the battery on my cell phone was finished and that was it. So I couldn't call anybody and nobody could call me and I was by myself for a couple of days. I go through many things in my mind during that time. I finally spoke with my mother and father about two weeks after the storm. My father said to me, "Your mom … she grew ten years older in the last two weeks."

Things seem to take so long these days in Cayman. It's so hard to get anything done. I'm still living in only the upstairs of my place. There's so much things in there that sometimes it's hard to find my bed. I am riding a bicycle to work now.

I had ordered a brand new car way back in July before the storm but it still hasn't been shipped yet. I still go through moments. Like some days, I am very happy but some days, I am very upset. It's hard.

I was very scared during this hurricane and had a very rough time after. Very! Honestly, I remember that as the worst and scariest experience of my life!

Father Knows Best
- Bel Air Gardens

Seven weeks after Hurricane Ivan hit Grand Cayman and held his family hostage in the garage of their home in Bel Air Gardens, little Michael Watler finally opened up and talked about his experience. He and his mother, Sophia, spoke of the horrors of riding out the storm with their family in a boat inside their garage:-

Sophia Watler, with her son, Michael
(in the boat in which their family stayed during the storm)

Sophia: On Saturday, 11th September, throughout the day, Daddy was calling, begging us to pack up and go to the shelter at the Family Life Centre off Walkers Road. We were all pretty adamant about staying in the house and he was angry with us. Reluctantly, he said, "Okay," and we all stayed together in the house.

We were fine Saturday evening. There were myself, my little boy, Michael, my parents [Donnie and Agnes], my brother, Rod, Mona Lisa (who was nine months pregnant), Uncle Lad, his son, Joe, their helper, Maureen, and her toddler daughter in the house. The place was a bit dark so we were just all sitting around. We had the lanterns lit.

When we woke up around seven in the morning, the wind was howling. It sounded demonic-like. It just sounded evil. By nine o'clock, the house started to flood. It was just so sudden! We didn't have time to save anything. The water came gushing through the front door and, in no time, it was up to my chest, and I'm about five foot eight inches tall. And, at the same time as the water came in, the ceilings came down! It all happened at the very same time – the ceilings came down and the water came up. Uncle Lad and Joe went to the back door but the lock wouldn't move. The knob and everything was jammed. They were working at that for about ten minutes. At this time, I had Michael on top of the kitchen counter. He was crying and I was trying to soothe him.

The wind sounded horrible. I have never heard anything like that before in my life! We were in Cayman for Gilbert and that was nothing compared to this. The plywood on all the windows was shaking and we thought it was going to fly right off! It was just horrible.

At one point, when Uncle Ladner was trying to get the door open, some of us were sitting on top of the kitchen counter and some of us were standing. We were kind of in a circle. We all just looked at each other for what we thought would be the last time. We honestly thought that was it. We thought, with the water coming in, we were going to drown. That was it. Dad was in shock. He just looked numb like he couldn't believe it. He and Mom ... they couldn't say a word. We all just looked at each other - it was like a silent goodbye, you know? Then Uncle Lad hollered for us to get in the boat. He and Joe got the life

Ladner Watler (whose grandfather, the late Joseph Rodriquez Watler, rescued many people in the '32 Storm), standing next to the boat in which he saved his own family's life

vests out of the boat and gave them to us. Uncle Ladner tied the boat to the ceiling beams. We all just went into the boat and huddled up with blankets. Michael was bawling.

Our heads were almost up to the ceiling. We watched my car float from the driveway to right up against the boat and the trailer, blocking us in so we wouldn't float away. That must've been God. In the boat, we watched the fridge and some furniture float out. We lost six vehicles in one shot. All of us lost our vehicles.

Michael: I thought the house was going to fill up all the way. It started to get worser. Then they got the door open. I went in that boat back there. I like that boat because it's big and can hold plenty people. All of my family went in it. The boat was in the garage. I felt good when we got in the boat but I was sad because it was too cold. It was cold and I could hear the wind. It sounded like "wh-ew-ew-ew-ew-ew-ew-ew-ew-ew-ew" for a long time. And I saw the wind! It was white!

The fridge started to float out and the chairs, the black chair too, and the T.V. all came into the garage. Plenty stuff was floating, and fish too. The fish were floating under the T.V. I have a pond over there that came right up into the house. The sea and the pond were all mixed together. The ducks were thinking they wanted to come into the house but they couldn't. There was no space. They looked in the garage but there were too many things in it. I wanted to save them because they were in the storm.

The water was filling up. It was low. Then it come up high. My Uncle Lad tied the boat onto the ceiling so it couldn't float away. I couldn't see all the ducks. They were hiding in the bushes. I felt safe because the boat saved me.

Sophia: We were in the boat from after nine in the morning until around four in the afternoon when Uncle Ladner and Joe swam and got Uncle Ladner's rescue boat which was hooked up to his Land Cruiser down our driveway. They waded to us and Uncle Lad took us two-by-two to DaDa's house. Uncle Ronnie and some of the others were there and they took us to Uncle Ronnie's house, which is much higher. Michael and I went first. Then they kept going back to get the rest. The men all went last. Women and children first, you know!

I don't know what we would've done if Uncle Lad hadn't been there because he's into rescuing. He saves lives for a living so he knows what to do.

We stayed at Uncle Ronnie's that night, but, after all that, who could sleep? And the wind was still strong.

The next day, when we woke up and looked around, I was speechless. It was unbelievable. Everything was barren, desolate looking. It looked like an atom bomb had hit Cayman!

Michael: Our little dog, Gizmo died. He drowned in the storm because he couldn't swim anymore. I don't like Ivan. He was the worstest!

Sophia: When the house flooded and the ceilings came down, we were all looking at each other and saying, "We should really have listened to Dad!" After all, *father knows best*!

A Mother's Love
- Randyke Gardens

Tina Dixon with her children, Nathan and Nalya

A young mother and her two small children, Nathan, age 7, and Nalya, age 4, stayed in their apartment in Randyke Gardens during the hurricane. They re-live the horror of it each day and told their story several weeks after the storm:-

Tina: Everything started about two o'clock in the morning. The wind blew the board from my bedroom window off so we ran downstairs to where my sister was sleeping. Then we went back upstairs and put the bed against my window so that it wouldn't cave in. Where my other sister, her baby and her baby's father were sleeping, the boards stayed on okay.

Everybody was up at two o'clock that morning. After about an hour or so, the boards on the downstairs windows blew off. But we were all right until about six o'clock in the morning when the wind started to really pick up. That's when we had the kids downstairs. We didn't want them upstairs because of the windows. Around ten o'clock, the water really started coming in and Nathan was playing right by the front door where the first pieces of the sheetrock fell. It almost hit him so we sent them upstairs. Once the water started coming in, it never stopped.

Nathan: I went to sleep at nighttime and then I waked up and everybody was awake because the water started coming in the house. My mommy told me and my sister to stay on the stairs because the water kept getting higher.

Nalya: The water was all over the house.

Nathan: Everybody was there. We were moving up and down and they said, "Don't move." The water was dirty – it was like poop. It came from a pond and the sea.

Nalya: I kept thinking my bike was gone.

Nathan: I was thinking of nothing. Only the grownups were thinking about it. They were thinking of how to clean all these things up in the water. Then the whole place popped open with water. The water kept getting bigger and bigger. It was up to the downstairs ceiling but our house is big and we had stairs.

I was on the stairs with the bed on top of me because everything was dropping down from the ceiling.

Nalya: Everything was mashed up.

Tina: We had about six to eight feet of water inside the apartment. On the outside, the water covered the whole first floor. So we called 911 and they said that no one could get to us because of the wind but that, as soon as everything calmed down, they would send someone. They said to go into the bathroom, but as soon as we opened the bathroom door we saw that the ceiling had caved in there too. In all the rooms and in all the bathrooms, the ceilings had caved in so we had to sit in the stairway from about ten that morning until six o'clock that evening. It seemed as if time had stopped and things just kept getting worse. The water kept rising and the wind kept picking up.

I started to panic and called my parents. I said, "Please help us. The water only has to come up seven more steps before it reaches us. The only way we can get out of here is by boat because the water outside is so deep." I was calling everybody I could think of to get help only to find out they were in trouble too. At that point, I lost it! I was really scared. I cried and prayed, "Dear Lord, I am responsible for my children and their lives are in my hands right now. I don't want them to perish like this. Please help us!"

Nathan: There was a lot of furniture and things floating and some things got mashed up. Our glass tables got mashed up in the water. I had the mattress over my head a long time. When the roof blew off, we had everything coming down. It was very windy and very yucky.

Tina: Around six o'clock that evening, when we looked through the window, we could see the lights of the fire truck up on the road and, by now the water went down enough for us to open the door and we hollered out to them. They said, "We're the firemen – we've been sent in." We told them we had kids so they said, "Put them on your backs. You're going to have to swim for it so that's what we did." They told us to grab up whatever we could, clothes or anything. Then we had to swim out for it. When we got to the road, they took the kids.

Nathan: When the fire engine came, it was very deep out there. We had friends with us and we went to the truck on their backs. I was on Randy's back and my sister was on Mommy's back.

Nalya: The water came up real high on Mommy. It came way up here [pointing to her chest] to her and I was sad.

Nathan: The water was going "Z-z-z-z-z-z-z-z-z" like waves. It looked bad! I never took nothing with me. An old woman was screaming for help. She was in Randyke Gardens too. The firemen were helping everybody and telling everybody to get out and go but one guy didn't want to go. He was next door to me. He didn't want to go because he was afraid of the water.

We went to the fire station in the fire truck. I don't know what time it was. I think we were there before things had started to calm down. I had prayed for God to stop the storm but He wouldn't. One day it stopped and I was happy, but I'll never forget. I thought the fire truck was cool but I think Ivan was very bad. I never want to see him again.

Tina: They took the kids to the fire station but left us at the top of the road with some other firemen and two vehicles. They said they would come back for us but, because it was really, really windy and the wind started to pick up and it started getting bad again, they took us to the Enchenique house. I didn't stay there though. I called my children's uncle, Prentice Panton, and told him I had got separated from the kids. He said he would come and get me. When he got as far as Jose's Esso, he couldn't go any further because the roads were flooded. I had to swim out again to meet him.

Across the street, the fence around the airport was down so we drove through the opening which took us onto the airport runway. We drove straight down the runway until we could see the back of the fire station and that's where I and the others got out. We got out at the runway, as Prentice couldn't go any further because of the flooding. The water was to our knees so Prentice spotted his lights to guide us as far as he could. When I got into the fire station, a fireman asked me, "How did you get here?" I replied, "Never underestimate the strength of a mother's love. They are my kids. They need me. No one could come back for me so I came to them!"

Nathan: I used to have a fireman truck and a shovel that I played with but now they're gone. At the fire station, I was sad and was going to cry. The firemen gave me Milo. When I grow up, I want to be a fireman so I can rescue people.

Chest Deep
- East End

Although Mr. Vernon Dixon's children tried to coax him to go with them, along with his wife, Cora, to Bodden Town, he insisted on staying alone in his own home in East End for the storm where he bravely waited in water for hours to be rescued and taken to higher ground:-

Vernon Dixon, inside his grocery store in East End

It was only me one there in my house for the storm. My wife and two boys had gone there to our daughter's place down in Bodden Town. They coaxed me to leave and I tell them I wasn't leaving. I was staying right there. Later on in the night, I heard a noise on the east side of the house and I open the door and I looked out and saw that the lime tree was up against the window. It came up against my glass window so I shut that door and went out into the sitting room and I sit down there and heard a noise in the next room. When I opened the door, the water was pouring down like a river from the top and the zinc was blowing off. I shut that door and went down to the bathroom where I saw there was about a foot of water.

I had a big tree on the north side of the house. That fell down across another house. It had sounded like thunder when it fell.

We had one tub filled with water, just in case, but now the saltwater was coming through the north room and it was *chest deep* on me. The wind was blowing hard and the water was going right through the house. So I sit down in the kitchen all morning and waited. Two guys came then and rescued me. These guys were in a house up the road and they were using my boy's jeep. They had that there waiting on me and I get in and they took me up to the Civic Centre. That was when the weather was breaking in the afternoon. But the water was still coming and going back and forth. The next morning, my boy and daughter came from Bodden Town to look for me.

After I come out the next day, I saw that a coconut tree had fall down across another house and destroyed it. I had an upstairs building that my son and his family lived in. The storm demolished that. There was seven foot, two inches of water in that house and my son and his wife and daughter never saved nothing from it. There was so much water coming from the east that people were coming in boats.

There was sand piled up in my store but I had a lady working here and we came day after day and cleaned it up. What was dry, we saved. What was wet, we throwed out.

I didn't intend to open my store again because the things that were all right, I was sharing up and giving to my good customers. I was just giving them away. But then the representative for East End came to me, on more than one occasion, telling me I must open because there wouldn't be nowhere else for the people to get anything. I'm glad I opened up though, to help the people.

All of my places are in a mess. Half the top went off my main house. The next house to that was damaged. The top went off the next house to that. Then the next one to that, the downstairs was totally condemned and upstairs, only the frame was left. I had six buildings altogether and only two had survived. It's a lot of work. After the storm, I had three women and three men helping me clear up because I didn't know that the Government was going to send people around. I was trying to help myself. The Government done good though. They sent a bulldozer and they clear all around the place.

I can remember the '32 Storm and it was nothing like this. I was a little boy then. I was ten years old in 'thirty-two so I remember it. But Hurricane Ivan was one hundred per cent worse - one hundred per cent!

Torment under the Kitchen Table
- Bodden Town

Several weeks after Ivan wreaked havoc in Bodden Town, Wilston Levy and his helper, Monica Dehaney, recalled the long morning they spent caring for Mr. Wilston's elderly wife, Frances, while Ivan raged all around them in their flooded home, with no roof over their heads:-

Mr. Wilston: Well, we had it bad! I'm diabetic and have to take insulin every day, which made things even worse.

On the morning of the storm, the house had full up with saltwater. We had to put my wife underneath the *kitchen table* so nothing would drop on top of her from the ceiling. The roof had gone somewhere early in the morning. So I put her under there and the lady who stays with us was minding her until I could get her over to my sister's place. By that time, all the roof had gone. There wasn't no roof left!

Miss Monica: My employers are old and they didn't want to go to a shelter or anything so we stayed in the house.

Mr. Wilston Levy, in the doorway of his Bodden Town home

On Saturday, everything was all right. Then on Sunday morning, I get up and give Miss Frances her breakfast. About nine o'clock, everything started to come off and

264

the ceiling started to cave in. After Miss Frances eat, she was lying down sleeping in her room and then I heard that side of the roof fly up. I went in there and wake her up and tell her to get up because the roof had cave in. After I bring her out, everything is flying off! The zinc and everything start to fly so I take her and put her underneath the table and we sit down under there on the settee cushion, right in the water, as the storm pass right over us, through the house. It was so scary!

Mr. Wilston: From early on, the water came in. It was coming down from the top and all the house was full up. When the water hit the sheetrock in the ceiling, every bit of it let go. Inside the house was piled up with stuff, piled up with junk! It was a big mess.

I was just scared for my wife that everything was going to drop down and kill her. That's all I was scared of.

Miss Monica: The wind was blowing hard. It was blowing so hard all day that we couldn't come out. We were sitting there with the rain falling on us. The zinc was blowing all around us. It was terrible and I was praying to the Lord to stop it.

It was a sight to see! The wind looked almost dark. It looked like fog. It was blowing, blowing and we had to just sit under there until it calm down. We were under the kitchen table from eleven o'clock in the morning until about eight o'clock that night. That's when Emilio come to get

Monica Dehaney, in Bodden Town

us. Him come and help us to get out and carry us over to next door.

Mr. Wilston: On Sunday night, I was sitting out on the porch but I couldn't go anywhere because zinc was still flying all about. All over the place, zinc and the gutters was blowing and licking up against the house. I couldn't take the chance to go and get help because the zinc might have hit me and cut me up so I just sit out on the porch in one chair, right in the water, till morning! Water was all through the house. The sea was breaking right there and coming right in.

On Monday morning after the storm, the weather broke and I get my wife over to my sister's and we stayed there for about two days. My wife has to walk with a crutch. I got a little wheelbarrow that I could carry her in. I have to carry her, you see, so she won't fall down. I tell you, we had a rough time.

That sea coming in was something. That had only happened one time before; that was in 1932. I came back three weeks after the storm from Honduras. I was young. I'm eighty-eight years old now. I was born in Cayman on 10th October 1915, the day the first World War started, in that old house right next to where mine is now. I was born in Bodden Town and I'm still living in Bodden Town. I don't see anywhere else for me to go.

That hurricane was the biggest thing I have ever seen in Cayman in my life. I was quite a young boy when the '32 Storm came but it wasn't as bad as this. No sir! The 1932 storm wasn't nowhere as bad as this. I can tell you because I know!

The Great Escape
- Ocean Club

After making every possible preparation for the hurricane, Lindsay Wright and Robert Parr saw no reason why they should leave the comforts of their newly refurbished luxury home at Ocean Club. Little did they know, they would be spending five hours during the height of the storm fighting tidal waves and struggling for their lives in the bed of the only room of their home left standing.

Robert and Lindsay, standing in what once was the hallway leading into their master bedroom and spare bedroom

Their neighbour, Garry Bosley, had only been living in Cayman for two years when he got the chance to do something he had always wanted to do – experience a hurricane. Maybe it was crazy. Maybe it was fate. Whatever it was, it is no doubt that if Garry and his friends had not made the decision to stay in his condo at Ocean Club that night, Robert and Lindsay would never have survived the storm. The following is their amazing story of survival:-

Garry: My friends, Randy and Audrey, had planned to spend Saturday night, 11th September, in their home in North Side but they got evacuated. We thought that if the storm was going on the north side of the island the south shore should be the

267

safest place. So they came and spent the night with me on the south side. I had phoned my wife that morning and told her, "The storm is going to hit sometime tonight but don't worry about me. I won't be able to phone you probably for a few days because the phones will be down. I'm living in a concrete house and it's a two storey so, if the roof comes off, I can go downstairs and if it floods, I can go upstairs." I always thought that if you lived in a concrete house you're safe … but you're not.

Lindsay: I think the terrible thing about it was that Robert and I had centered our lives for the last year and a half on re-building our house and getting it back to all its glory. We spent every waking moment on doing up the house. I had not seen my family in two years and so I decided it would be lovely if they came here. Back in August, my brother-in-law's sister was tragically killed in a car accident in Arizona so my sister and her husband went through all the trauma of that so I was pleased that they were coming over to us so they could have a well-earned holiday. That gave us the incentive to make sure the house was perfect and that's what we did. We restored the house …

Robert: … and all the treasures. Since I have traveled around the world for decades, I have been collecting artifacts and old antiquities - just priceless stuff, like all these beautiful jade pieces. We had this walk-in vault that was six feet tall by four feet wide. It was bolted to the floor and, had I known, I would have put all my jade pieces inside there, but as it was, I just put the small figurines in, just in case the shutters blew off and the wind came into the house … we just never thought this would be so bad. We thought it would be a bit worse than Mitch. Up until about eight-ten when our power went off, I was looking at the Internet at NOAA and it was still showing that the projected path of the hurricane was the north side of Cayman.

Lindsay: My sister and her husband got in on the Friday, a week before the storm, and we had a lovely evening at the Cracked Conch on the Sunday. When the proprietor of the Cracked Conch was saying, "Oh, you know we've got Ivan coming along now," I was like, "Yeah, right, whatever." I had my family here so I didn't care about a hurricane.

I didn't think too much about it until Friday, the 10th, when they were trying to leave and I had to find out from British Airways if there was a plane and what they were going to do. Everybody I knew in the world was trying to get on planes. So when my sister and her husband were leaving, she begged me to go with her. She said, "Please come with me. I don't have a good feeling about this. I don't think you should be staying here," and I said, "No, this is God's country. Nothing is going to happen here. We're going to be safe." She kept saying that she wanted me to get on the plane, but right up until the last minute I wouldn't go. I will always remember standing at the airport with her that Friday night. Robert was busy at home securing the house.

Robert: I was cutting trees down and strengthening the panels that Ocean Club's manager had put up that day. I cut down seventeen trees but I didn't need to cut them because they would have come down anyway. There was one tree that I left …

Lindsay: Saturday morning came and Robert came running into the bedroom and woke me up. He said, "My God, Lindsay, Ivan has changed course. It missed Jamaica and it's heading west, straight for us." My mind was still in England with my sister. It was only when he told me that I had to come and see what he was on about, that I saw Ivan. It was when we looked at that photograph on the computer. Immediately, he was back in action working to secure the house…

Robert: I still thought it was going to go like Hurricane Mitch, maybe a bit closer, but it was still to the north. I thought we would be okay on the south side.

Lindsay: I used to work on cruise ships. We were trained for anything that would happen on a ship … for bomb scares, fires. We had to do a basic sea survival, a fire-fighting course. We had to be able to launch a lifeboat. You had to know what to do. You have to learn not to panic and to take control and so, on Saturday, when Robert was doing all the preparing, I was going around Ocean Club and trying to find out what everybody else was doing. There were people that were leaving. There were people that were staying. I just thought it was like all the other hurricanes and we would be fine. But I made a point of finding out about all the houses that were around us and who was staying and who was going. I wasn't really thinking, well, maybe I might need them, but it's that security of knowing who's around you.

At seven-thirty on Saturday night, the waves started coming up over the front of the seawall and around the back of the house.

Robert: The seawall ends right at our balcony and the water was already coming up where I had been standing in the morning, cutting down trees on the adjacent empty lot.

Lindsay: Around this time, I came out to keep Robert company because he was still busy and he said to me, "Take a last look at this, darling, because I don't think the jacuzzi's going to be here tomorrow."

During the day, I had met this guy in the next house when I was finding out who was where. I actually met and chatted with this guy, Garry, who is a beautiful Canadian, when he was wandering around Ocean Club with a coffee cup in his hand - very laid-back guy.

So I asked Garry what he was going to do for Ivan and he goes, "Well, I'm going to stay here and have me a hurricane party, eh." He was almost like someone pouring oil over troubled waters. He was so laid-back. So I thought, What in the world am I worried about? Why are all these *other* people evacuating?

Robert: The other thing … that unit where Garry lives was owned by a lady I know and respect, who has been in Cayman for a long time. And the couple that was staying with Garry had asked her, "Are you putting up shutters?" and she said, "Oh, no, it's going to be fine. It's going to the north of us." She left and Garry wasn't worried. He invited his friends for the 'hurricane party'. The Ocean Club manager put up our shutters but did not tell us to leave when we saw him on Saturday morning.

Lindsay: When I met this lovely Garry, I said, "If you're having a party, keep some for me and I'll drop by later on," not realizing what was to come.

Robert: I put our passports in our filing cabinet in the computer room. This filing cabinet weighed eight hundred pounds because it was solid concrete, with four legal size drawers. The great room had all our treasures; jade and artifacts, fossils, petrified wood, three hundred million year old trilobites and ammonites, a dinosaur bone with the spinal cord still in it that was one hundred and forty million years old – real museum quality pieces. I was really a big collector and got my collection from all over the world. I had a Ming vase from the Ming Dynasty and a Nine Dragon vase. There was no way to protect them even with a vault like we had, it could not all fit inside there.

Lindsay: Robert had worked solidly securing the house the whole of Friday and Saturday and then he watched a few minutes of the storm on the Internet. So, when the power went off Saturday around eight, he wanted to go to bed. But how could I sleep? I was stressed out. I couldn't go to sleep.

Robert: The last report from NOAA, at eight-ten, was telling us, and I was reassuring her, that the storm was going to start at two in the morning. The eye was going to pass at six. Then we were going to get tropical storm winds again at eleven. The storm was going to leave us by eleven. And that was the last news we had.

Lindsay: He was relaxed and he went off to bed. So I called my shop manager, Jean, from Kirk Freeport, and it sounded like a party was going on in her house. Everybody was laughing and you could hear glasses going 'ching, ching' and I was just there in our house feeling empty.

Robert: Each room in our house was done in a theme. The hallway leading up to our master bedroom was medieval. In that hall, we had seventeen real swords from Toledo, Spain. They were beautiful.

The master bedroom was oriental with oriental carpets. In there we had my Samarai swords and my jade. My father was born in China and we had all his stamp collection in our vault, which was in this bedroom.

Lindsay: And we had this beautiful screen with the Ching Ming River, my jewellery box, and a hundred and eighty year old antique wedding cabinet from China, which had been converted into a wine chest. So the whole of that section was Chinese and it was beautiful.

The great room was the prehistoric room with all the fossils and teeth. The spare bedroom was done in a Caribbean theme with these gorgeous Bird of Paradise flowers that we had bought at Vigoro Nursery. It was a very Caribbean, sunshiny room and I thought, what a positive room to be in so that's where Robert went to bed but I felt ill at ease so I didn't go to bed until later on.

With no electricity, it was so hot that we went to bed in our swimsuits. It took me awhile to get to sleep but, when I did, I dreamt that I was in the kitchen baking cakes and I could smell vanilla. Then I woke up and realized the reason I smelt vanilla was that the vanilla-scented candle next to me was burning at a dramatic rate. So I got up and went into the other room.

Garry: I think it started getting bad in the apartment about two or three o'clock on the Sunday morning. The water started to come up to the window outside and then inside onto the floor. We were downstairs and I was on the couch closest to the kitchen, Audrey was sleeping over by the window and Randy was on the couch against the wall. Then, all of a

Picture taken by Garry Bosley

View from Ocean Club looking towards Mariners Cove early Sunday morning, 12th September 2004

sudden, a big wave hit the patio door, knocked it out and the water came bursting through. There was an air conditioner behind the couch that Audrey was sleeping on. She was sound asleep when this wave hit and knocked the air conditioner out of the wall. She came shooting across the living room on that couch and hit the couch I was lying on. That's when we decided it was about time we went upstairs.

Stuff was piling up in the living room and it was all filled up with water. We didn't have just floodwater rising. We had big waves coming in. We took the air conditioner and put it at the entrance door to relieve the pressure of the water so that it just kept running out the back door but the water kept coming up higher and higher. Then Ivan took the door so we didn't have to worry about that anymore!

Lindsay: Robert had told me there were going to be stones banging and whatever. So I was thinking about sounds. I wasn't thinking of sight. It was now about two-thirty. Everything was pitch black and I was like a cat by this little window in the master bedroom.

In order to look out the window, you have to stand on this sunken tub. So I was peering out and none of the outside lights were working because there was no power. But what I could see was like a mass of white and everything else was pitch black. Then, when I looked over at the next houses, what I saw took me back to when I lived in England. It took me back to the Salisbury Plains and it just looked like the breeze was going through a cornfield with that kind of movement as the corn bends. I was standing there thinking that wasn't right. Then I realized that that was not wind either. That was the sea and it was breaking and going past our house onto the front line of houses.

I knew at that point that we were surrounded by ocean and we had no way out! There was no wind, no noise, no banging or anything - just the sea. So I thought, Okay, Lindsay, okay, don't panic. Let's get Robert up and let's go back and check everything. So I went into the bedroom and I woke Robert up and said, "Come on, darling, you've got to wake up. I think things are getting bad now and I need you to be awake and to help me." So he got up and we went round and checked things.

Robert: I had my headlight and my mag light, with another headlight. We could see the flooring and, with the candles, we saw a bit of water. Then Lindsay slipped and fell.

Lindsay: My head whacked onto the tile! My arm whacked onto the tile! My hip whacked! He tried to get me up. I said, "Please don't touch anything. Just let me lie here and think about the pain and when I'm ready to move I'll move." I got up and then I realized that we actually had water in the house so he said, "Let's get the towels from the linen closet," and I said, "I just washed them. I don't want to get them all dirty. Can't we find something else to use?" But we got them and put them down. Robert was by the patio window, wringing out the towels into buckets. I was picking up the buckets then walking to the laundry room, emptying out the water and going back to him when I finally said, "I am not doing this all night! You can forget this!" And he said, "You have to." "Well, I'm going to have to have a tea break," I told him.

Robert: I said, "If it doesn't get any worse than this, we can hang on."

Garry: The next thing that happened in the apartment was that our fridge flipped over in the water. Randy was standing on the fridge, which was floating in the kitchen, and he was passing all our hurricane supplies to me. I was standing on the kitchen counter passing them to Audrey who was standing on the stairs until the impact of the waves hit the cupboards and started taking the cupboards out. Then we KNEW we had better go upstairs.

The waves kept pounding and bringing everything in. All of the furniture and everything was piling up in the kitchen, tighter and tighter. By then, I was standing in water on the stairway landing which is about four feet up, watching the waves go through.

I watched the waves push the living room furniture, the dining room furniture, the kitchen cupboards, the fridge, the stove, the washer and dryer, and pound it all through the concrete wall on the front of the house. Everything just went out - just like that. I have no idea what time that was. It was so dark. I lost all concept of time. I was relieved when that front wall went out because then I didn't have to worry about the pressure of the water anymore. Now it was just flowing through the house and we were upstairs.

Robert: I was trying to caulk the patio doors from the great room inside the house like I had done in Mitch but it wasn't working because the tidal waves kept coming and the caulking didn't have a chance to dry. Debris, seaweed and crabs were going between the steel shutters and the windows. We had our headlights and we could see it all going up and coming back down. My caulking just washed out. It wasn't holding.

Lindsay: Then Robert was back to wringing out the towels. He had a little stool that he was sitting on. I was still going back and forth with the buckets and the next minute there was a BANG! Then my ears … you know, when you dive into a swimming pool and your ears fill up with water and you've got that strange sound going on? It was just like that. We were underwater! The whole of the patio door had exploded when this tidal wave hit and it took us both underwater. It was the whole of the sea coming into the front room. It was us and the furniture. Everything was floating to the back of the house.

A piece of furniture hit the back of my head. I don't know if it was a chair or a table or what and, all of a sudden, I started to get this floaty feeling where I was drifting off and I thought to myself, Lindsay, you can't drift off because, if you drift off, you're not coming back. You're underwater, love. You've got to keep your head awake. Then I felt the waves start to go away from me, to go back out again, and my first thought was 'Robert'. He got the main brunt of the window. At least I was pushed out to the side. When the patio doors exploded, he hit this built-in cabinet, which was just in front of the kitchen cabinets. He hit that and, because he is a solid guy as he works out everyday, he folded up and used all his muscle power to protect himself. He took that whole four foot cabinet and himself all the way back through the kitchen. I was screaming his name and I heard him say, "I'm okay, I'm okay."

Robert lost the torch, which he had on his head. I had a Glade four dollar candle sitting on the very thing that his body hit and that little candle moved from there to there but it didn't move out. If that candle had dropped to the floor into the ocean, I wouldn't have known where I was going because everything was pitch black! That candle was our beacon that showed us to the French glass door that led through the hall to the spare bedroom. I said to Robert, "Follow me, follow me, we have to go this way."

Robert: We were both right in front of the patio door and it was like a scene out of a bad movie. I was looking at it and I couldn't believe what I saw. The steel shutters and the patio glass were hit by what seemed like fifty thousand tons of water. I don't know how tall that wave was but I know that the shutters and the patio glass just exploded on us and, for some reason God sent Lindsay off to the side. If she had got one cut, I don't think she would have made it because she's so tiny. I was sitting more to the side of her when the wave hit. I went straight with the wave and couldn't, with all of my strength, stop it. I couldn't fight it so I got into a ball and just went right

Lindsay Wright and Robert Parr, with their newfound friend, Garry Bosley (left)

through this cabinet and all the way into the kitchen past the fridge. It was quite a long journey. I didn't know I had gotten cut. I just got up and my first thought was, "Oh, Jesus, she must be dead. She couldn't have taken a hit like that and have made it." "Lindsay," I shouted, and there she was in the dark. I figured she must be all broken up and everything.

When we finally got into the spare bedroom, furthest away from the ocean, I couldn't shut that door to keep the water out. I tried to shut the computer room door but I couldn't because the furniture was up against it too. Then I realized that, despite the heavy jacuzzi being in front of that patio glass, the window to that room had blown out also. The computer room was flooded with all the computers and furniture as well so I couldn't shut that heavy oak door to try and keep the sea away from us.

Lindsay: He put the ladder up against the bedroom door and the dressing table and he said to me, "Come on, we're going to have to put some clothes on," because I just had on a bikini. We were like Ursula Andress and 007 coming out of the ocean, you know. Then Robert shone a torch to look into the spare wardrobe to see what we could put on and all we saw was blood and I didn't know if it was mine or if it was his. I had been hurt. He had also been hurt but that could've been where I fell over. I mean, I kept falling over and I didn't know whose blood it was and I was thinking, Oh, my God, this is serious!

He was looking in the spare wardrobe and there weren't practical clothes in there. So he took out these Latin American trousers, the ones that are tight, with bell bottoms and holes in them and gave them to me to put on because that's all that was there and he was putting on clothes he had never worn before in his life. He was dressed up like a commando, like Arnold Schwarzenegger, with this bandana around his head and he had all this camouflage gear on. It was like a fancy dress. I was dressed like Jennifer Lopez ready for a night out in these tight clothes. We were just wearing the strangest of gear.

While we were dressing, I could see that he was badly cut. There was a cut on his stomach and I could see the outside of the subcutaneous layer. It looked like bacon. It was all white where it cut right through – right down to the raw flesh. It took us a long time to get dressed.

Lindsay: When we'd got the clothes on, Robert said, "Come on, let's get on the bed." On the cream-coloured sheets, which we had only had about a week, there was blood pouring everywhere.

I kept thinking to myself, We've got to get some help. It was pitch black, although we had this little candle burning which was giving me a lot of comfort. So I said to Robert, "Have you still got the torch?" He had lost the torch off his head but he still had his little doctor's torch. He gave me that and I said, "There's a guy in that house over there. Let me use the torch to try and get hold of him and let him know that we're still here." So Robert gave me the torch. Of course, I had worked at sea, so I knew how to do Morse code. So, in the pitch black, I was doing Morse code with the torch. They had actually seen what I was doing but I had no way of knowing so, just like they did on the Titanic, I just kept doing it and doing it until I couldn't do it anymore.

Garry: After we got upstairs, we were watching Robert and Lindsay whom we had met earlier in the day. They were flashing lights at us but we couldn't go downstairs because there was furniture floating around and we were in trouble ourselves, at the time.

Lindsay: The next tidal wave came and took the whole of that oak door off its hinges and back underwater we went again.

Robert: With each wave, we saw more furniture coming in with it. Our eight hundred pound cabinet with our passports in it, which had been in the computer room, actually went across the hall, still standing, and it ended up in the bedroom where we were lying.

Lindsay: Every time a wave came, he was like, "I love you," and I couldn't argue. When somebody tells you they love you, you don't want to start an argument. You've got to say, 'I love you' back, haven't you? So I was concentrating on that but then I realized that the reason he was saying "I love you" was because he knew at any moment we were both going to die and what I'm going to remember is him saying: "I love you."

It was very romantic and it was a little bit like the Titanic when you see that old couple and they're lying

Picture taken by Garry Bosley

Dr. Robert Parr's house at Ocean Club early Sunday morning, 12th September 2004

in bed and everybody's manning the lifeboats and this couple decides to spend their last few moments in bed together and that's where they're going to die. The bed cover was over my head. Robert had hold of me and there was a lot of debris on top of that, which was weighing the bed down.

Now it was getting very light. Thank goodness! I was looking out to the ocean, facing the tidal waves as they were coming in and gauging which one was going to be the wave that was going to take the whole of the room and fill it up with sea and underwater we would go. I could see by the way the wind was going through the hall that the wall must have been completely exposed because I could see that the wind was picking up the saltwater and pushing it right across to the back end of the hall and it looked like 'horizontal smoke'. That was the most amazing thing to see – the water going along like that.

I started to get, from inside out, this cold feeling. My body was starting to go very, very cold. We had been in completely wet clothes since three o'clock and I think shock must've set in. I started to get the shivers coming through me and I thought, I've got to try to get out of here. I've got to try and make my way out before I lose all of my energy. I was trying to reason with Robert, telling him, "We've got to leave." But as he had been told and, as everybody had been told, you must never leave your house. But the house was disappearing and I thought, There's going to come a time when, if we don't go, that's it.

It was difficult to get out of the bed because the bed was so wet and soggy. It was folded like a pancake with us trapped inside it. I somehow managed to crawl out from under him and I got to the left-hand side of the window and said, "If I can get through this window, we can get out." It was the type with the crank opening thing and I started to get the window open and then it just stuck. It just seized on me and the handle broke off in my hand and I thought, Oh, great. We can't get out this way. It's not going to work. I told Robert that and crawled back into the bed with him.

We had an alarm system to the house for intruders and that was out in the hall.

Robert: The battery was way up in the rafters and the tidal wave shorted out the battery and it turned on the siren.

Lindsay: So the alarm was going off. It was like, "WAO, WAO, WAO, WAO, WAO," and I was thinking, Oh, great! Somebody is going to find us and rescue us. That was so wonderful! Just imagine. It was like being in a situation where there's a murder or something and all of a sudden you hear that police siren. You get quite a relief through you because you think someone is going to come and rescue you. For that brief moment in time, I thought, I'm safe because somebody's going to hear that siren and come and get us. But it took me a good ten, fifteen seconds to realize, you stupid person, nobody's going to come out in the middle of a hurricane just because some alarm system has gone off.

Robert: That alarm lasted through several cycles of tidal waves. When the tidal waves came, the house filled up with water and it drowned the battery and the siren so you couldn't hear it but then, "gurgle, gurgle, gurgle … WAO, WAO, WAO," you'd hear it again.

Garry: We could hear their security alarm going off for about an hour and that, combined with the howling of the wind, was awful. We were just wishing it would quit and thought the batteries were never going to die on it.

Lindsay: I made a conscious decision then, rather than keep going under the water and die by drowning, I'd rather get hit by something and get taken away that way. That was my choice. Robert didn't want that but that was my way out. I couldn't lie there and wait to be covered up with more debris.

Robert: The house was a very well-constructed house. It once was the developer's house so all the inside walls were solid concrete block. There were only two walls that were plaster and those were the hallway walls. By the time the alarm started going off,

Picture taken by Garry Bosley

Ocean Club mid-day, Sunday, 12th September 2004

some of the furniture and seawall had actually knocked a big hole through the drywall so, from that bedroom, we could actually look through the hall and, beyond that, we could see the sea and we could see that there were no computers or anything in the computer room. But we did not know that the house was breaking apart.

Garry: Out of our upstairs window, we watched Lindsay and Robert's house throughout the rest of the morning. We could only see the front [road side] of their house and we watched it for hours before we realized that it was falling apart. That's when we saw the corner of the wall that faced us start to crack. At that time we could see Lindsay at the bedroom window. So we were hollering down to them, "Your house is falling down. You've got to get out of there. We'll meet you at the bottom."

Lindsay: The next tidal wave came and took me underwater again but, as it took me under, there was a piece of plywood from somewhere that came in on top of the wave and pressed me down so not only was I going underwater but I had this piece of plywood on top of me which was pressing my head up against the concrete wall and it felt like my head was in a vice. I had the wall on one side and the sea was pushing the wood up against my face. There was no way I could get away from that to get above the water and, at that point, I didn't know if there WAS an 'above'. As far as I knew, the water had come up to the ceiling. All I knew was that I was underwater and this piece of wood was up against my head. Then the wave receded and the pressure subsided. So, as soon as the pressure went, I grabbed the piece of wood and threw it and struggled like a cat to get above water to get my next breath. When I came up, I noticed a piece of hurricane shutter that was right in front of my face that was all twisted metal and I thought, The next tidal wave that comes, that's what's coming at me. So I was thinking, Right, well, this is it ... this is it. And I was thinking that, okay, okay, you know, my mum died two years ago. She was my 'be all and end all'. She was what kept me going through everything in life. When she died, if it wasn't my belief in the fact that one day I would meet her again, I couldn't have got to the point where I was now. My sister is a spiritualist and she has a lot of faith in spirits and she has said that in the hereafter what you do on this earth you take into the next cycle of your life and it's a continuing thing. I didn't really feel frightened and I thought, If I'm going to meet my mother, surely this isn't going to be that bad. It's going to be uncomfortable. I'm going to die but, at least, I'm going to meet my mother at the other end. So I said to my mum, "Is this what it's all about? Is this what I'm meant to be?" I said, "Mum, if this is the way it is, please be there for me at the other end."

At this point, I looked out the window and I saw the body of a dead man. It was a dead body and it came from the side where the seawall had been and it floated out and just lay there floating outside the window. The head was down, the arms were out and it just floated and floated and floated. At one point, I used to work at a hospital in a mortuary so I know about dead bodies. This was not a body that had been in a grave for years or something. It was a fresh body. So I was looking at this dead body and thinking, How is that body just floating there? It wasn't moving about. It wasn't being bashed about by the two hundred mile an hour winds that everybody had talked about.

So the body was just floating and I thought, If that body is just floating and I can get into that water, I can survive. The one tree that Robert had not cut down was left between our house and the front row of houses that were still there at Ocean Club. And I thought, That's a fresh tree. It's not a dead tree, so it can hold my weight. The water there is protected between the two buildings. If I can get out that window and grab onto that tree, I can get to the next house. So, while all this was processing in my brain, I was saying to Robert, "If we can get out, we can get to the next house," and he's like, "Darling, come on, you don't leave the house. How do you know that you can get into that house?" And I said, "Robert, Robert, look. The window in that house is smashed in. The curtains are blowing out. There is no patio there. If we can get in there, we can get up the stairs. See, in the upstairs, the window is intact. We can do it, Robert. If we can get out into that water, we can grab onto that tree and somehow get into the next house and, from there, we can move on." When I said to him, "There's a dead body," it spurred him on. But we couldn't get out because the window was blocked. So that was all fairytale thinking because we couldn't get out that window.

Garry: All we were looking at was Lindsay in that window and thinking how to get to them.

Robert: Then the biggest tidal wave we were to survive came and God blew out the centre window.

Lindsay: I thought it was my mother that blew it out. She had said to me, when she was on her deathbed, "Don't you ever worry about yourself. I will always make sure that you will be all right and, if you can't be all right, then I will come and get you." So I had the knowledge that if I was going to die my mother would be there. I knew she would hate it, because she hated the sea, but I knew she was there.

Robert: When this tidal wave hit, it took us literally all the way up and we hit the ceiling and, when it receded,

Garry Bosley leaning against his damaged car at Ocean Club

that centre window was gone and the other two were still intact. It was like God was telling us, "Go out this window." I couldn't believe that He had not only blown out the window but He had blown out the entire frame. There was no broken glass so it was the perfect way out.

Lindsay: I was shivering so strong that it was almost violent. That was when Robert said, "Well, look, I'm bigger than you. Let me go out first. If there's another wave, I can use my strength to hold you." So I said, "Okay, Robert, there's a tree. If you can grab onto it, then we can make the next move."

The sea that had been going back and forth past our window had taken all the earth and everything from it so when Robert jumped, he was up to his neck in saltwater. He had put a lifejacket on me so after he jumped in he held me and I went in. Then the next tidal wave came and underwater we went again!

Garry: Randy and I ran down the stairs and, right as we got down to the bottom, a big wave came and my thought was that they'd never survive it.

Robert: That wave took us up against the side of the building and then it washed us out but, thank God, the wall of the house was still there and stopped us.

Garry: So, when the wave passed through, Randy and I went out and they were there, hanging onto a tree between their house and ours.

Lindsay: We grabbed the tree and held on and out of nowhere these two guys came and made this human chain. Although I knew Randy, and I had met Garry the day before with his cup of coffee in his hand, at that point in time I had no recollection of who they were or what they were. It was now about eight-thirty on Sunday morning.

Randy took hold of Garry, Garry took hold of Robert's hand and Robert had hold of me. They were taking their own lives into their hands to come out from where they were upstairs in the other house. The whole of their downstairs was completely gone and looked like an open garage so they had to come down those stairs into the hurricane to rescue us off this tree.

I was just like a cat who was struggling, trying to find her feet and find her bearings, you know. I was coughing and spluttering. Everything was just a tangled mess of concrete and debris and when we put our foot out, we didn't know what we'd step on next. We sort of staggered towards Audrey, Randy's wife. She was halfway up the stairs. There was a part of a sofa that was still there that we had to climb over and there she was.

Robert: She was so polite. She put out her hand and said, "Hi, I'm Audrey."

Lindsay: She was so wonderful. She was so calm and compassionate and I never thought I would actually be able to touch another human again because I really didn't think I was going to make it. I just didn't think I was.

Audrey grabbed us and took us up the stairs and I was shaking. It was a violent shake. It wasn't like a shiver. The whole of my body was shaking and Audrey put her arms around me and I put my arms around her and all I kept saying was, "I'm alive! I'm alive! I'm alive!" because I couldn't believe that I was alive. I really had accepted I would meet my maker. I really didn't think I was going to actually be able to walk away from that.

Audrey kept saying, "You're fine, you're fine," and, although I didn't really smoke much at that point in time, I said, "Could I have a cigarette?" and she said, "Sure, and here, have a drink." It was only eight-thirty in the morning and she gave me a can of beer and a cigarette but I couldn't find my mouth to put anything in because my hands were all over the place. Robert had just fallen into a heap in the corner.

Garry: When we got them upstairs, they were absolutely in shock. Robert was hurt fairly bad from being tossed around in the waves in his house and was in shock from that.

Lindsay: He was pretty calm just sitting there and he was like, "Okay, we're here now but this house might not survive much longer. Okay, everybody, get sheets together. Tie them in knots. We're going to put belts on and the five of us together can try and find a safer place to go." I was at the point where I was saying, "I'm alive, I'm alive," with this euphoria that I was not dead.

The whole of the building was shaking. Robert was over there in a heap and Garry and Randy went over to the window. This was the first I had actually seen the hurricane because, up until then, our house had been covered with the shutters. Being on this second floor now, with no shutters, we had a full view of what the hurricane was doing. So Garry or Randy said, "Oh, my God! Your house is going!" I had to see what was going on and I got up and Garry and Randy were saying, "No, no, stay where you are," and I said, "No, I've got to see what's happening." So I went over to the window and looked down at the house and I could see the window where we had escaped from and I could see all the debris coming out – the cushions, the books and everything were coming out the window. Then there was this big huge crack in the house and the next minute I saw the roof, which we had just put on, come off. It was as if a little five year old had a ribbon on a stick and he let the ribbon go and the ribbon just flew away. That's how the roof went. It just went right across in strips … one … two … three … four. I just stood there and I saw the house go. I watched the house disappear.

Robert: It was a 'standing seam' roof. Each section was twenty-five feet long and the one in the back was about forty feet. The super structure of the house collapsed. So now, the roof had nothing to hold on to and twenty-five foot sections of roof flew off.

Lindsay: Luckily, it went in the same direction the dead body went, and not towards the house we were now in. The wind was going south.

At that point, when I saw the house going, I said to Audrey, "What's the time?" and she said, "It's a quarter to nine," and I thought, My God, we had twenty minutes to get out of that window. Twenty minutes … twenty minutes.

After I watched the house disappear, I came back to Robert and I said, "Well, that's it. That's it, gone." And Robert was then saying, "We need to start thinking about moving on to the next house," because we could see that the downstairs had gone and we didn't know how long the upstairs was going to hold us but we were reassured because there were five of us then and because the others hadn't been through what we had been through they were a lot calmer. They were a little more jovial, or at least Garry was. Robert however was sitting over there bleeding.

Robert: I was lying in a pool of blood. I made her go to the back because I was worried the front windows would blow out. But she kept going and looking out those front windows and going down the stairs to look.

Sunday afternoon, the wind was just unbelievable, and at that point we were praying, "Please let it end by six, so that when it gets dark we don't have to go through this again with this noise." It sounded so bad that I said, "God, whatever I did bad, please forgive me. I know that you are the most powerful thing there is in the universe. You've proved your power. Please, just end it. We just cannot take any more of this."

Garry: We spent the rest of the day hoping that our place wouldn't go down like theirs did, checking our building out every time something crashed into it. We took the attic access door out and took mattresses and leaned them up against the windows where

Lindsay and Robert, standing amidst the debris, including Robert's black Porsche, at Ocean Club

the wind was coming from and opened the windows on the downwind side to relieve the pressure in the house.

When it had calmed down to about sixty mile an hour winds, Randy went out and down to the next unit to us and saw that that was in worse shape than ours.

Then he went to the one after that and decided that if we had to move, we would go two doors down.

In the afternoon, the water receded and that was a big relief but then the wind picked up again and was hitting us harder than before. It started picking up from the other way and we thought, Oh no! That means we're only halfway through this thing! We had water coming in but we never really lost much of the roof. At times, we were scared but nobody panicked. We were especially scared after watching Lindsay and Robert's house fall down. The force of the waves was absolutely unbelievable. A big section of their roof landed in front of our door. So we thought, Well, that will keep the waves away from our house. But, in about an hour and a half, the waves tore that roof up and pushed the whole thing through our living room. You cannot stop the force of those waves. It was just unbelievable.

Lindsay: Robert was very quiet. I knew he had lost a lot of blood. He was having fever. He had slept a little that night and so had the other two. Then Audrey went to sleep. It was amazing. Everybody was lying around and I could hear them breathing. But I was terrified to sleep because I kept having double vision. I was looking at things and seeing them moving and I didn't know if it was the hurricane or if it was a concussion.

I had no idea what was going on and I was freezing cold. I had wet clothes on and they wouldn't dry. Then Audrey was up and she said, "I hope the lady that lives here doesn't mind, but let me see if I can find some dry clothes." So she managed to find this little coat with fur around the edge on the hood. I remember smelling it and it smelled so clean.

I kept going and checking each room and everything was so bleak. There was no light inside. There was the sea completely surrounding the whole of Ocean Club. There were broken tree stubs and, then, in the distance, I saw this house on the other side of Mariners Cove with its lights on and it was lit up like a Christmas tree! It just mesmerized me. I just sat there with these wet clothes on, looking at that. Audrey had given me these cigarettes and I'm trying to count them because I wanted them to last for the rest of the time I was there. I could see this little house with lights on and I was like, "Oh, God, there's other people alive."

Robert: Garry's apartment unit where our lives were saved was on the end, next to our house. The unit on the other side had no stairs left in it. We can't help but wonder how we ended up in this unit and why there were people in it. What if it hadn't been that way?

Garry: At the height of the storm, the waves in the ocean were over forty feet. Our windows weren't boarded so I could see out. When I was looking out the upstairs window, I was looking way up at these waves and I thought they were going to wipe us out for sure because there was no way that any building could survive waves like that.

Randy and I had talked about the storm before it came. Randy and his wife, Audrey, had been here for seven years and have seen a little bit here and a little bit there but we both said before the storm that we wanted to be close enough to the storm to actually experience it but just far enough away to live. I think I accomplished that. Ivan was the first hurricane that I have ever seen and I don't really care if I ever see another one!

Lindsay: Robert had to go into the hospital on the Monday and stayed overnight. He had over a hundred stitches. He was badly cut up and Dr. DeAlwis stitched him up. My cat had stayed at my friend's at Reef House. I was like, "What do I do?" I had an animal at one place and Robert was severely injured. He was like a patchwork quilt with stitches all over.

I was still in overdrive. I hadn't slept Saturday night. I didn't sleep Sunday night. I got Robert into hospital and he wanted me to stay with him on Monday but I had to go back to Reef House to check on the cat. I knew Robert was safe but I didn't know about the cat. Of course, when I walked to Reef House, I saw that the house was underwater and the windows were broken. Somebody saw me in distress and said, "Let me take your cat," and I thought, I have to spend the night here, because it was the only place that remained of my past or that resembled anything of my past. But, of course, I had to walk back to the hospital to see Robert and I told him, "Look, I have to go back there." He was upset because I was leaving him there and I was like, "This is something I have to do." So back again I went to South Sound and into the house and I spent the night in that house just talking away to my mum and asking her, "Where do we go from here? Everything I have is gone."

After Robert got out of the hospital, we spent the next few days trying to find people to help us get the safe open. We had no generator, no electricity, and how do you get into a blooming Fort Knox safe without somebody to help you? All we had left in the world was in that safe so we had the next few days trying to get people to help us to open it.

Robert: The Stadtlanders were very nice to us. Dr. Stadtlander and Ronnie let us stay in their house with the use of their car so we could get around. Our two cars had flooded.

Lindsay: Robert had a black Porsche and a lovely yellow Porsche, which 'drove' itself to Durty Reid's about half a mile away! Before the storm, it was parked by our tennis club.

Robert: We had spent five hours, from three-thirty until eight-thirty, in that spare bedroom taking the brunt of the storm. Later, I saw our mattress over by Rex Crighton's yard across the road. I touched the mattress and I said, "Hey, I feel for this bed. I think it saved my life."

Lindsay: Cracking that safe open was not like I was Catherine Zeta-Jones with Sean Connery. I had to crawl in there and I was covered head to foot in dirt and sand and it smelled like one hundred year old eggs. I had to crawl in there to find bits and pieces of my jewelry but my jewelry box had exploded and I lost most all of it.

Robert: I had done everything I could to preserve my dad's stamp collection. I had bought a huge, two thousand pound fire vault, six feet tall and four feet wide, and it was bolted to the floor. My father died when I was ten years old and I told him then, "Daddy, I am going to preserve this for you forever." But the hurricane took that vault out of the bolts on the floor and over Rex Crighton's wall. The water was so high that it didn't even damage the wall. That two thousand pound vault ended up in Rex Crighton's yard. We broke into it about ten days later and found that everything was soaking wet. Even though the stamps were wet, I took them out. I had tears in my eyes and broke down because I thought my father would never forgive me because he entrusted me with that and I had lost it. I had bought the biggest vault I could find to keep those stamps in but nothing can stop the power of nature. Nothing can stop the power of God.

Garry: One thing that's hard to believe was that it wasn't until three weeks or a month after the storm when we were talking to Lindsay and Robert that we found out that they never heard us hollering down to them during the storm because the wind was howling so loudly. We always thought that they had heard us, which we thought was why they had come out the window when they did. But they didn't. It just worked out that way.

Lindsay: I tell you, with God as my witness, we never heard a word. We did not know, when we climbed into that ocean, what we were facing. I just knew I had to go in. I had no idea that those men were on the other end. Neither did Robert.

Garry: I turned into a wino after the storm. I was still staying at Ocean Club and all of our water and supplies were gone but there were wine and champagne bottles, still full, lying all over the yard from everybody's liquor cabinets. So every night we had a bottle of wine. The night after the storm I found a nice bottle of champagne. Randy, Audrey and I popped open the champagne and some Pringles chips and had a nice candlelight dinner.

Lindsay: Although I need a vacation, I will not be leaving Cayman. But I can honestly say that I will never, never, never stay for another hurricane!

We sleep with the lights on now. The light is still a comfort to us. Robert is healing more quickly than me. I haven't healed as well as I would've thought. I woke up the other night and I was back in my kitchen at Ocean Club and I was cooking. When I woke up, it was so vivid. I woke Robert up and said, "Robert, get up. We have to go back to Ocean Club to the house. The house is there. What are we doing here?" and Robert is going, "Darling, it's not there and he had to convince me." I just felt I was physically in that kitchen and it scared me so much that I couldn't go back to sleep. I had to go outside. It's all over now but I still sleep with the light on.

South Sound Sunset

Ivan

Ivan Ivan
what a lion
like a flying
piece of lightning.

Waves crashing
waves splashing
people slipping
roofs dripping.

Raining down
dripping down
people slipping down.

Hurricane Ivan
Bad Ivan
Killer Ivan … Ivan.

Shona McGill (age 10),
Bodden Town resident

287

Shake, Rattle and Ripple
- West Bay

Ken and Grace Wright of West Bay

Although it has been said that West Bay was not hit as hard by Hurricane Ivan as some areas on the island, perhaps long-time West Bay resident, Grace Wright, would beg to differ. The following is Miss Grace's amazing tale of survival:-

I am Grace Ebanks-Wright, a fifty-nine year old wife and mother. All people in this story live in the district of West Bay. On Saturday morning, September 11, 2004, I helped my husband, Ken, with hurricane preparations on our own home in Mount Pleasant. We nailed plywood on some of our windows, and secured and put away some patio furniture. Later on that afternoon, we placed important documents (like passports and bank books) in Ziploc bags and packed them in a waterproof backpack. This was important, as by this time we had decided to leave our home and ride out the storm elsewhere. We made this decision, as we feared we might lose the wooden staircase of our own home in Mount Pleasant. Since our home is at second storey height, this staircase would have been our only means of exiting our house once the storm had passed.

On Saturday night, with driving rain blowing and wind gusts beginning to pick up, we drove to our daughter Kimberly and son-in-law Albert's apartment, which was located on Ernest Jackson Road, in the general area of the West Bay Fire Station. Shortly after we arrived, the electricity and water shut off, and we settled down to ride out the storm, happy to be together whatever lay ahead. All through the night we kept listening for updates on Radio Cayman, plotting Ivan's course as it resolutely and determinedly turned closer and closer towards Cayman.

Around four a.m. on Sunday, September 12th, we heard a loud crash on the corrugated iron roof. What a noise! We only found out later that the crash came from the tall T.V. cable antennae being ripped off. This blow to the roof caused water to come in through the bedroom and bathroom ceilings. Drip…drip…drip…drip…with every drop trickling through the ceiling and down the walls we became wetter and wetter and our anxiety rose higher and higher. Using garbage bags to protect the bed mattress, we shifted everything else of value into semi-dry closets in other rooms. By five a.m., heavy rain was gushing through cracks in the rear wall and we took turns mopping up water. We kept hoping and praying that this was the worst that was going to happen.

As daylight came in around seven a.m., we looked out the glass windows of the living room to see a lake of water to the south moving closer and closer to the front steps; as well as waves coming from the east from the vicinity of Salt Creek. Higher and higher the water crept, engulfing the wheels and then creeping over the dashboard of every car in the yard. Sections of neighbouring roofs were ripped off by the hurricane force winds and hurtled through the air. A two-by-four beam from a neighbour's roof hit the east wall of the main bedroom like a flying missile, and gouged a large hole in the wall. We quickly pushed the bureau against the hole to prevent anything else from flying through it. The wind was blowing so hard and so fast by now, it sounded like it was wailing, keening, and screaming. As more and more damage was being done to the apartment, and as the storm winds grew fiercer, we wondered whether the house would be able to withstand the storm for many more hours.

Suddenly, around ten-thirty a.m., we heard a loud rumbling noise. The whole roof began to *shake, rattle and ripple*. We could see cracks of the eerily dead gray sky as the rafters began to lift and re-settle on the outside walls. With a great RRRRRRRRRRRRIIIIIIIIPPPPPPPPPPP, the roof was GONE and the cold gray light and driving rain of Hurricane Ivan poured through the air conditioning vents in the living room ceiling. What should we do? We had to act quickly! The glass light fixture in the living room was dismantling and falling off the ceiling so we ran into the front bedroom. The four of us debated cramming ourselves into the clothes closet, but quickly realized it could not hold four people. Instead Ken and Albert grabbed the bed frame and turned it on its edge; next they placed the mattress over the frame and bureau – in this way creating a protected shelter in the smallest corner of the room. Kim and Albert crouched under the mattress shelter. Ken and I stood under a door frame that connected this bedroom to the living room. We were frightened and upset; the men were silent but Kim and I were praying out loud, asking God to protect us and provide safety until the hurricane passed.

Suddenly, some ceiling boards started to heave up and down, and one split from the rest spiking into the bed mattress which was protecting Kim and Albert. With each change in wind pressure, the ceiling boards were heaving up and down, and it felt like the entire house was *shaking and rattling*. The bedroom light fixture was slowly filling with water and threatened to collapse on to the floor below. By this time (around eleven-forty a.m.) the wind was so strong we could not see fifty feet to the adjacent house.

We realized that where we were had risks, that we were not safe, but it would be more dangerous to venture outside in the wind (which was around one hundred and fifty miles per hour – gusting to one hundred and eighty miles per hour at times). We all felt terrified and uncomfortable; there was very little room to move our legs or arms in the cramped quarters, and by this time, Kim and Albert were sitting in water. Ken and I were at greatest risk of being hit on our heads by the ceiling boards that continued to split and give way. How much longer would this situation last, we wondered?

At approximately twelve forty-five p.m., the wind died down enough that we could see the next house. Tap-tap-tap!! What was that? More debris hitting the window? Was a window about to break? BANG BANG BANG and then a shout! The two brave men who were trying to rescue us were my cousin, Dalkeith, and his son-in-law, James. Our neighbour had seen the roof fall but was unable to come until the wind had died down. The hurricane winds had blown over trees into the normally cleared driveway between the two houses. Dalkeith was forced to clear a path with his machete so we could all achieve safe passage through the debris. As we tried to step out of the house, we realized that the storm surge was at its peak and we were confronted with waist deep water. All of us in our group are swimmers, but we still needed to cling to each other and walk single file in a human chain – one behind the other.

Dalkeith's home had an intact roof, but was flooded. As we crawled through his living room windows, we noted fifteen inches of water outside his home and approximately eight inches of water inside his home. What a relief – sopping wet, but with a roof over our heads, and good company with which to share the ordeal! Once we had rested for a few minutes and drunk some clean water, Dalkeith noticed that the storm surge was receding. "Quick!" he said, "if we don't get this water out now, it will never leave the house!!" Kim and Albert got to work, helping Spurgene, Wendy, Dalkieth and James sweep water out of the house. Ken and I helped mop up the standing water on the floor. By mid-afternoon, the water had receded, bringing some relief; exhausted but a little drier, we were feeling better now. Dalkeith cooked some turtle meat on his propane barbecue – which tasted simply delicious after our tiring ordeal! He invited all four of us to stay with them through Sunday night and we accepted the invitation.

It felt wonderful to be inside a building that was not losing its roof and ceilings. We were so grateful to Dalkieth and James for coming to rescue us, and for Spurgene and Wendy noticing that our roof had blown off. We thanked God that none of us had been hit by flying objects, or injured as we walked in high winds through the muddy, debris-filled water. We were successful in saving our wallets and passports.

It was now Sunday night and the winds were slowly dying down. After talking for awhile we went to sleep (some on sofas, some on chairs) with very thankful hearts.

The next week brought improvements as we cleaned up and salvaged whatever we could in our yards and homes. We found out that we had not only survived a hurricane, but a tornado as well! CUC reported that three cement electrical poles in West Bay had been felled by a tornado. As we revisited Kim and Albert's apartment in the days after the storm, we found things that seemed inexplicable, except by a tornado having hit the apartment. For example, full propane tanks had moved against the wind and nestled themselves between a car and the apartment without damaging either the house or car … and at the end of the driveway, the mangled remains of the three cement power poles lay as twisted monuments to our ordeal. Hopefully, time will help us all to recover, but we will never forget Hurricane Ivan!!